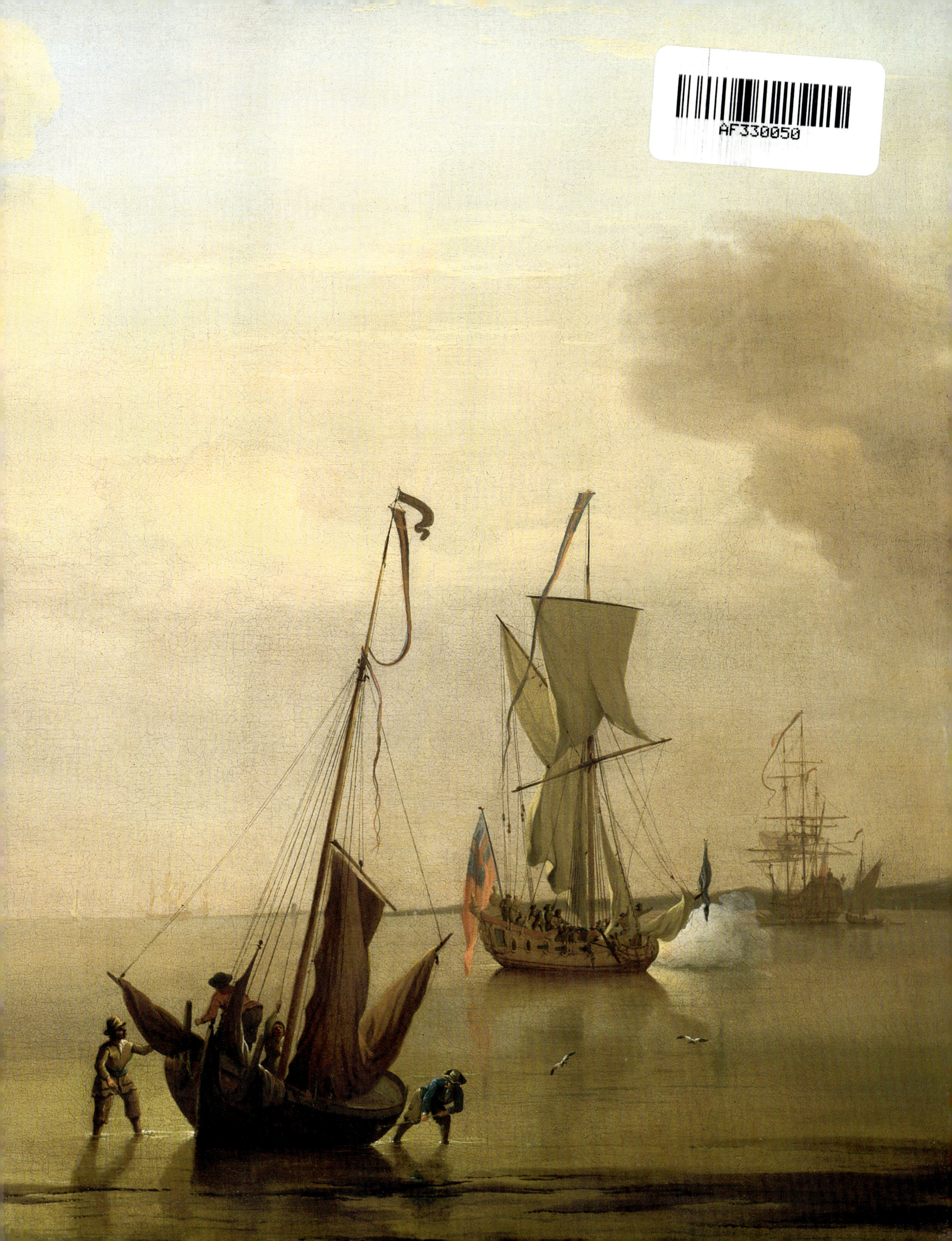
AF330050

PETER MONAMY

1681 – 1749

AND HIS CIRCLE

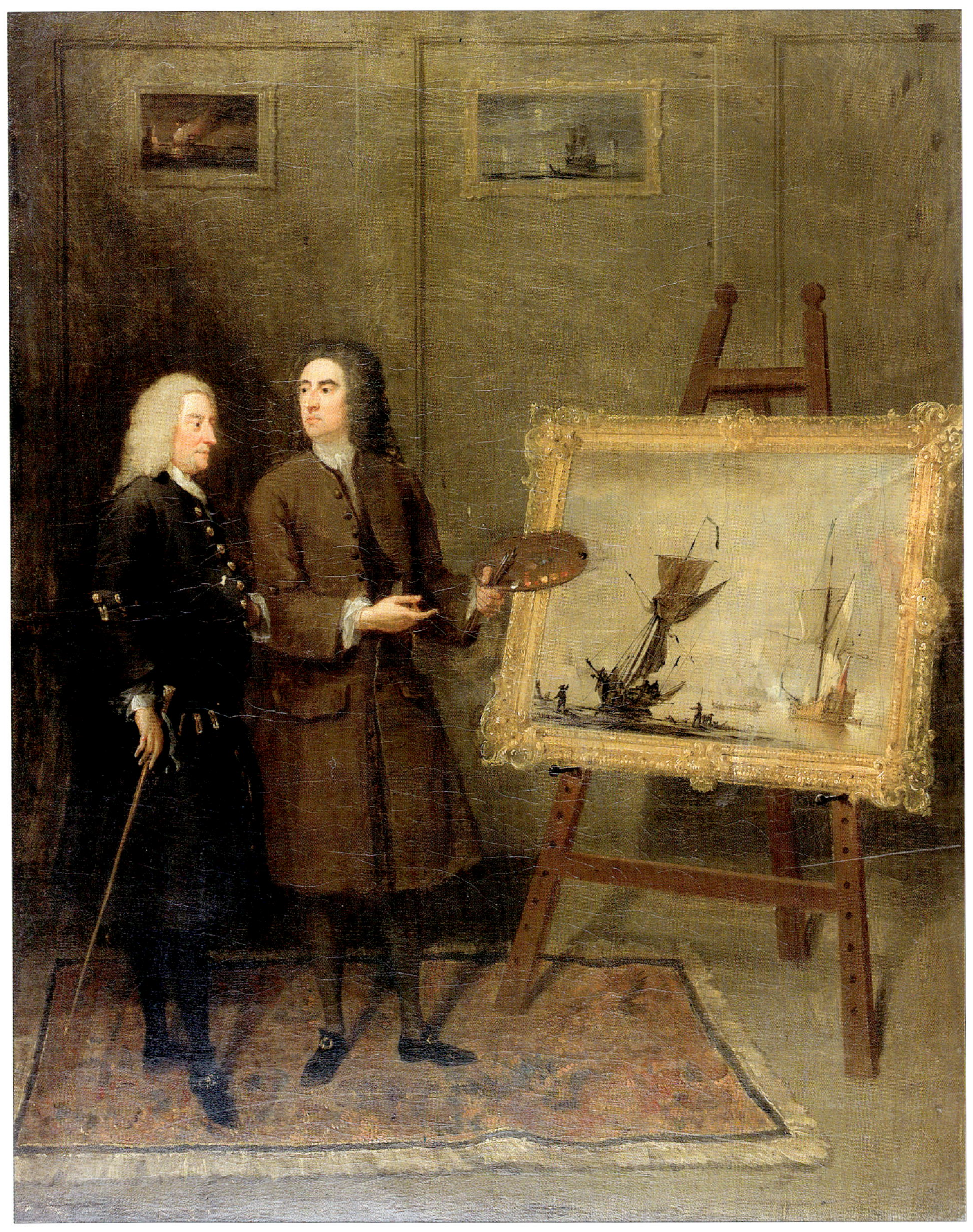

Frontispiece: *Monamy, the painter, exhibiting a sea piece to Mr. Thomas Walker, his patron. Oil on canvas. 24in. x 19in. By William Hogarth.*　PRIVATE COLLECTION

The painting on the easel is a good example of one of Monamy's 'commercial' calms and is signed by him. Hogarth did this painting about 1730. On the wall in the background there are two other small seascapes by Monamy. Mr. Walker was a Commissioner of Customs and a noted art collector. Monamy and Hogarth were friends and contemporaries, and they collaborated in producing this picture.

PETER MONAMY

1681 – 1749

AND HIS CIRCLE

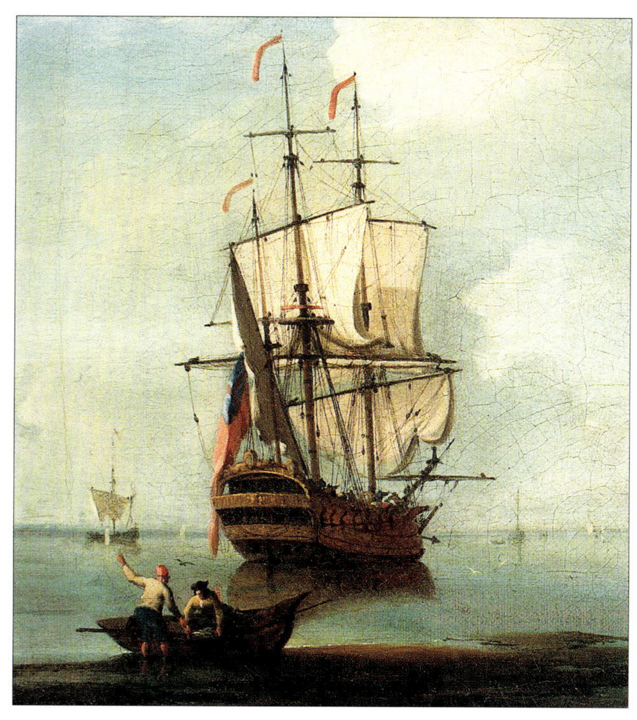

F.B. COCKETT

ANTIQUE COLLECTORS' CLUB

British Library Cataloguing-in-Publication Data
A catalogue record for this book is available from the British Library

Printed in England
by the Antique Collectors' Club Ltd., Woodbridge, Suffolk
on Consort Royal Satin paper
supplied by the Donside Paper Company, Aberdeen, Scotland

Contents

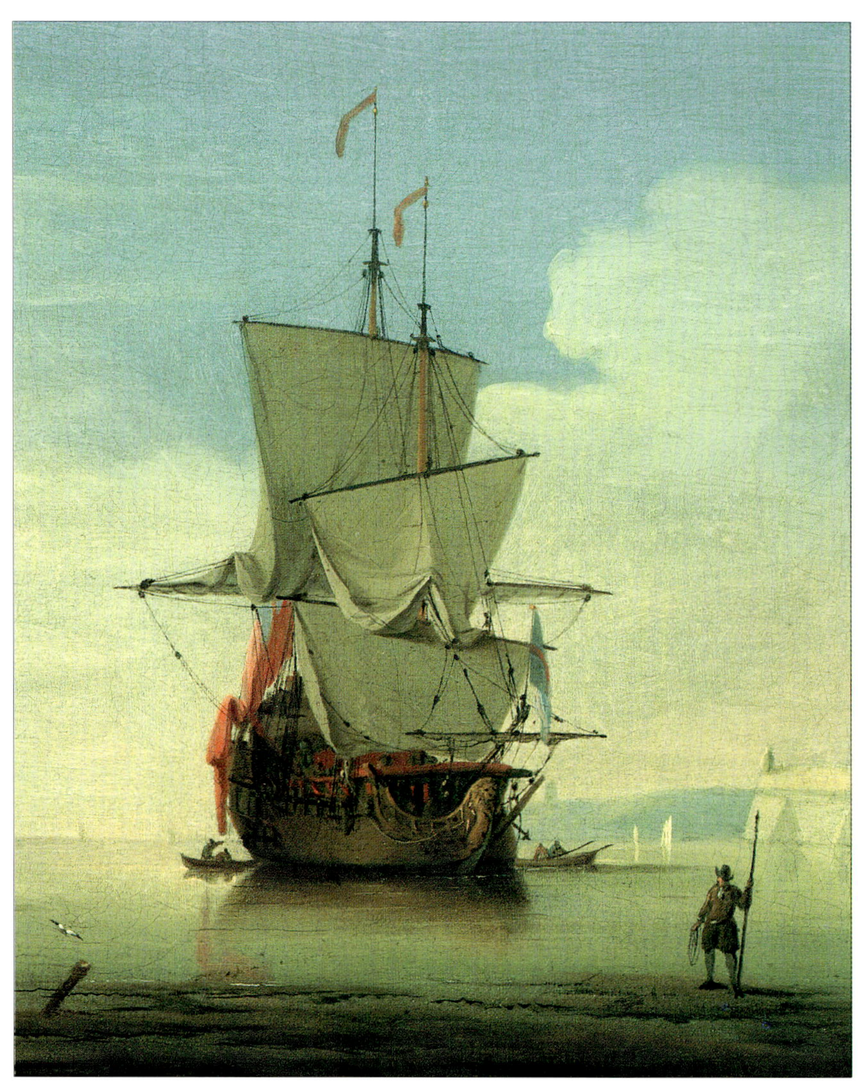

Detail of Colour Plate 35.

Acknowledgements

In the course of hunting for Peter Monamy's paintings, and trying to obtain either good photographs or, even better, colour transparencies, I have had wonderful cooperation. A wide variety of museums, salerooms, private owners, picture dealers and special collections have been involved, and it is a pleasure to mention them here and to thank them.

I am most grateful to Her Majesty the Queen for permission to illustrate a Monamy from the Royal Collection. The collection of the Earl of Derby and the Whitbread Collection at Southill Park have also been most cooperative.

As usual, the National Maritime Museum at Greenwich has allowed me unlimited access to their files, and they have been very generous in allowing me to use a number of their colour transparencies.

The British Museum Print Room has also been a mine of information. The Jersey Museum and Société Jersiaise have both contributed illustrations for this book.

The Worshipful Company of Painter-Stainers and the Company of Watermen and Lightermen of the River Thames have both lent important illustrations.

The Courtauld Institute of Art, and its photographic survey department, have been most helpful in taking photographs in some private collections – such as those at Goodwood House. The Witt Library also has, as usual, been a fruitful field for research.

I must add my thanks to the picture departments of the four major salerooms of London – Bonhams, Christie's, Phillips and Sotheby's.

I have had a great deal of help from picture dealers who have lent many of their colour transparencies to illustrate the book. Particular mention must be made of Richard Green, Agnews, Parker Gallery, Lane Fine Art, O'Mell Gallery, David Messum, Hahn and John Appleby of Jersey.

I owe a particular debt to Mr. Charles Harrison-Wallace, for access to his monumental research on Monamy and also for many stimulating meetings and conversations. Mr. David Cordingly and Cdr. David Joel have been very helpful in the same way.

Mr. James Taylor's recent book on marine painting has been very useful reading, as also have been E.H.H. Archibald's *Dictionary of Sea Painters* and Mr. M.S. Robinson's great two volume work on the Van de Veldes.

Finally I must thank Mrs. Doris Toms for producing a beautifully typewritten copy from my handwritten script.

My wife, Dorothea, has been a great support at all times, ranging from coming with me to see Monamy pictures all over the place to incessant proof-reading and interested criticism.

Introduction

This book is a follow-on from my first book, *Early Sea Painters,* which charted the period in England between the Van de Veldes and Peter Monamy (roughly 1680-1720). This was a time when a small wave of Dutch and Flemish marine artists came to live and work in England in the wake of the Van de Veldes. It was while pursuing the research on these rather rare and obscure early sea painters that I realised what an important figure Peter Monamy was.

He was the first English marine artist of any stature. Looking for his pictures, over about thirty years, gradually convinced me that here was a home-grown marine painter of the early eighteenth century who was immensely prolific and, more importantly, accurate and attractive. Very little seemed to be known about him and his pictures were not to be seen in our great national collections, with the sole exception of the National Maritime Museum at Greenwich. By far the greatest number of his works turned up in the salerooms, particularly the auction houses of London (Bonhams, Christie's, Phillips and Sotheby's).

By following these sales, year by year, a good photographic library of his works could be built up. Unfortunately it was soon apparent that there was a difference between many works merely 'attributed' to Monamy (which were of very uneven quality) and those which were signed and of obviously better quality which were 'true' Monamy pictures. It seemed to me that a proper study of Monamy was overdue.

The difficulty of researching an English artist of the early eighteenth century is considerable as there is very little contemporary writing about him. This was a particularly turbulent, unorganised, and chaotic period of our history. There were no organised artistic societies where artists could show their work (the Royal Academy was not available until 1768). They were completely dependent on wealthy patrons and dealers of doubtful integrity.

For many years the occasional remarks on Monamy and scraps of information found in the notebooks of Mr. George Vertue, which are fortunately preserved in the British Library, were almost the only contemporary documentary source for him.

It was not until 1983 that a serious exhibition devoted entirely to Monamy was organised and held at Pallant House Gallery, Chichester. The research for this exhibition took up a number of years and was done by Mr. Charles Harrison-Wallace. His industry and enthusiasm in searching out the details of Monamy's life and work was stimulated by the fact that he is himself a direct descendant of Peter Monamy. Mr. Harrison-Wallace has kindly made available to me the results of his research. Also our personal meetings and talks have been a powerful stimulus to me to get on and complete this small study of Peter Monamy. I have unashamedly plundered his encyclopaedic knowledge for a great deal of the information laid out in this book.

Peter Monamy's legacy to us is, of course, his actual paintings, and the best way to judge him as an artist is to look at and think about his pictures. For this reason I have assembled here a unique series of photographs of forty-five or so of his paintings, covering all his working life and the variety of his subjects. Particular care has been taken to ensure that all the photographs are of 'true' Monamys. Photographs of 'attributed' pictures, and unsigned pictures have on the whole been excluded. It is hoped that by surveying all these pictures the reader will be able to make up his or her own mind as to the competence, accuracy and attractiveness of his works.

Most of his pictures are in private collections, which is not surprising because they are so 'liveable with'. This is also the reason why his paintings turn up so frequently in the salerooms and why it is almost impossible to contemplate a full catalogue raisonné of his works at this stage.

The last two chapters of this work are devoted to 'Monamy's Circle'. This was a small group of marine artists who worked during the last years of Monamy's life and for several years after his death. They were influenced by Monamy and some of them may have actually worked in his studio in his later years, although there is no documentary evidence for this supposition.

Francis Swaine is the most important of this group and there is much evidence that he was closely associated with Monamy in his last years. Certainly Swaine absorbed a great deal of Monamy's technique and also used the same palette of colours. He was very prolific and in many cases, with unsigned works, it can be difficult to differentiate between the hand of Monamy and Swaine. However, a close study of their painting techniques and of certain tricks of composition does make this possible in most cases and these chapters do go into these aspects of recognition problems in some detail.

The same remarks apply to the four much less well-known painters who are dealt with in the last chapter. These were Thomas Mellish, T. Leemans, Thomas Allen and J. Cook. All these painters tend to appear in salerooms under the blanket attribution of Peter Monamy and it is hoped that these photographs and remarks about them may help in their future identification.

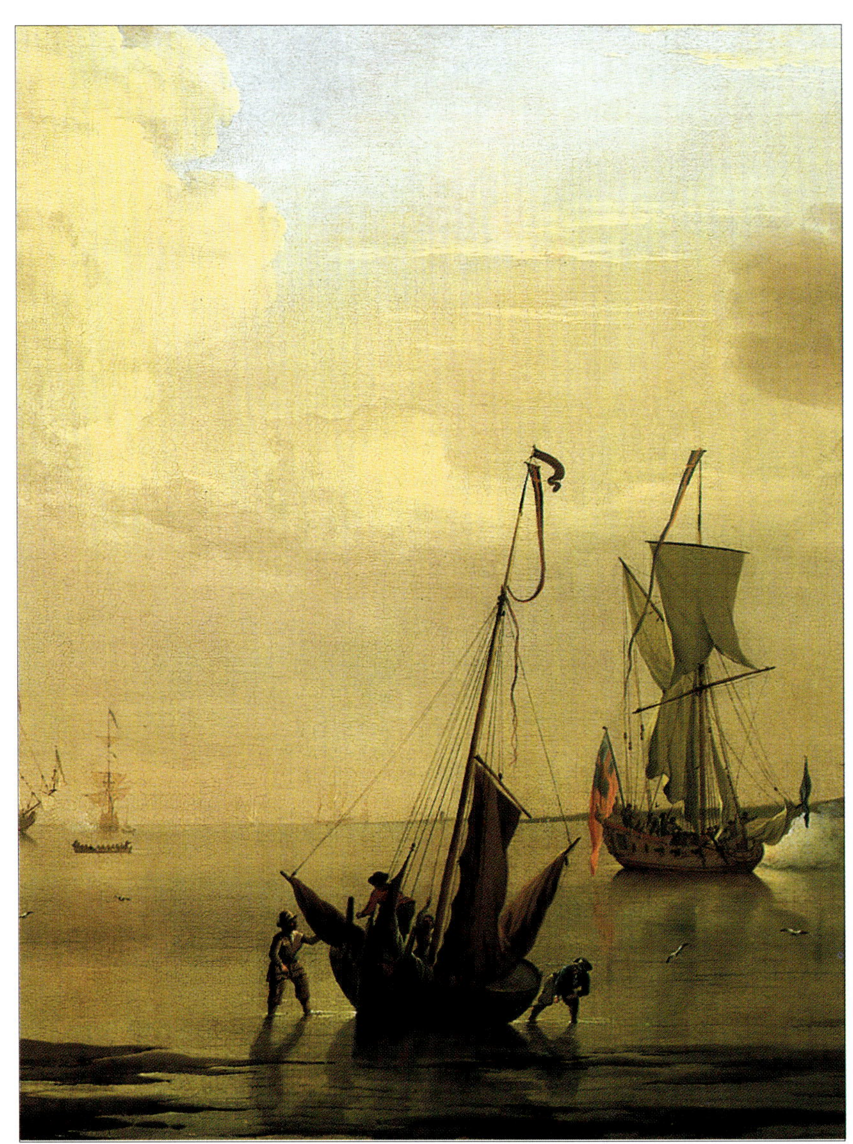

Detail of Colour Plate 34.

CHAPTER 1
Biography, Origins and Artistic Development

Peter Monamy is of considerable importance in the history of British art as the 'founding father' of British marine painting. A contemporary and friend of William Hogarth, he developed into the most attractive and competent recorder of the marine scene of the first half of the eighteenth century. In his 'great years' (roughly between 1725 and 1740) his fame was universally acknowledged.

The only contemporary manuscript references to Monamy's life and work are to be found in the notebooks of an engraver called George Vertue (which are held at the British Library).[1] Vertue was a delightful and chatty art dilettant of those times, but a little vague on matters of date and fact. He, it was, who supposed Monamy to have been born in Jersey, and indulged in conjectures about his early life. Unfortunately these mistakes and conjectures were copied by Horace Walpole in his immensely influential *Anecdotes of Painting in England* (Volume 4) published in 1780.[2] This work became the source book for nearly all subsequent art histories of those times and so these early mistakes were perpetuated for nearly two hundred years.

In 1981, however, Charles Harrison-Wallace – a direct descendant of Peter Monamy – published the results of several years of painstaking research on the family, forebears, and early life of Peter Monamy in the *Annual Bulletin of the Société Jersiaise*.[3] In 1983 he wrote the introduction and catalogue for the pioneering exhibition of Peter Monamy's works which took place at the Pallant House Gallery in Chichester that year.[4] Most of the information in this chapter is taken directly from these two publications, and the author is also indebted to Mr. Harrison-Wallace for much information imparted verbally in several conversations.

Peter Monamy was born in the Minories, a London City street running north from the Tower of London and the waterfront Custom House up to the church of 'St. Botolph's without Aldgate', where he was baptised on 12 January 1681. He was the fourth and youngest child of a certain Pierre Monamy and his wife, Dorothy.

The Monamy family history up to this point is full of variety, adventure and a certain amount of illegal entrepreneur activity (commonly known as smuggling!). The Monamys first appear in the Channel Islands records in 1540 in the person of Etienne Monamy of St. Saviour's Parish, Jersey, and it seems that they may have been early refugees from the counter-reformation in France. Etienne had two sons, Clement and André. Clement remained in Jersey, but André moved to Guernsey and founded the Monamy family there. He was a very successful Elizabethan merchant and in 1569 he bought a house which is now the Savings Bank in the High Street, St. Peter Port. He had two sons, both of whom had died by 1613, but not before one of them had fathered a son (born in 1612) who became the second notable André Monamy of Guernsey. This André grew up in puritan Guernsey and pursued the Parliamentary Cause with vigour, becoming a commissioner and Lieutenant of Militia. He was a successful merchant, with his own merchant's mark and seal dated 1654. Unfortunately, he got into financial difficulties, and on Charles II's restoration he fell from grace. His eldest son was named Pierre and he was the father of our painter – Peter Monamy.

Pierre was what one might call a 'colourful character' and, being a merchant by heredity and upbringing, he ran a sort of import-export business between the Channel Islands and Great Britain, Unfortunately he became involved with the issue of forged customs clearance documents for a ship called the *Rose and Crown* in 1676. This was the subject of an enquiry, as a result of which Pierre landed in prison for two months at the age of twenty-four. On release he appears to have continued with these activities and there are some more stories about disagreements and skulduggery among his associates. In the course of combing London for handy counterfeiters, Pierre came to mix with a number of individuals involved with the graphic arts. While consorting with these characters he met a young girl called Dorothy Gilbert who was to become his wife and our artist's mother. Since there is no hint of the smallest tendency towards art in the Monamy family before this, we may suspect that Peter inherited his talent from the Gilberts.

As Pierre had no fixed address at this time it seems likely that he and Dorothy moved in with the Gilberts and lived with them in the Minories during their early married life. They had four children: one son, who died during infancy and then Ann born 1678, James born 1680 and finally Peter in 1681. They were all baptised in the same church in the Minories.

Little is known about Peter's childhood until 1696, when he was fifteen. In this year the Binding Book of the Painter-Stainers Company records: 'Peter Monamy, Son of "Pierre" Monamy of London, Merchant, bound to William Clarke for seven years by indenture'.[5]

His father, Pierre, whatever the legality of his activities, seems to have been prosperous enough to place his son as apprentice in this prestigious city company, to ensure that he got a good education and grounding in his chosen career. At this time the status and power of the city livery companies was very high and there was no better way of ensuring a good start in life than an apprenticeship of this kind. William Clarke, who was actually Master of the Painter-Stainers in 1687, was well known and respected, having two trade establishments, one on London Bridge and another in nearby Thames Street, in which Peter would have worked. He is sometimes described as being a 'house-painter', but the modern meaning of this term, envisaging repetitive laying on of paint on walls, ceilings and window frames etc., gives an entirely false impression. His work would have involved elaborate decoration on ceilings (such as Thornhill's work at Greenwich), paintings on canvas inset into wall panelling or mirrors, painting on wood panels on coaches and inn signs, and possibly some decorating and even gilding in ships in London docks.

Seven years' apprenticeship under such a master must have given him great experience in the technical basic skills of an artist such as the handling and mixing of paints, simple rules of drawing and picture design, and a certain commercial awareness. Apprentices were not free to marry until completion of their term and soon after Peter was 'made free' on 1 March 1704 he married a girl called Margaret. A daughter was born in 1706 and christened at St. Olave's church in Bermondsey. Both mother and child must have died because on 9 January 1707 Peter married his second wife, Hannah Christopher, at Allhallows, London Wall. He was aged twenty-six at this time.

George Vertue's notebooks make reference to Monamy's early interest in marine subjects. He speaks of Monamy's 'early affection to drawing of ships and vessels of all kinds' and goes on to say: 'by constant practice he distinguisht himself and came into reputation − besides his industry and understanding in the forms and buildings of shipping with all the tackles, ropes and sails etc. which he thoroughly understood made his paintings of greater value besides his neatness and clean pencilling of sky and water by many was much esteemed especially sea faring people officers and other marchants'. These 'seafarers and marchants' were particularly Channel Islanders, with whom he had a strong connection, through his family background, which he maintained throughout his life. In particular there was the remarkable Durell family of Jersey, who produced seven Captains, a Lieutenant and a Vice-Admiral of their name during the eighteenth century alone. They intermarried with the Saumarez family of Guernsey who also were a distinguished seafaring family. From 1726 onwards, for over two hundred years, there was always at least one officer on the Navy List named Saumarez.

Scions of these distinguished Channel Islands families served in all the main naval actions of the early eighteenth century (Philip Saumarez was Lord Anson's First Lieutenant on his famous voyage round the world, 1740-1744). As Peter Monamy came into artistic reputation, they would have been his friends, supporters, collaborators and patrons.

The years between 1704, when he was 'made free', and about 1720 or so are often referred to as his 'journeyman years'. There is much speculation but little well-documented knowledge about what he was doing during those years. He emerged in his middle and later period (roughly 1720-1740) as the most accomplished and famous English marine painter. How did he acquire this superb ability and technique?

Being a journeyman means that he was free to hire himself out for his skills to whoever wished to employ him. There was plenty of artistic 'house decoration' work going on at the time which required help from skilled young hands. Antonio Verrio was just finishing the decoration of Hampton Court; Sir James Thornhill (a fellow Painter-Stainer pupil) was busy on the great ceiling and wall decorations of the Painted Hall at Greenwich. Monamy might well have been employed on this sort of project, but we do know that at some time in his early years he became fascinated with the painting of ships and marine scenes.

In 1707 the great Van de Velde the Younger died, thus bringing to an end the workshop at Greenwich known as the Van de Velde studio. His two main assistants here for the last ten years or more had been his son, Cornelis Van de Velde, and another Dutch painter called J. Van der Hagen. This studio had become a sort of picture factory during its last years, turning out large numbers of 'versions' and 'copies' of Van de Velde pictures which were very popular and commanded a ready market. After Van de Velde's death, both Cornelis and J. Van der Hagen left the Greenwich studio and worked in London as independent marine artists for many years, continuing to produce Van de Velde type pictures and many copies and versions of Van de Velde subjects. Young Peter Monamy must have known about them and may even have been associated with them in some way. In fact Vertue refers to his 'imitations of Van de Velde and other famous Dutch masters'. Certainly the evidence of his known paintings points to some influence from this quarter. Isaac Sailmaker was also active in London right up to 1721 when he died at the great age of ninety-one. He lived and worked at his house at Kings Bench Walk, as Vertue put it, 'where he painted to his last'.

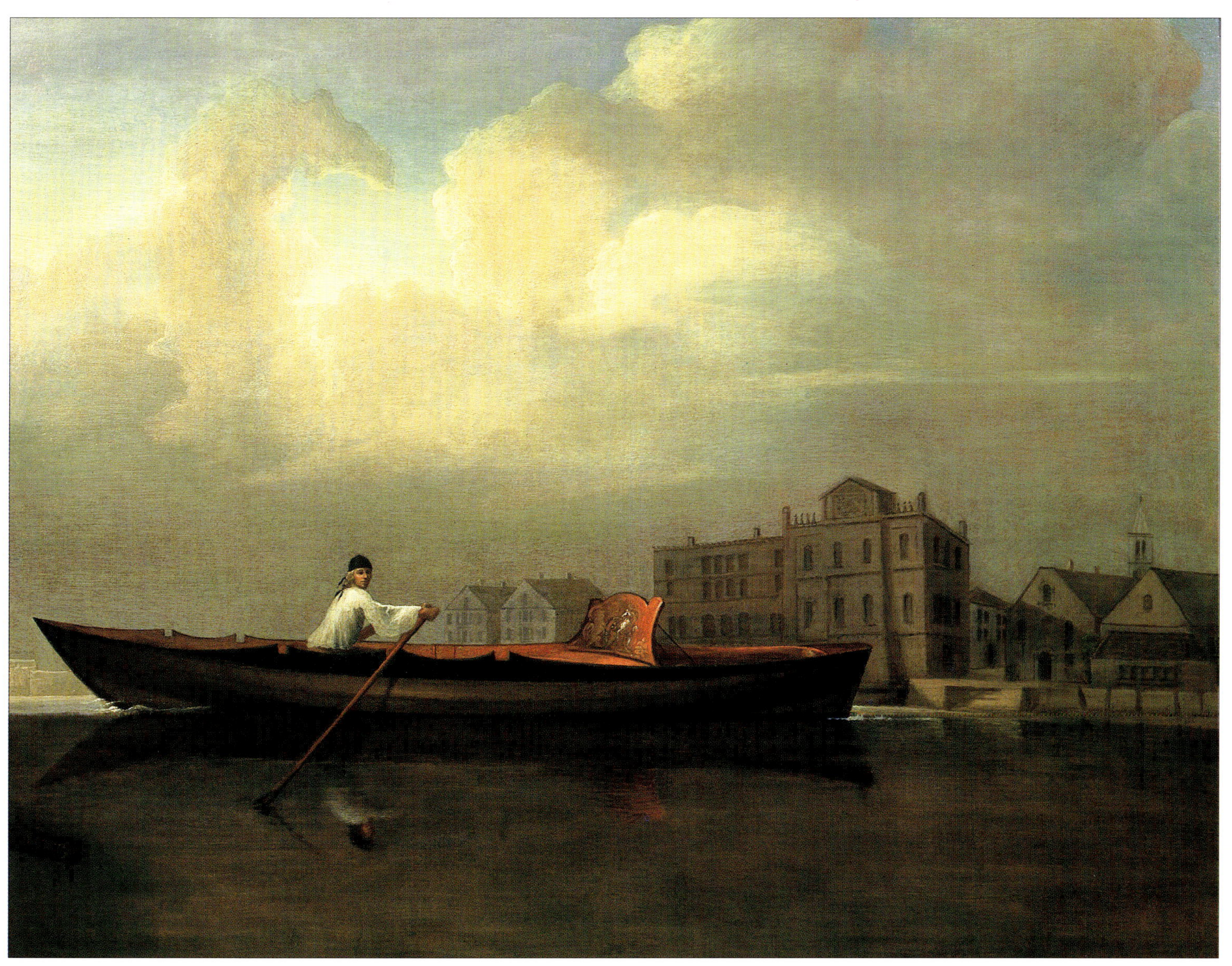

Colour Plate 1. *First Winner of Doggett's Coat and Badge Race, 1 August 1715. Oil on canvas. 33in. x 42in. Signed P. Monamy.*
COMPANY OF WATERMEN AND LIGHTERMEN OF THE RIVER THAMES

This little picture is the first signed and definitely known painting by Peter Monamy and is still in the Watermen's Hall in London. In the background is the original Watermen's Hall which the company moved to in about 1701.

Thomas Doggett was manager of the Haymarket Theatre and in 1715 he gave a prize to commemorate the accession of George I on 1 August. A traditional waterman's coat and badge was awarded to the winner of a race from London Bridge to Chelsea in a waterman's skiff against the tide! In the painting the arms of George I (Hanover) are prominently displayed on the backrest of the skiff. A skiff in those days weighed at least a ton, and the race took about five hours. The race is still held every year, but in a modern light rowing skiff.

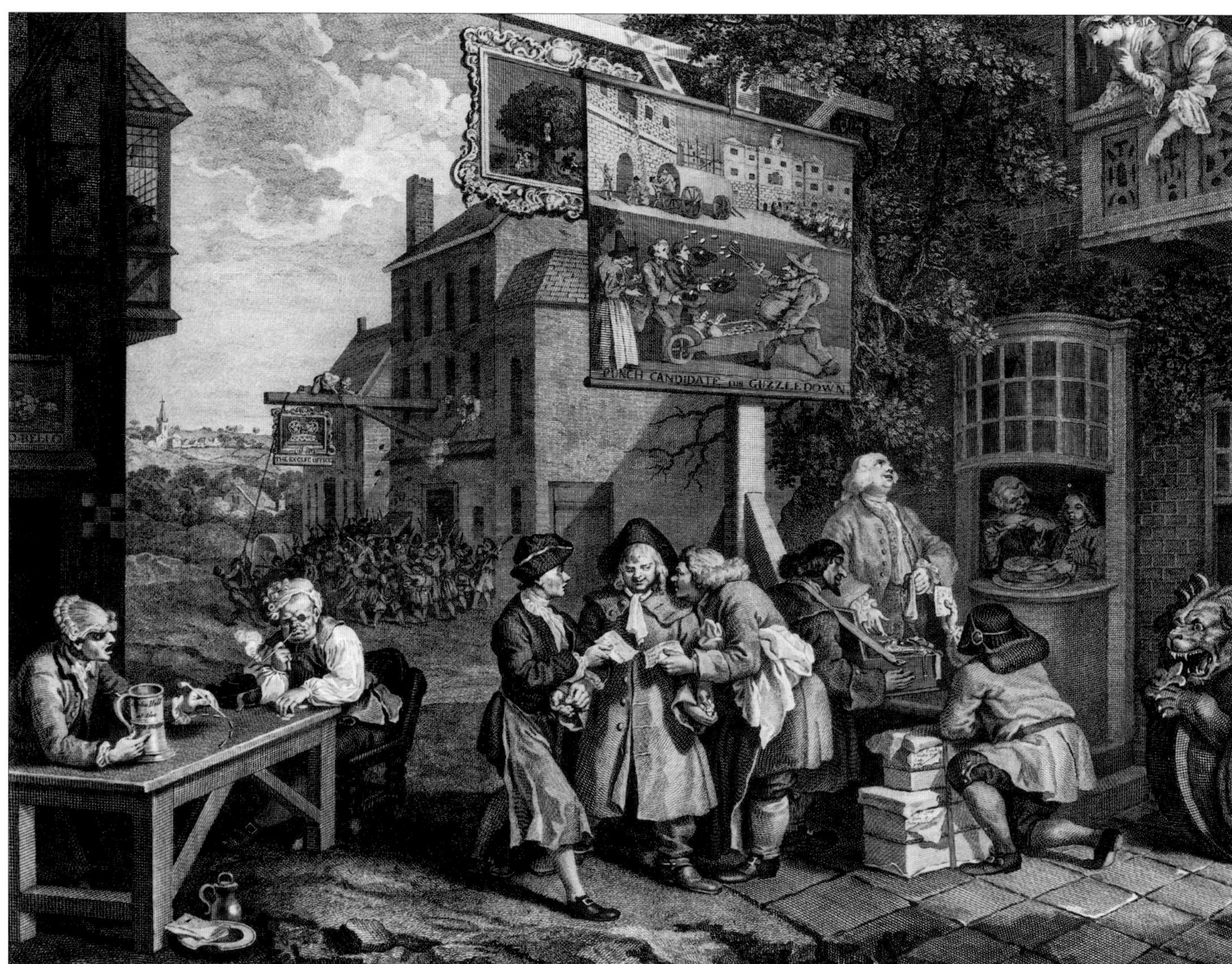

Plate 1. *This is No. 2 of Hogarth's 'Four prints of an election', issued in 1757. It is included here to illustrate the importance of the painting of inn signs and shop signs generally. These would have been an important part of Monamy's work, especially in his early days. On the left of this print, in the margin, is an inn sign of the 'Porto Bello', with a ship painting which may well have come from Peter Monamy's studio!* BRITISH MUSEUM

Apart from all these influences he must have had plenty of minor employments in the way of painting inn signs and house and shop interiors (Plate 1).

The most important landmark in his professional life was in 1726 when he became a Liveryman of the Painter-Stainers Company and he presented them with 'a valuable sea piece of his own painting'. This very large work on canvas (it is about 7ft. x 5ft.) hangs there to this day (Plate 2). It is of great importance in assessing the progress of Monamy's work because it is the first marine painting which we know is indubitably by him and was

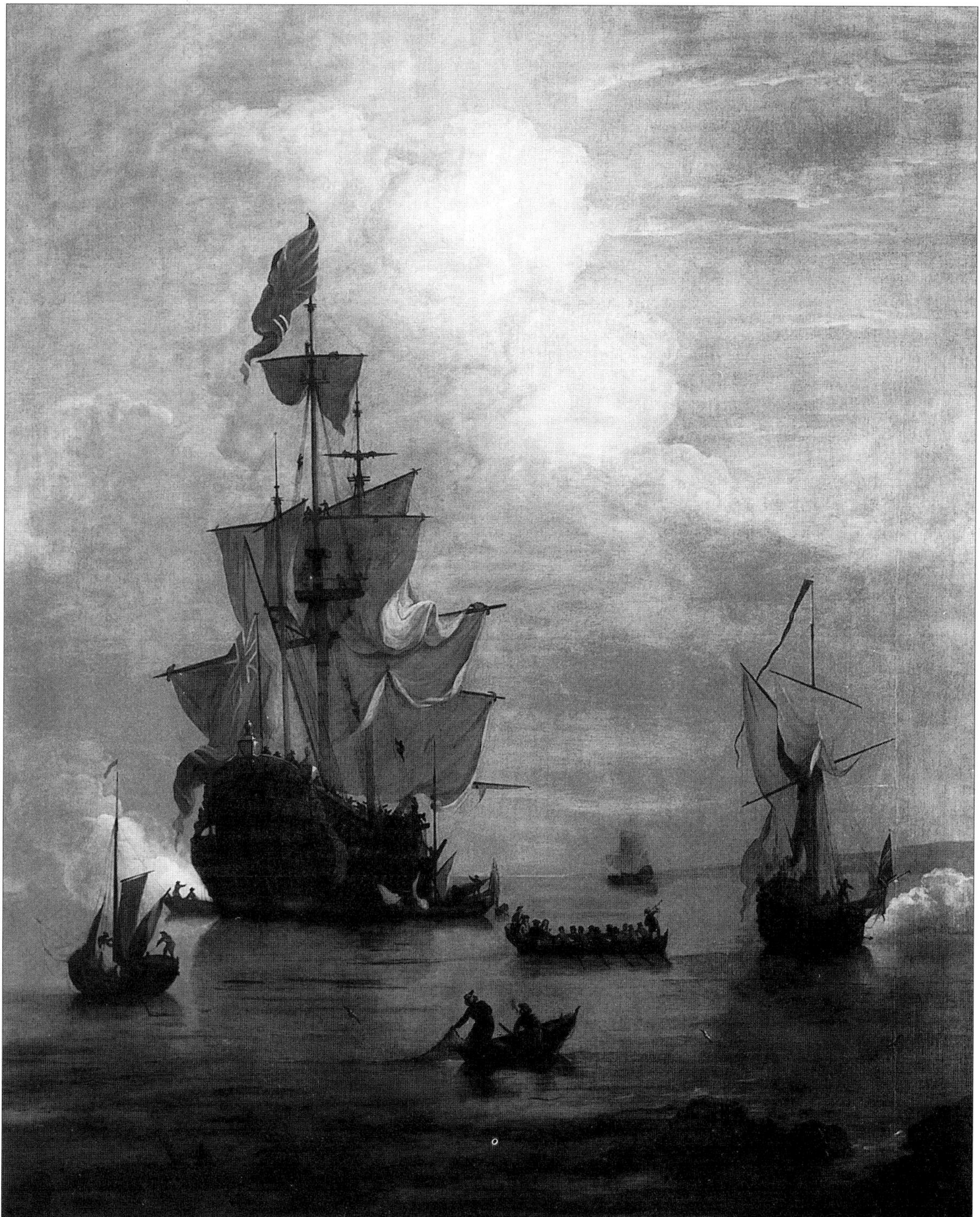

Plate 2. This is the large picture of the Royal Sovereign, *stern quarter view, which Peter Monamy presented to the Painter-Stainers Company in 1726 on the occasion of his being made a liveryman of the company. Oil on canvas, 7ft. x 5ft. Not signed. It is a very big picture indeed.*
THE WORSHIPFUL COMPANY OF PAINTER-STAINERS
The composition derives closely from the younger Van de Velde's painting of the Royal Sovereign of 1703. This painting, however, is conceived specially as a large decorative wall painting and the brushwork is very loose − it is designed to be viewed from a distance rather than close up.

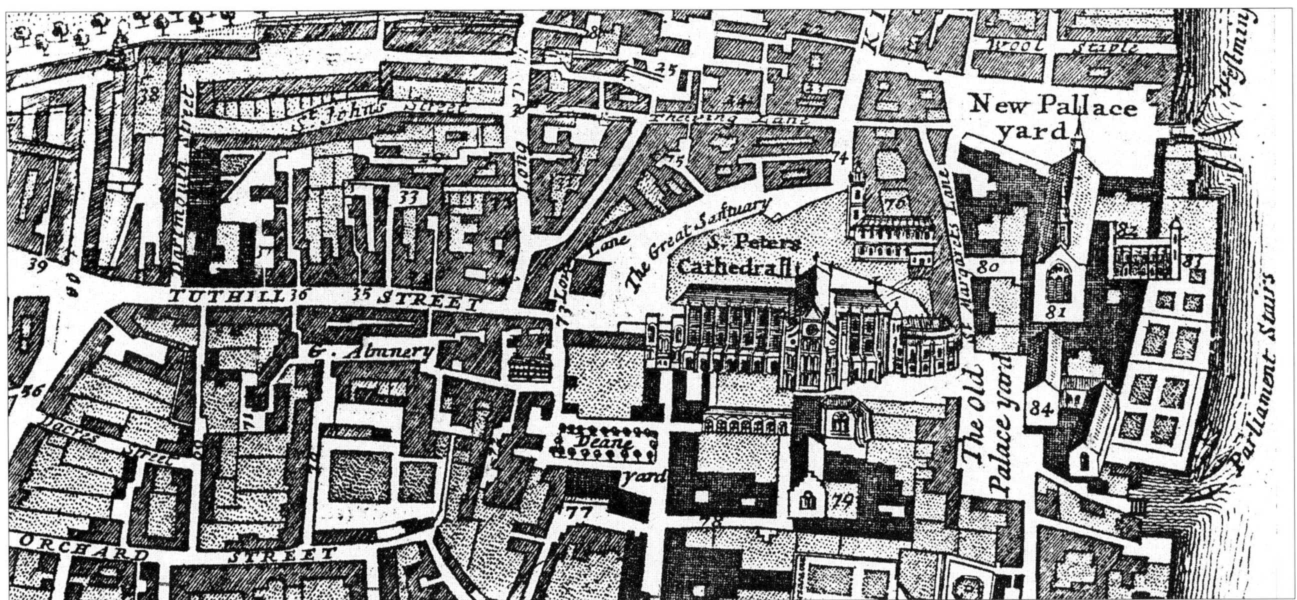

Plate 3. *Map of St. Margaret's Parish, 1720.*
73: The Gate House. 76: St. Margaret's Church. 80: Fish Yard. 81: Westminster Hall.
82: The Exchequer. 83: House of Commons. 84: House of Lords.
Peter Monamy's house was almost exactly where Oliver Cromwell's statue now stands
outside the House of Commons.

done when he was aged forty-five. It marks the period when he was 'coming into fame' as the country's best and most well-known marine painter. From about 1720 onwards signed and occasionally dated pictures by him begin to multiply and his own painting style and palette becomes much more obvious.

During his journeyman years Peter and Hannah must have moved lodging more than once. A first child was baptised at St. Botolph's in 1708, then another in 1709 at St. Mary, Whitechapel, Stepney. A third child was baptised in 1712 at the same church. All three must have died young, an example of the appalling infant mortality of those days. Between 1712 and 1720 they had one daughter, Mary, who survived. Then in 1723 the Westminster rate book records the appearance of a certain 'Peter Monyman' in 'Fish Yard' near Westminster Abbey. Shortly after this, in 1725, the St. Margaret's parish register records the baptism of Ann, the last child of Peter Monamy.

Fish Yard, which has now disappeared, was within the precincts of the old Palace of Westminster, very near the spot where the statue of Oliver Cromwell now stands (Plate 3). It is interesting to note that many of his Channel Islands relations and friends, particularly members of the Durell family, lived nearby in Westminster, which provides the possible motive for his choosing to live there. This was where he lived, with his wife Hannah and his two daughters Mary and Ann, until his death in 1749.

At this time (c.1725) his reputation was spreading and he could afford to

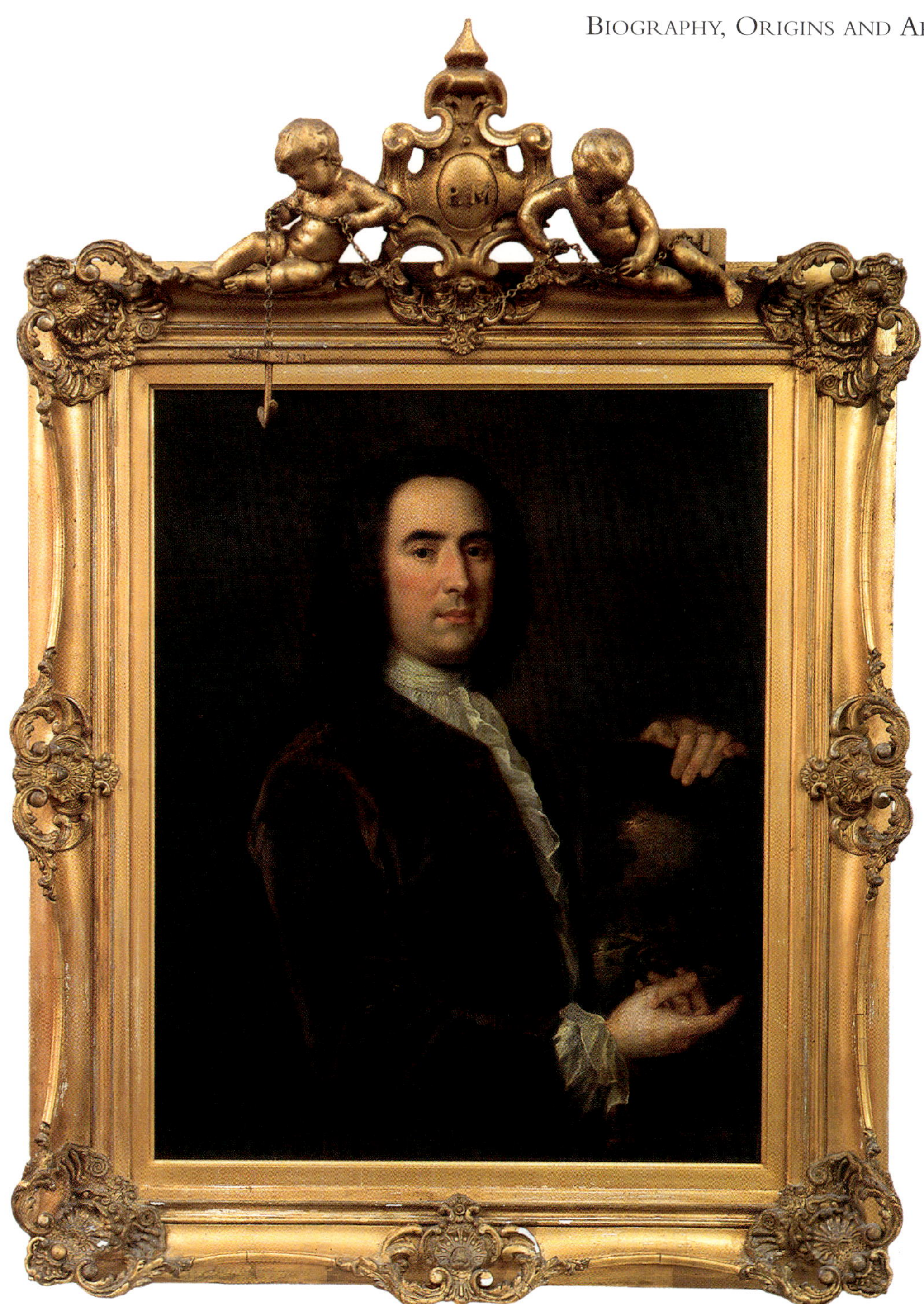

Colour Plate 2. *Portrait of Peter Monamy by Thomas Stubley, c.1730. Oil on canvas, in its original profusely carved frame.* PRIVATE COLLECTION

travel. Vertue records that 'he made many excursions towards the Coasts and Seaports of England to improve himself from Nature…'.

At the age of fifty Monamy was uniquely famous, and 'to remember his fame', says Vertue, 'his picture was painted and done in mezzotint print'. This portrait, an excellent work by Thomas Stubley, now hangs in a private collection in Jersey, in a rather spectacular frame adorned with appropriate maritime type carving (Colour Plate 2).

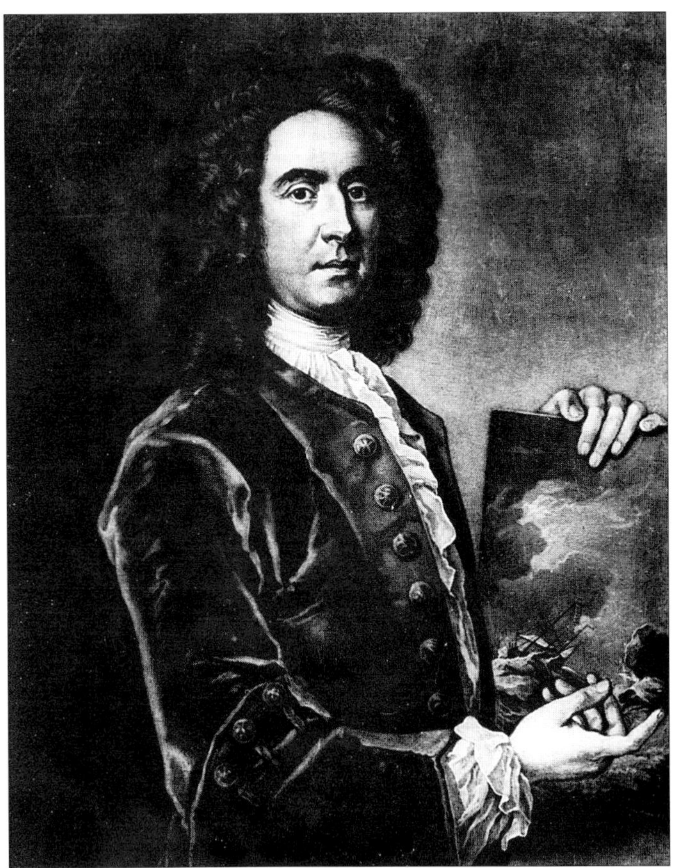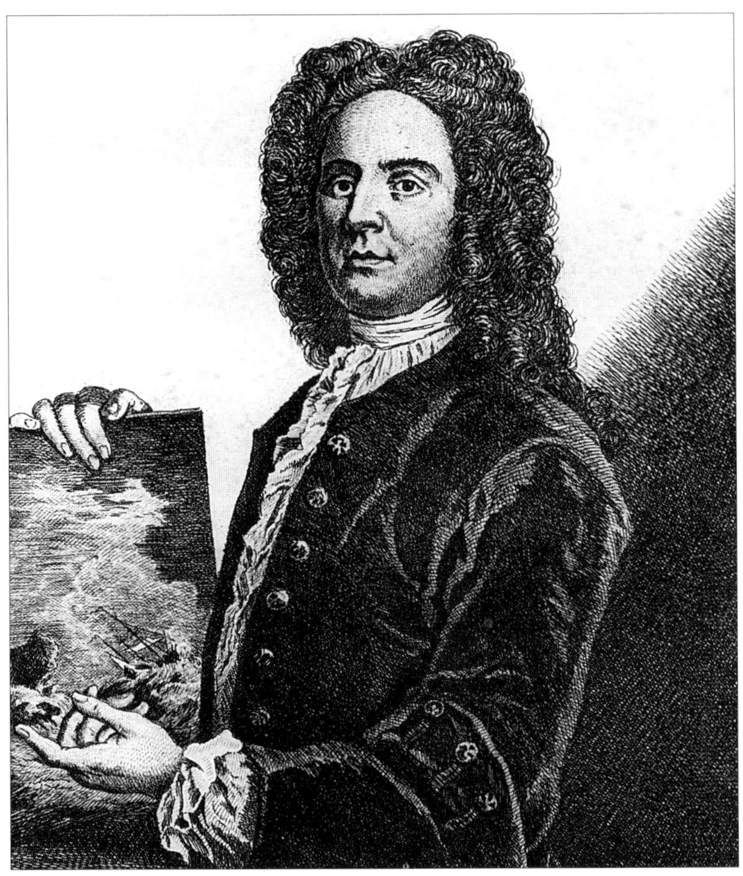

Plate 4. *Prints of the Monamy portrait.*
On the left is the fine mezzotint engraving, taken directly from the portrait, by John Faber junior, the most prolific and famous mezzotinter of the day. Done in 1731. The legend below reads 'Petrus Monamy / Navium et Prospectum Marionorum Pictor: / Vandeveldo Soli Secundus'. Monamy holds his own typical rough sea painting in his hands.

On the right is the later etching (1771) done by James Bretherton, taken in reverse from Faber's mezzotint, to illustrate Walpole's Anecdotes of Painting *(published 1780, fourth volume).*

FABER PRINT MR. HARRISON-WALLACE, BRETHERTON PRINT SOCIÉTÉ JERSIAISE

The mezzotint print was done by John Faber junior, the most prolific and prominent mezzotinter of the day. It shows a handsome man, and the legend below it reads 'Petrus Monamy / Van de Veldo oli Secundus' (Plate 4). The claim, second only to Van de Velde, was not unreasonable, more or less stating that he was *first* among living marine artists.

Very soon after the production of the portrait and mezzotint, William Hogarth, then aged thirty-three, collaborated with Monamy in producing a very interesting and now well-known painting entitled 'Monamy the painter showing a sea-piece to his Patron, Mr. Thomas Walker' (see Frontispiece).

Monamy himself painted and signed the 'sea-piece' on the easel in the picture. Mr. Thomas Walker was a Commissioner of Customs and a noted art collector of that period who owned several Van de Veldes and

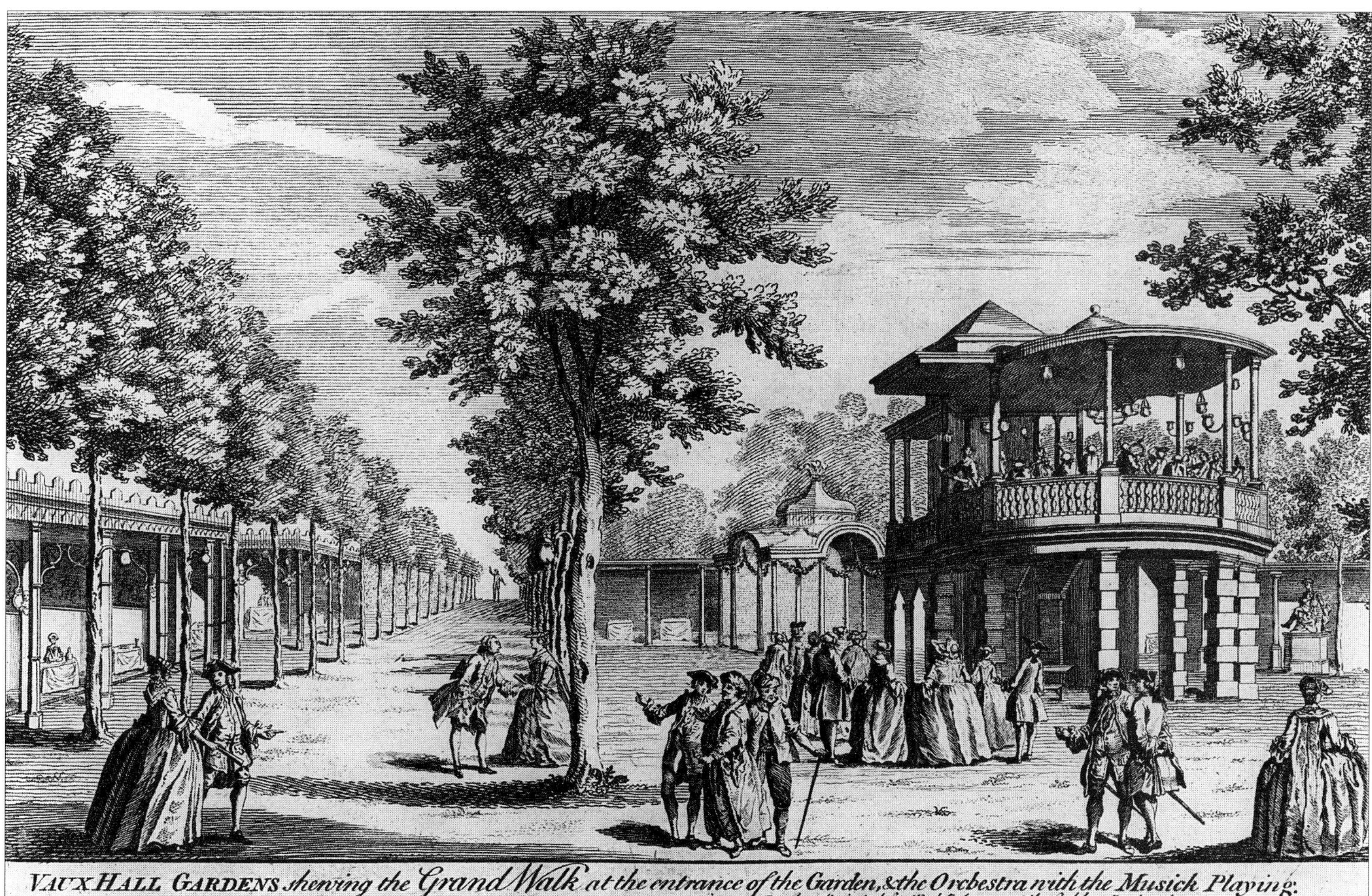

Plate 5. *Print showing the 'Grand Walk' of the new Vauxhall Gardens, about 1750. Notice the little 'Pavilions' or 'Boxes' on the left. These were where fashionable patrons could sit and have drinks or a meal and generally see and be seen by the promenading crowd. In the three 'boxes' on the left a large painting has been hung on the wall for decoration, and this was the way in which Monamy's four 'Vauxhall' paintings would have been hung.* BRITISH MUSEUM

who probably commissioned this picture. It was once owned by Horace Walpole, but is now in the collection of the Earl of Derby.

By this period (roughly 1730-1745) Monamy was at his peak and his paintings were much in demand. He had by this time developed his own recognisable mature style (and the proliferation of prints and engravings after his pictures attests his success). The next major episode in his professional life was the invitation to provide four paintings for the new Vauxhall Pleasure Gardens which had been reopened in 1736. These gardens were immensely fashionable, lavishly laid out, and had as part of their design a number of 'pavilions' or 'boxes' where patrons could meet or sit and dine while watching (and being seen by) the passing throng (Plate 5). These boxes were partly enclosed and each one was decorated

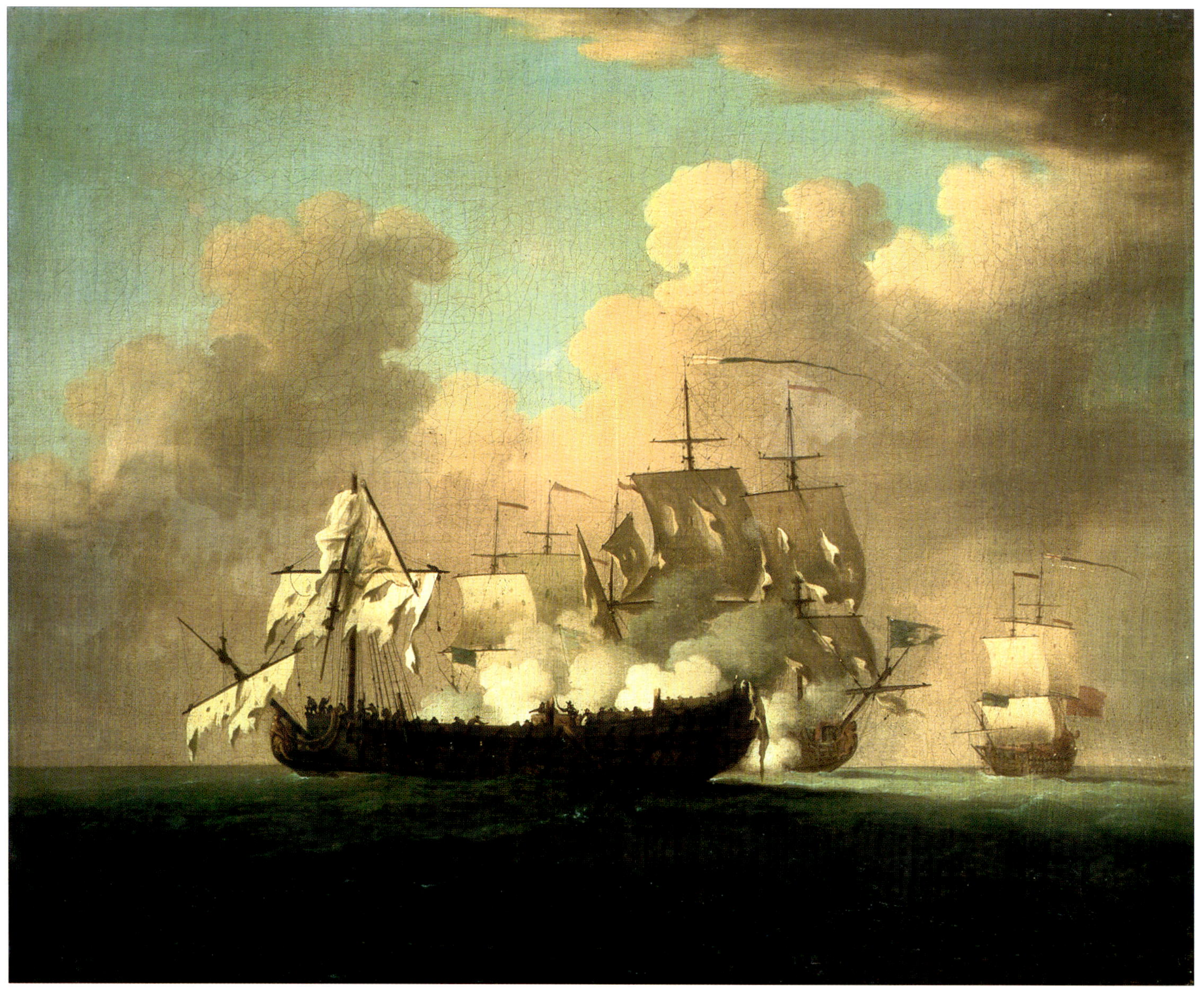

Colour Plate 3. *The Capture of the* Princesa, *1740. Oil on canvas. 15in. x 20in. Signed P. Monamy.* PHILLIPS, THE INTERNATIONAL FINE ART AUCTIONEERS, UK/ BRIDGEMAN ART LIBRARY

This painting is one of at least three known versions, one of which is in the National Maritime Museum Collection.

Captain Thomas Durell of the Kent *fought a historic duel with the* Princesa, *one of the larger ships in the Spanish Navy. This action was much acclaimed and was the subject of a popular ballad at that time.*

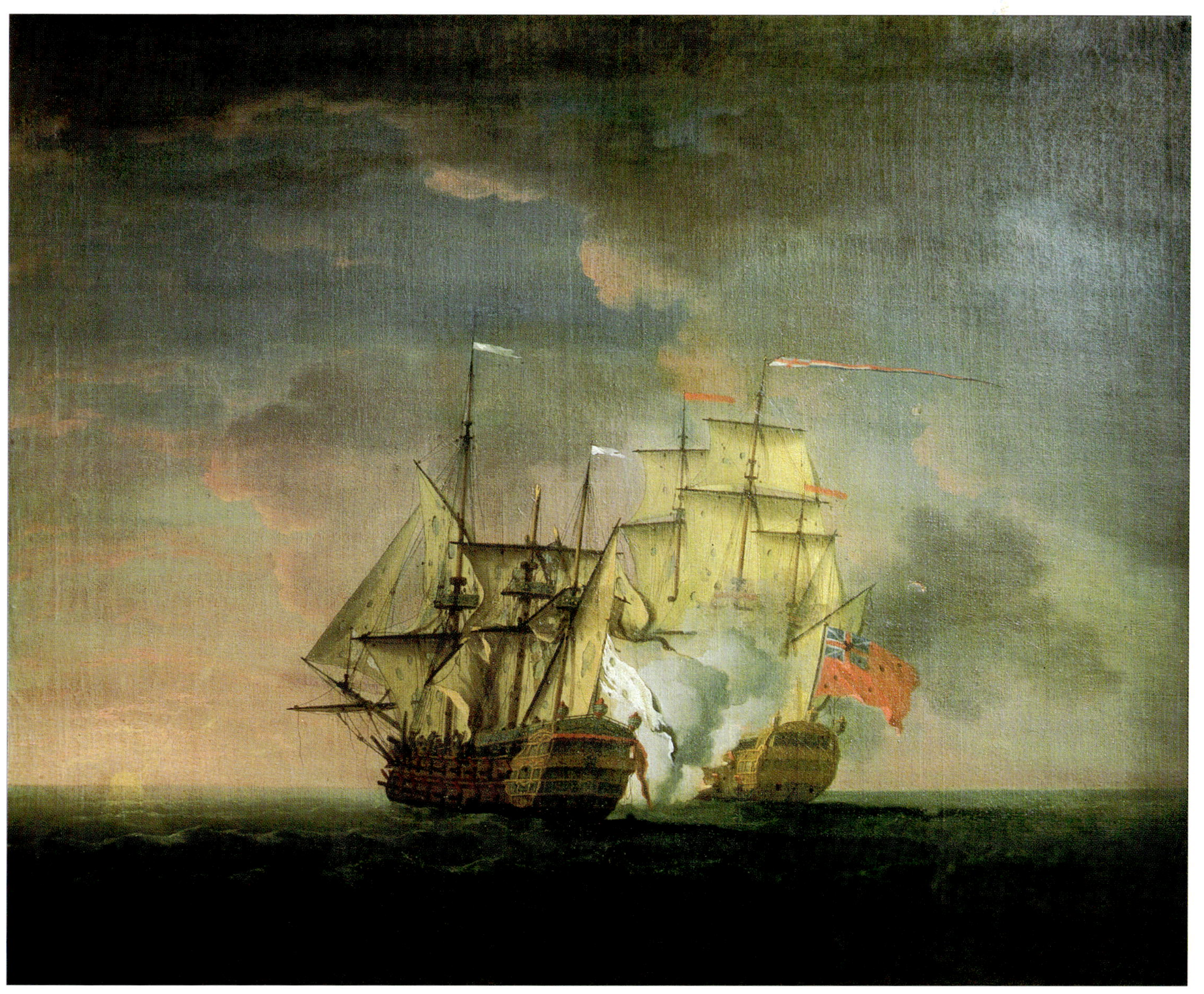

Colour Plate 4. *Capture of the French ship* Mars, *64 guns, by H.M.S.* Nottingham, *60 guns, commanded by Captain Philip Saumarez, 1746. Oil on canvas.*

PRIVATE COLLECTION

This was probably the last painting done by Peter Monamy before he died. Although ill and infirm, he must have made a special effort to do this as Capt. Saumarez was a Guernsey man, friend and remote connection of the Monamys.

with a large painting by a notable English artist of the time. Peter Monamy (aged fifty-five), William Hogarth (aged thirty-nine) and Francis Hayman (aged twenty-eight) were the three artists asked to contribute works.

Peter Monamy contributed four important paintings: 1. 'A sea engagement between the English and Algerine pirates'; 2. 'The capture of the San Joseph, a Spanish ship, in 1739'; 3. 'Sweet William's Farewell to Black Eyed Susan', an illustration to a song by John Gay of *Beggar's Opera* fame; and 4. 'Admiral Vernon's Capture of Porto Bello, 1739'.[6]

These paintings were done as part of a sort of patriotic festival, as at this period nationalistic feelings and pride were running high. They also gave Monamy a much needed exposure to the general public and thereby helped his success. The paintings themselves have not survived but prints of all four were made and can be seen at the British Museum (see Chapter 4).

For the last ten years of Monamy's life England became engaged in a war which was very largely a naval war. In 1739 the so-called 'War of Jenkins' Ear' began, merging into the greater conflict known as the 'War of the Austrian Succession' (1739-1748). This at last brought a number of special commissions to Peter Monamy recording specific actions. Pictures of the taking of Porto Bello (1740) and various frigate actions, such as the taking of the Spanish ship *Princesa* by Captain Thomas Durell of the *Kent,* appeared from his studio (Colour Plate 3). It is notable that in most of the actions of this war either the Durells of Jersey or the Saumarez family of Guernsey were closely involved as naval officers. These families were friends of Peter Monamy and probably started most of the historic commissions flowing to him. Lieutenant Philip Saumarez was Commodore Anson's first lieutenant on his historic voyage round the world in 1740-1744 in the *Centurion.* Shortly after returning from this he was appointed Captain of the *Nottingham* and in October 1746 he fell in with a French ship, the *Mars,* superior in size and guns. He fought a memorable duel with the *Mars* and eventually captured her. Monamy's painting of this action was probably his last picture and it hangs in Saumarez Manor, in Guernsey, to this day (Colour Plate 4 and Plate 6).

By this time, 1741, Monamy was sixty years of age and was beginning to feel the weight of his years. Vertue records a note about Monamy a little later, saying he had 'run thro' his Time about 60 years of age being decayed and infirm some years before his death'. However, he was actively working right up to his death in 1749, with the two rising stars of the marine painter firmament, Samuel Scott and Charles Brooking, hard upon his heels.

Monamy's death, says Vertue, 'happened at his house at Westminster at the beginning of February, 1748/9 – leaving many paintings begun and

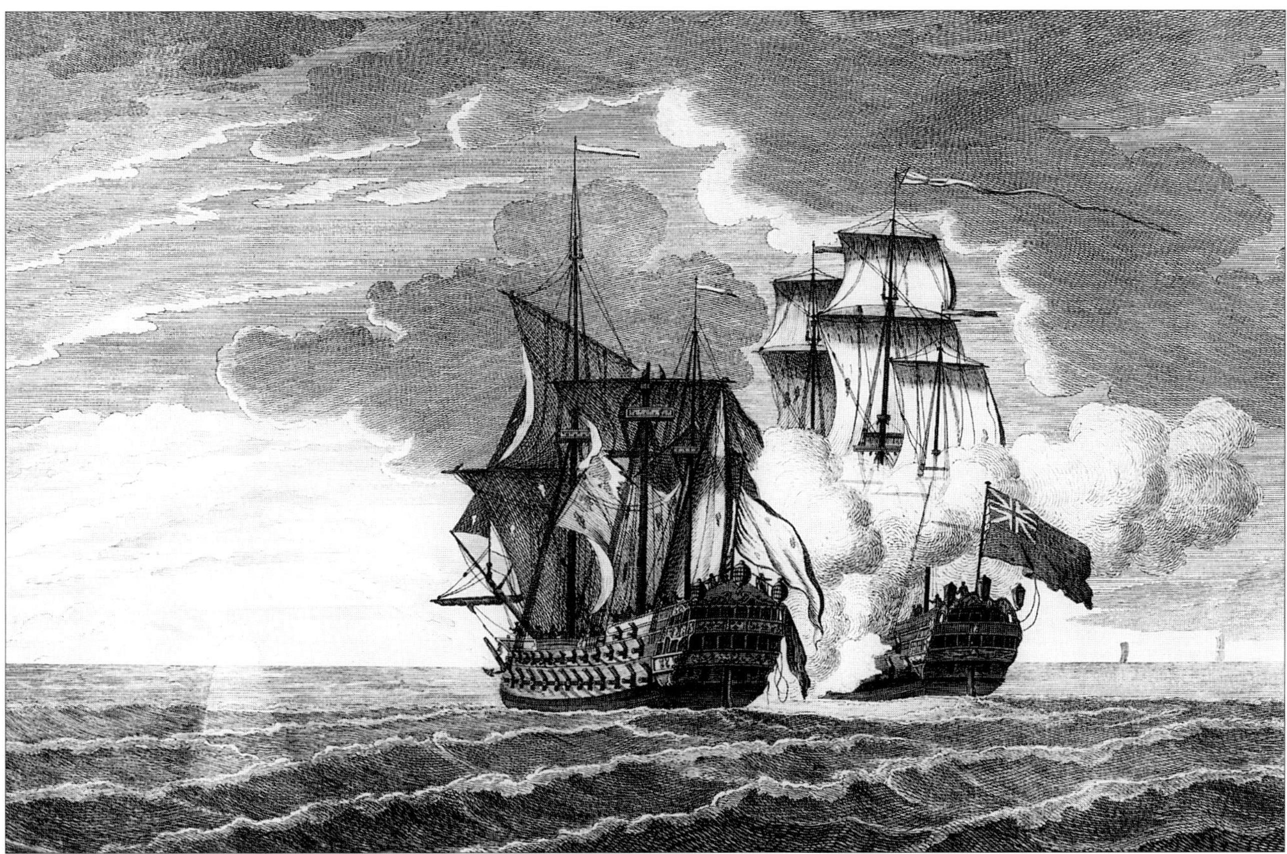

Plate 6. *This is the print of the action between the* Nottingham *and the* Mars *made by Swaine after Monamy's original painting. It was published in 1794, forty-eight years after the original action! This gives some indication of how these heroic single ship actions caught the imagination of the public.*   BRITISH MUSEUM

unfinished. His works being done for dealers at moderate prices – kept him but in indifferent circumstances to his end'. He was buried at St. Margaret's church on 7 February 1749.

A few months later, on 29 June, Mary Monamy, who was presumably Peter and Hannah's other surviving daughter, married Francis Swaine at Allhallows, London Wall. Their second child, a boy, was born in 1754, and was named Monamy Swaine. Both Francis and Monamy Swaine were marine artists and it seems likely that Francis in fact inherited Peter Monamy's unfinished works via Mary. He certainly continued to paint very much in the Monamy style.

Finally, we must quote a notice from the *General Advertiser* of 26 July 1750:[7]

> By virtue of a distress, tomorrow, the 27th. inst. the household furniture, pictures and china of Mr. Peter Monamy, sea painter deceased at his late dwelling house, next to King Henry VII Chapel in Old Palace Yard; likewise his collection of prints and drawings, amongst which are many of William Van der Velde Senior and Junior. The whole collection will be

> exhibited to view this day to the time of sale which will begin at 11 o'clock precisely. The whole to be sold in one day. N.B. the prints, drawings and models will begin selling at six in the evening. The house is to be let with good vaults opening in the street.

Although Peter Monamy enjoyed reasonable success in his lifetime, and was able to pursue an adequate life style, it is evident from the above that his fortunes declined somewhat at the very end and Hannah had money problems after his demise. It is nice to record that she was awarded a share of the profits of the first exhibition of the Society of Artists at Spring Gardens in 1754, amounting to ten guineas. The three children of Charles Brooking received a similar sum.[8]

A few years before he died Peter Monamy received the ultimate accolade for a British marine painter, namely an invitation from the trustees of the Foundling Hospital to become a governor and present one of his 'pieces' to be hung there. Captain Thomas Coram, a retired sea captain with philanthropic interests, set up the Foundling Hospital in 1739 and secured its Royal Charter.[9] William Hogarth, a founder governor of the hospital, conceived the idea of making the walls of its court room and public areas a sort of forum for distinguished English painters actively working at this period. It was in fact the first public gallery in England specifically for encouraging and showing the works of the rising new generation of English artists. Fifteen notable English artists were asked to contribute – amongst them were Hogarth, Gainsborough, Monamy, Scott and Brooking. Monamy delivered his painting the year before he died and it was duly hung. Unfortunately, it has been mysteriously 'missing' since 1909 and its present whereabouts is uncertain, whereas Brooking's masterly contribution is still there, in its original place, to be enjoyed by all and sundry.

——❖——

1. George Vertue's Notebooks – British Library.
2. Horace Walpole: *Anecdotes of Painting in England* (new edition London 1888).
3. Charles Harrison-Wallace: *Bulletin* of Société Jersiaise (1981, Vol. 23, Part l. pages 97-114).
4. Charles Harrison-Wallace: *Peter Monamy 1681-1749. Marine Artist* (Pallant House Exhibition Catalogue, 1983).
5. Minutes of the Society of the Company of Painter-Stainers, the Guildhall, London (M.S.S. 5667—9).
6. Alan Russett: 'Peter Monamy's Marine Paintings for Vauxhall Gardens', *Mariners Mirror* (Vol. 80, February 1994).
7. *General Advertiser* 26 July 1750. From *Mid-Georgian London* by Hugh Phillips.
8. *Marine Painting,* James Taylor, Studio Editions Ltd., 1995.
9. Ruth McClure: *Coram's Children. The London Foundling Hospital* (Yale University Press 1981).

CHAPTER 2
The Historical Background to Monamy's Life as a Marine Artist

Aknowledge of the main historical events and social background of the first half of the eighteenth century is a great help in understanding and appreciating Monamy's work.

The Monamy years (1681 to 1749) were turbulent times which saw the rise of England to the status of a world power. This was based particularly on her naval strength, her rapidly growing mercantile marine and thus her increased trading ability which led to the rapid growth of her vigorous colonies.

These colonies and trading posts, which had been established fairly recently in North America (Virginia, New England and Nova Scotia), in the Caribbean Islands and in India, were growing in importance. In addition, naval bases were established in the Mediterranean (Gibraltar and Minorca), in India (Madras and later Calcutta) and in odd islands such as St. Helena and Antigua.

This rapidly growing colonial expansion was, of course, disputed by other European powers, particularly Holland, Spain and France, and this led to numerous local quarrels and clashes of strength, apart from formal 'declared wars', which kept the navy busy, on and off, for most of the eighteenth century. In addition to this there was an increase in piracy (particularly in the Caribbean) and in smuggling of all sorts. All merchant ships embarking on long voyages therefore had to be armed and often were formed into convoys under naval protection.

Peter Monamy's working life spanned the first half of this rather lawless century. Born in 1681, during the last years of Charles II's reign, he was eight years of age when Catholic James II fled to France, to be succeeded by the invasion and accession of William of Orange leading to the Protestant reign of William and Mary from 1689 to 1702.

It was during this relatively peaceful interlude (at least in England) that Monamy was apprenticed to William Clarke of the Painter-Stainers Company at the age of fifteen for a period of seven years. When he was 'made free' in 1704 he was twenty-two years of age and now had the licence to work for himself and to give his own talent free rein. As we have

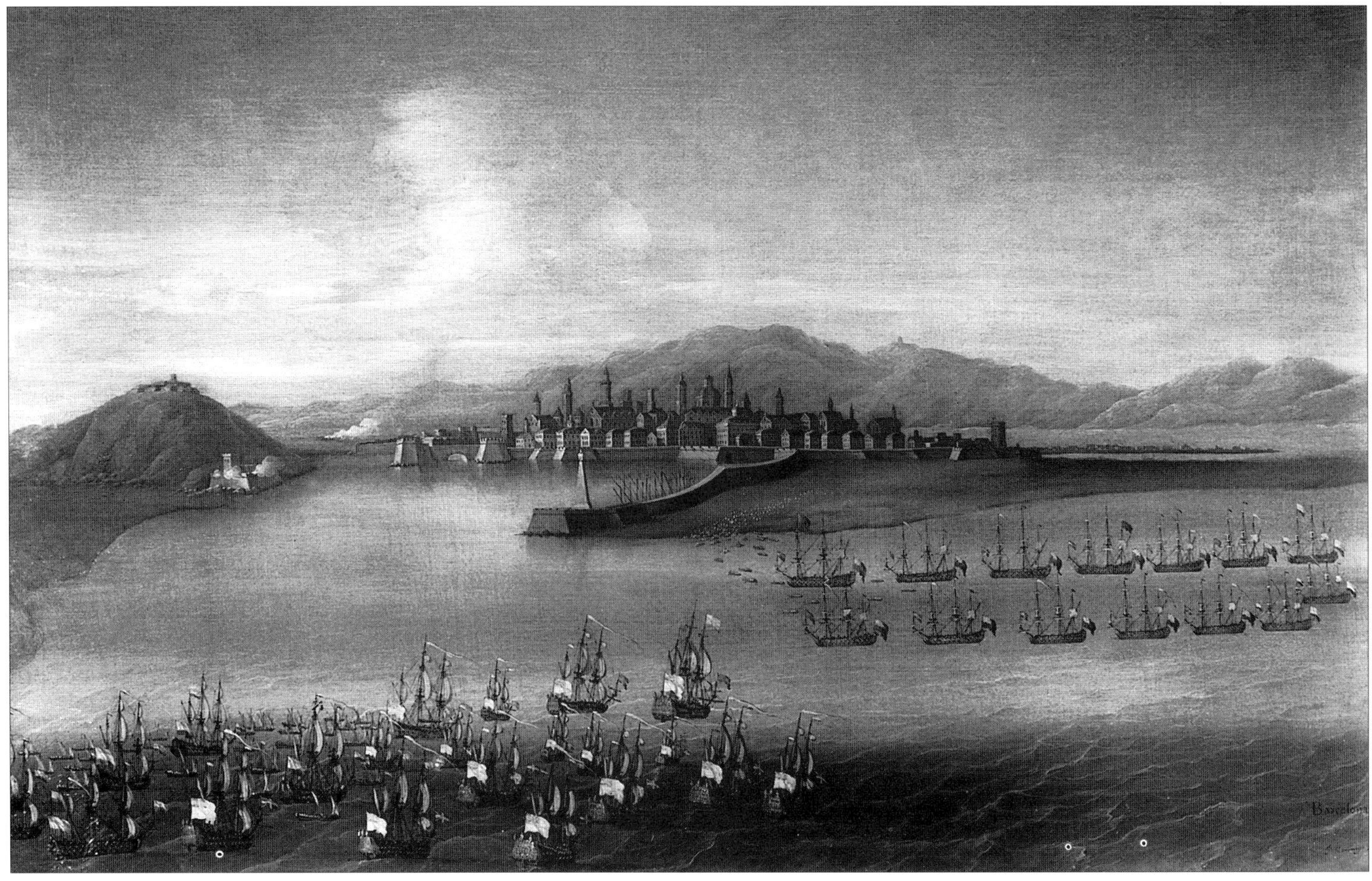

Plate 7. *The Relief of Barcelona, May 1706. Oil on canvas. 36in. x 53in. Signed P. Monamy Pinxit. and dated 1725.* PRIVATE COLLECTION.

PHOTOGRAPH COURTAULD INSTITUTE OF ART

This and the next three illustrations are scenes from the War of the Spanish Succession (1702-1713) and represent actions in which Admiral George Byng, later 1st Viscount Torrington, took part. The pictures were all commissions from Torrington around 1725, many years after the actions depicted took place. They were painted for Torrington (and were probably personally directed by him!) after he retired and bought a mansion at Southill Park, in which the paintings were to hang. They are still hanging there to this day.

This painting shows the relief of Barcelona after the French had attempted to retake it. Byng's squadron is seen lined up just outside the mole, landing soldiers in some small boats. Byng is about to round the mole and start his cannonade. There is an exceedingly detailed original description of all four paintings at Southill, giving the name and position of every ship taking part.

seen in Chapter 1, it is not known why or when he began to take an active interest in painting ships and marine scenes – it must have been fairly early in his career. The great Van de Velde, whose studio dominated the field of marine art in England, died in 1707. His studio continued to produce Van de Velde type pictures for a time, but inevitably there was an opportunity for a new younger artist to step in and produce marine pictures.

As a marine artist he would be expected to produce pictures of the great ships and of the naval occasions and naval actions of his time. This recording function of an artist was extremely important in these 'pre-photography' times and so we must take a look at the main political events during his working life, with particular reference to maritime events and sea battles.

The War of the Spanish Succession 1702-1713

In 1702, when Queen Anne came to the throne, the War of the Spanish Succession broke out and it dragged on until 1713.[1] This war is mainly famous in the history textbooks for the campaigns against Louis XIV's generals carried out by Marlborough and Prince Eugène between 1703 and 1706 which culminated in the great victories of Blenheim and, later, Malplaquet. This all had the effect of relieving the pressure on the Dutch Netherlands and generally curbing the aggressive power of Louis XIV of France. However, there was a series of quite major and successful naval actions during this war which were later to call for commemorative pictures from English marine artists among whom, of course, Monamy was prominent.

In 1702 a strong Anglo-Dutch fleet was sent to the Mediterranean with the idea of capturing a major port to act as a base for the Mediterranean fleet. This force, under Sir George Rooke, failed to take Cadiz, but shortly after this got wind of a large Spanish treasure fleet which had arrived in Vigo Bay. Rooke attacked and destroyed this fleet in an action known as 'The Battle of Vigo Bay'. (A picture of this action was painted by Ludolf Backhuysen.)[2]

The following year (1703) Sir George Rooke was again sent out and after combining with Sir Cloudesley Shovel's channel fleet he attacked and took Gibraltar, thus at last achieving the goal of having a strong British naval base in the Mediterranean.

In 1704, however, the French, under the Compte de Toulouse with fifty-one ships of the line, attempted to retake it. The combined Anglo-Dutch fleet under Rooke and Shovel met the French just off Malaga. This resulted in the only fleet action of the war – the Battle of Malaga.[3] After severe fighting the French were driven off and Gibraltar was secure for the British. (This action was later commemorated by pictures from both Monamy and Sailmaker.)[4]

Next, in 1705, Barcelona was captured after a short siege, supported by a

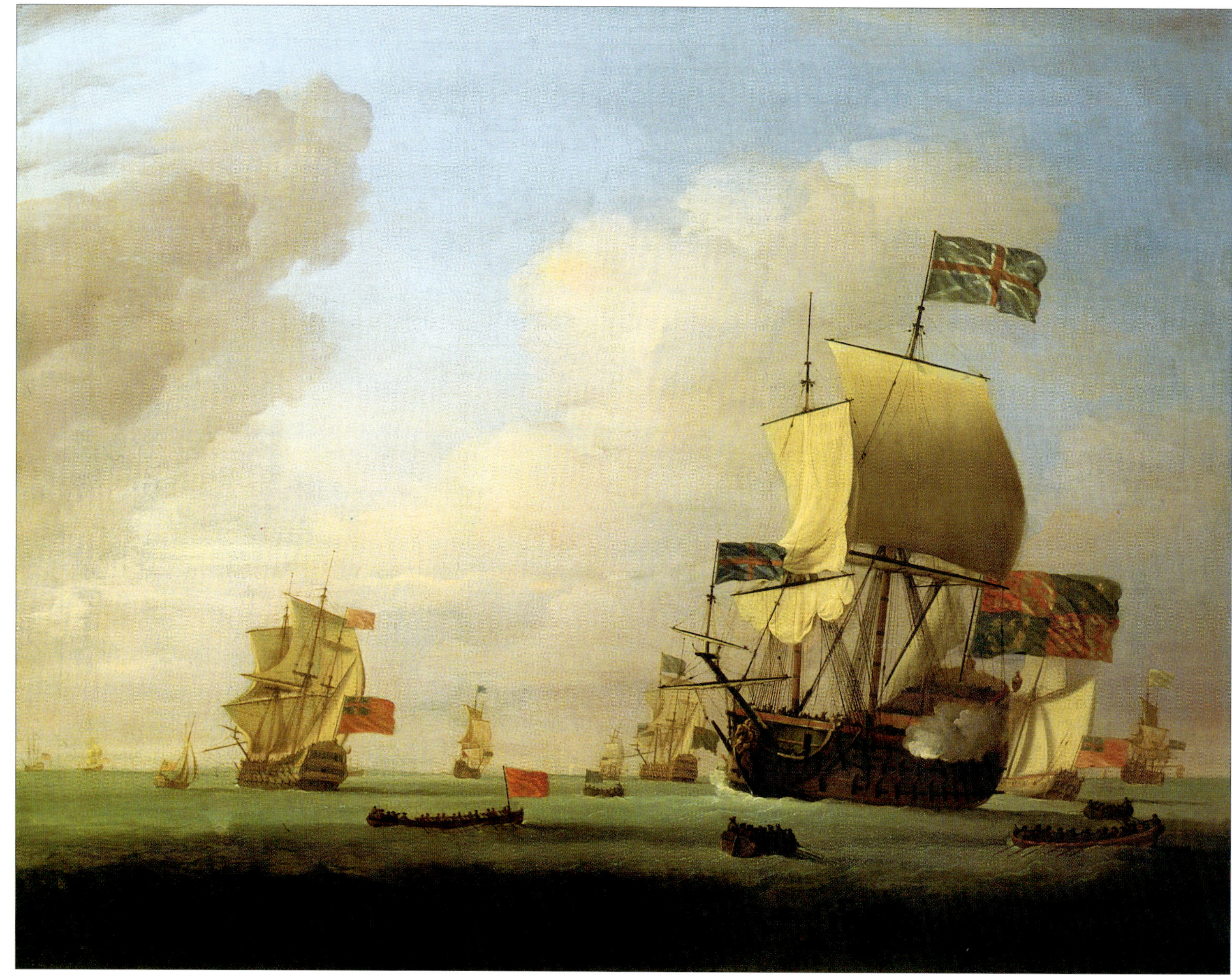

Colour Plate 5. *The* Albemarle *(80 guns), flagship of Sir John Leake, coming to anchor in the bay of Barcelona 15.5.1708, calling a council of war on board, prior to the capture of Minorca. The picture shows the Royal Standard hoisted on the stern jackstaff, which is the signal for all commanding officers to come aboard for a conference. 40½in. x 50in. Signed P. Monamy.*
SOTHEBY'S LOT 5, 3.5.95

strong fleet under Shovel. Again in the following year a strong attempt to retake it by the French was foiled by Sir John Leake's timely arrival with a fleet containing troop reinforcements. A little later there was an attack on Alicante, from the sea. Admiral Sir George Byng was prominent in all these actions and he later became an important patron of Peter Monamy. He gave Monamy commissions to paint pictures commemorating all the

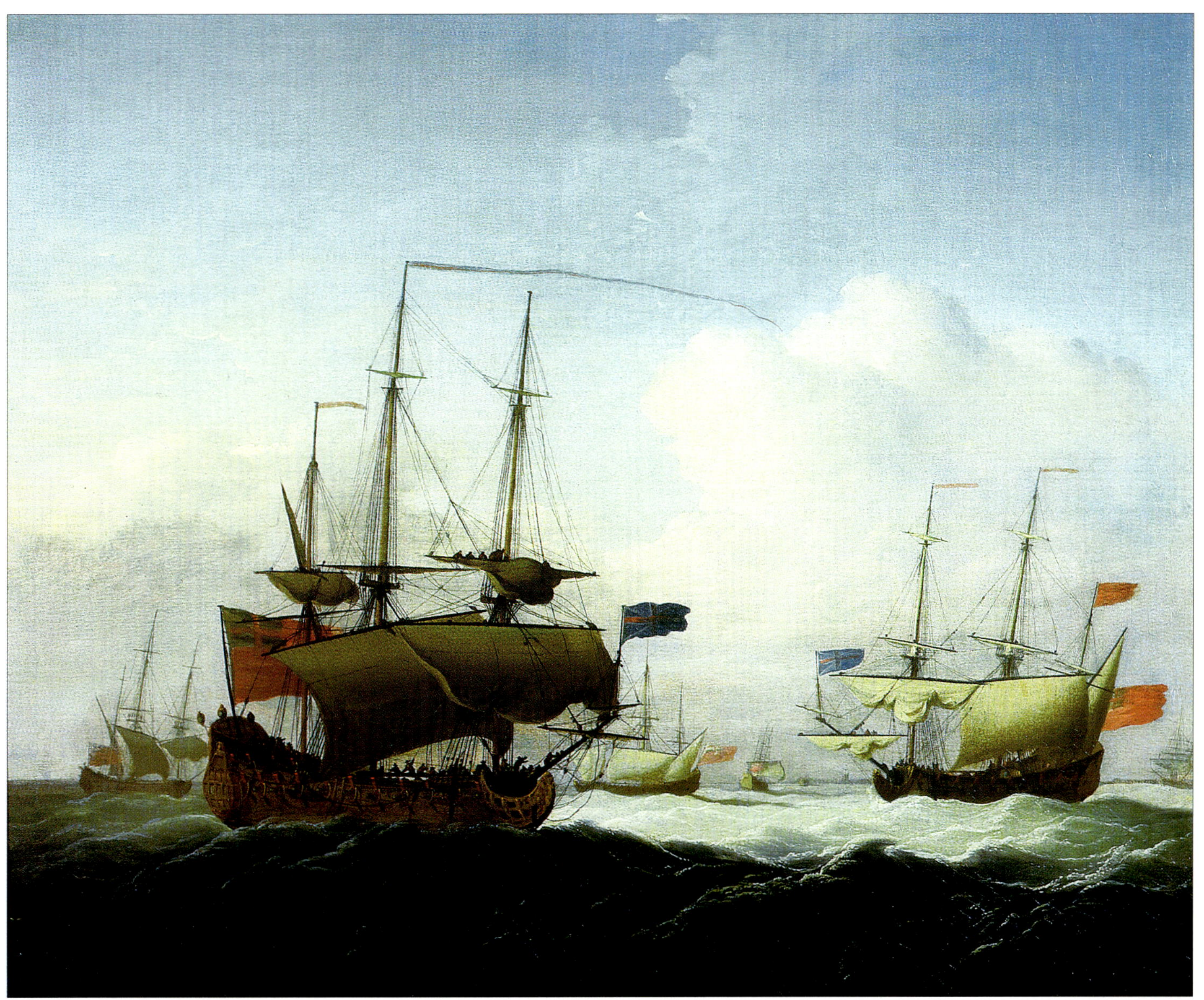

***Colour Plate 6**. 'The Privateer Squadron, known as the Royal Family, raised by a syndicate of London merchants in 1745 and commanded by Commodore James Talbot in the* Prince Frederick *of 32 guns. The profit resulting from the initial cruise was £200,000.' This was the inscription on the original frame of the picture, oil on canvas, 23in. x 28in. Signed P. Monamy P...* DAVID MESSUM
A fine example of the semi-piratical activities during the wars of that period.

actions of this part of the war (Gibraltar, Barcelona, Alicante, Dunkirk and later Cape Passaro) to decorate his country seat, Southill Park,[5] in about 1725 (Plates 7 to 10). He was created K.C.B. in 1725 and a little later became Lord Torrington. (Previously Vice-Admiral Leake appears to have given commissions to H. Vale to paint some of these events and one of the Vale pictures is now at the National Maritime Museum.)[4]

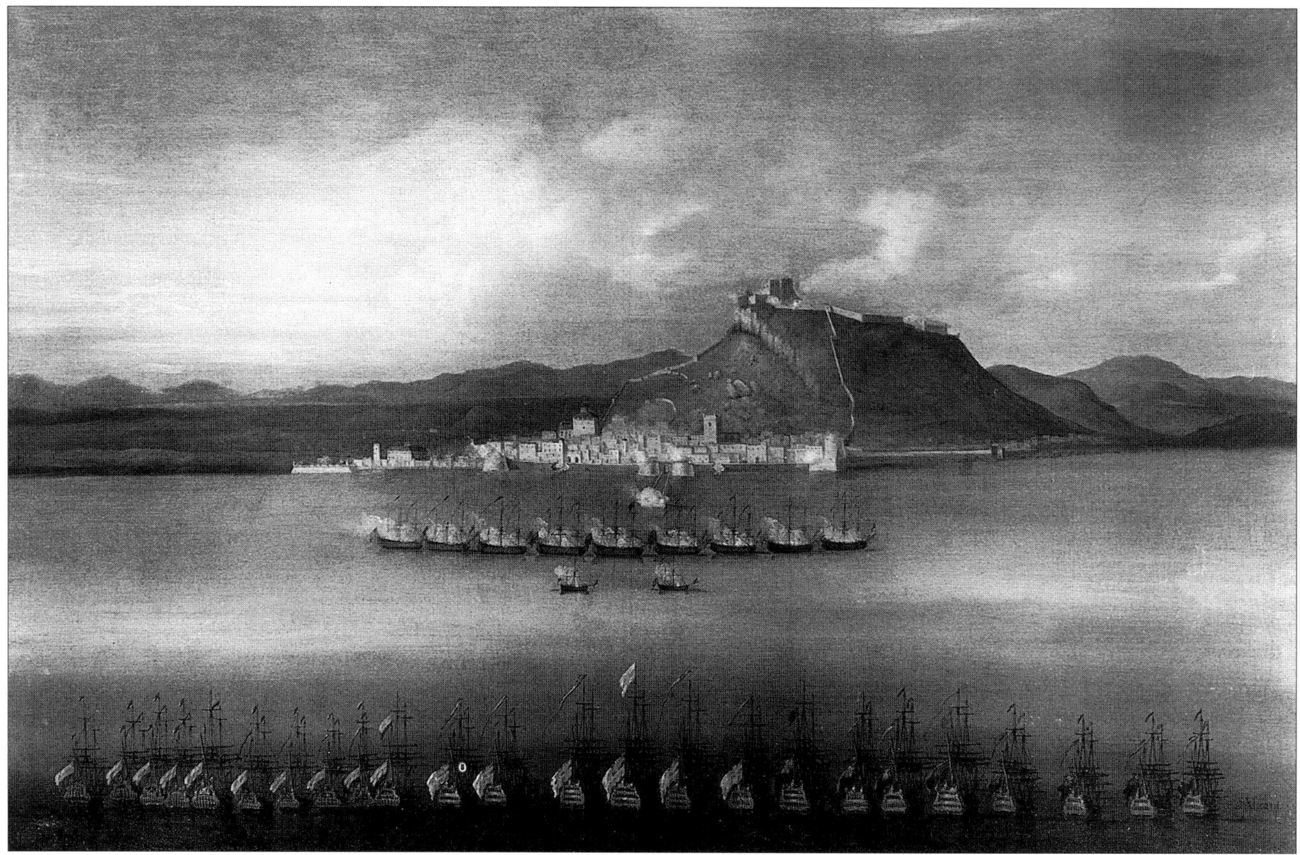

Plate 8. *The Bombardment of Alicante, July 1706. Oil on canvas, 36in. x 53in. Signed P. Monamy Pinx.* PRIVATE COLLECTION. PHOTOGRAPH COURTAULD INSTITUTE OF ART
After the relief of Barcelona, Sir John Leake and his fleet went on to reduce Cartagena and then Alicante. Here, after some delay, an assault was mounted, but first Admiral Byng's squadron was ordered to advance close to the mole and reduce the forts by direct cannonade. The picture illustrates this part of the action. In the foreground, drawn up in a straight line, is the rest of Sir John Leake's Anglo-Dutch fleet.

Plate 9 (Opposite above). *The Blockade of Dunkirk, February to March 1708. Oil on canvas. 36in. x 53in. Not signed.* PRIVATE COLLECTION. PHOTOGRAPH COURTAULD INSTITUTE OF ART
In February 1708 Sir George Byng, Admiral of the Blue, received orders from Prince George of Denmark (Queen Anne's husband) to take some ships to prevent the intended invasion of Scotland. The French scheme was to sail from Dunkirk with a picked fleet of fast vessels carrying the Old Pretender to Scotland, where a rebellion would be raised in his favour. It is noticeable how heavily Dunkirk was fortified at this time.

Plate 10 (Opposite below). *An Action at Gibraltar. Oil on canvas, 27½in x 36½in. Signed P. Monamy Pinx.* PRIVATE COLLECTION. PHOTOGRAPH COURTAULD INSTITUTE OF ART
This view is perhaps the earliest English painting of the famous Rock. Admiral George Byng, acting under orders from Sir George Rooke, in 1704 directed a cannonade and landed seamen who obtained the surrender of the Governor on 24 July. It is quite likely that this painting records this incident in Byng's career, although there were several other similar actions later during Byng's active service.

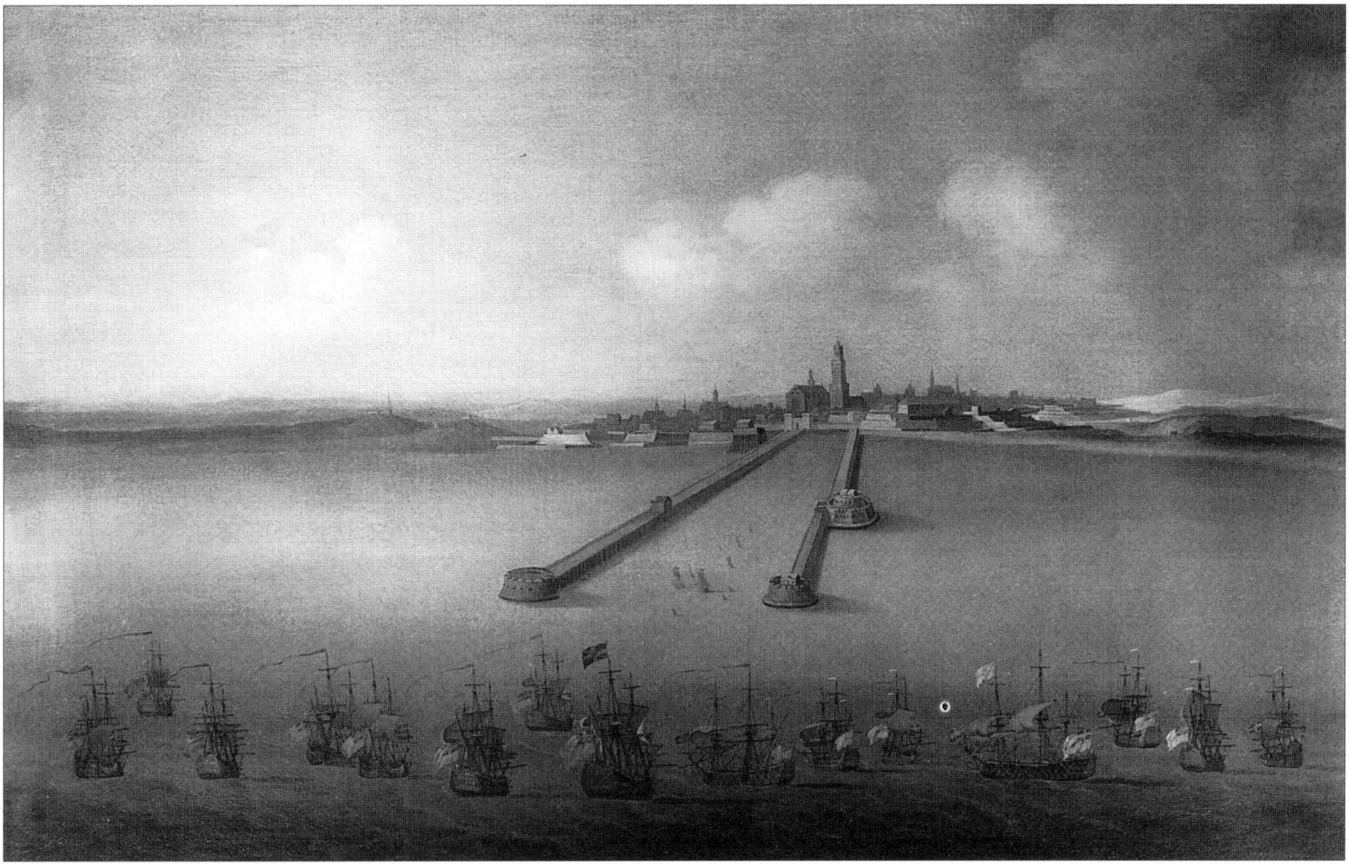

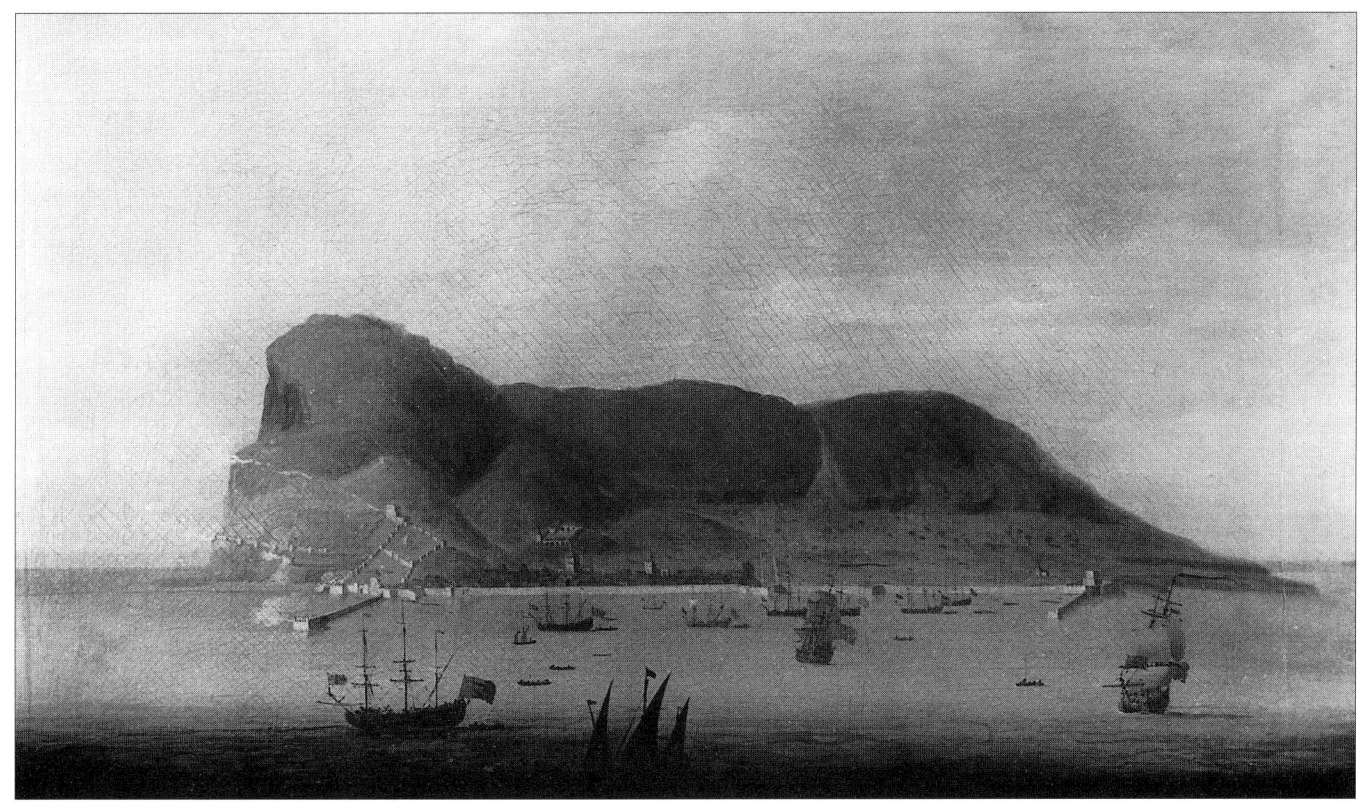

Although this war officially ended with the Peace of Utrecht in 1713, the peace was temporarily disturbed in 1718 when a large force was sent to the Mediterranean, under Sir George Byng, to prevent Spain from occupying Sicily. Relieving troops were embarked at Naples and the fleet then caught up the Spanish fleet off Cape Passaro and a major action took place. This battle, which resulted in the destruction of most of the Spanish fleet, caught the public imagination and was certainly the crowning achievement of Admiral Sir George Byng. It was recorded by a number of marine artists, particularly Peter Monamy and R. Vale.[4]

Following this there was a long period of relative peace at sea (nearly twenty-one years) until the 'War of Jenkins' Ear' broke out in 1739, but in spite of these officially peaceful years there was considerable lawlessness at sea and both piratical exploits and privateering actions in the Channel and in the Caribbean, particularly, were not uncommon (Colour Plate 6).

It was during these twenty years of peace that Peter Monamy's art and

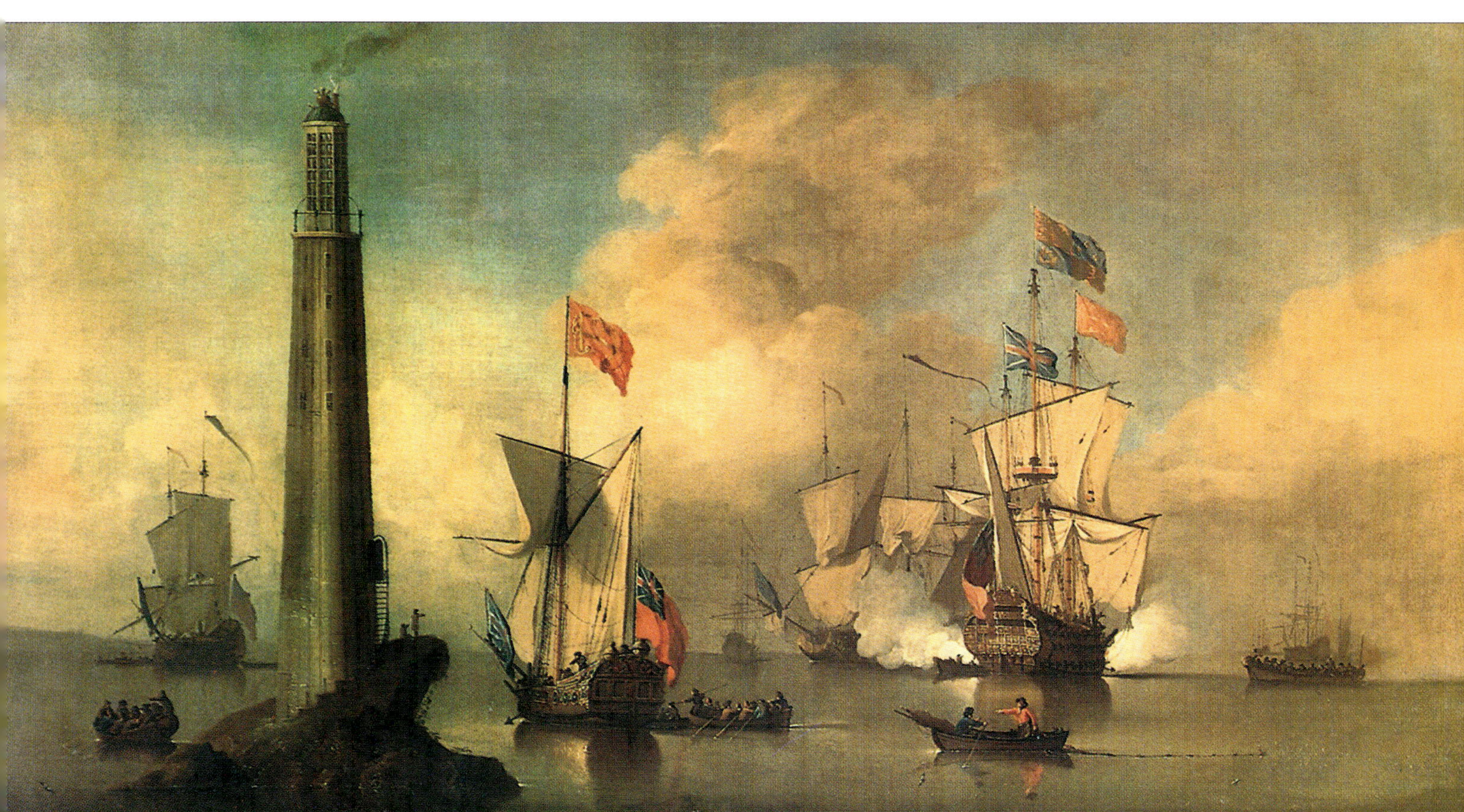

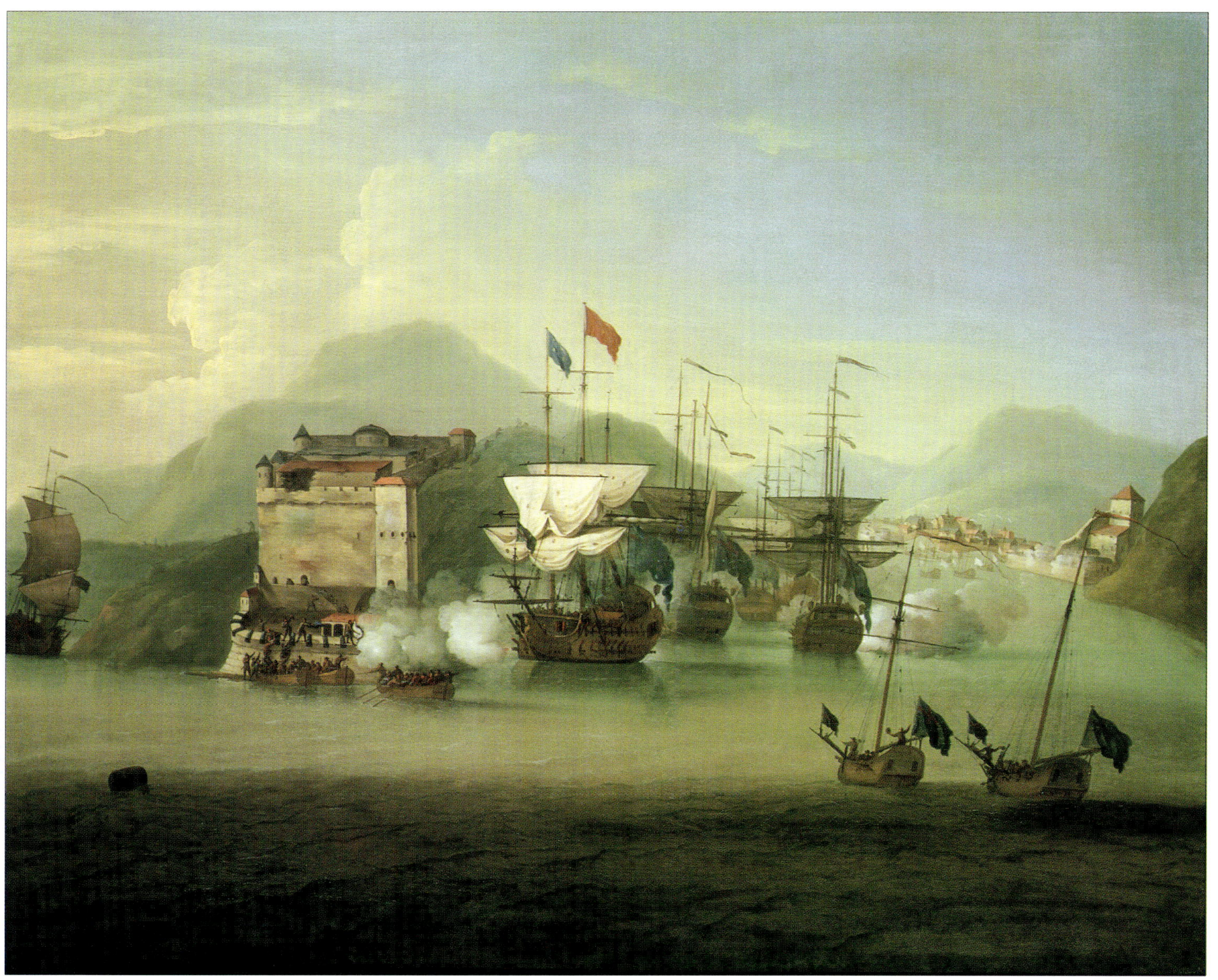

Colour Plate 8. *The capture of Porto Bello by Admiral Vernon, 21 November 1739. A drawing of this action was sent back by Capt. Durell, a friend of Peter Monamy, and it was from this that a series of paintings of the action were made. This painting is one of the series and shows Commodore Charles Brown in the* Hampton Court *bombarding the so-called Iron Castle at the entrance to the harbour. Samuel Scott also made several paintings of this scene. Oil on canvas. Signed P. Monamy.* RICHARD GREEN GALLERY

Colour Plate 7 *(Opposite). The second Eddystone Lighthouse, 1709-1755, known as Rudyard's Tower. Signed P. Monamy.* SOTHEBY'S LOT 64, 1.11.95

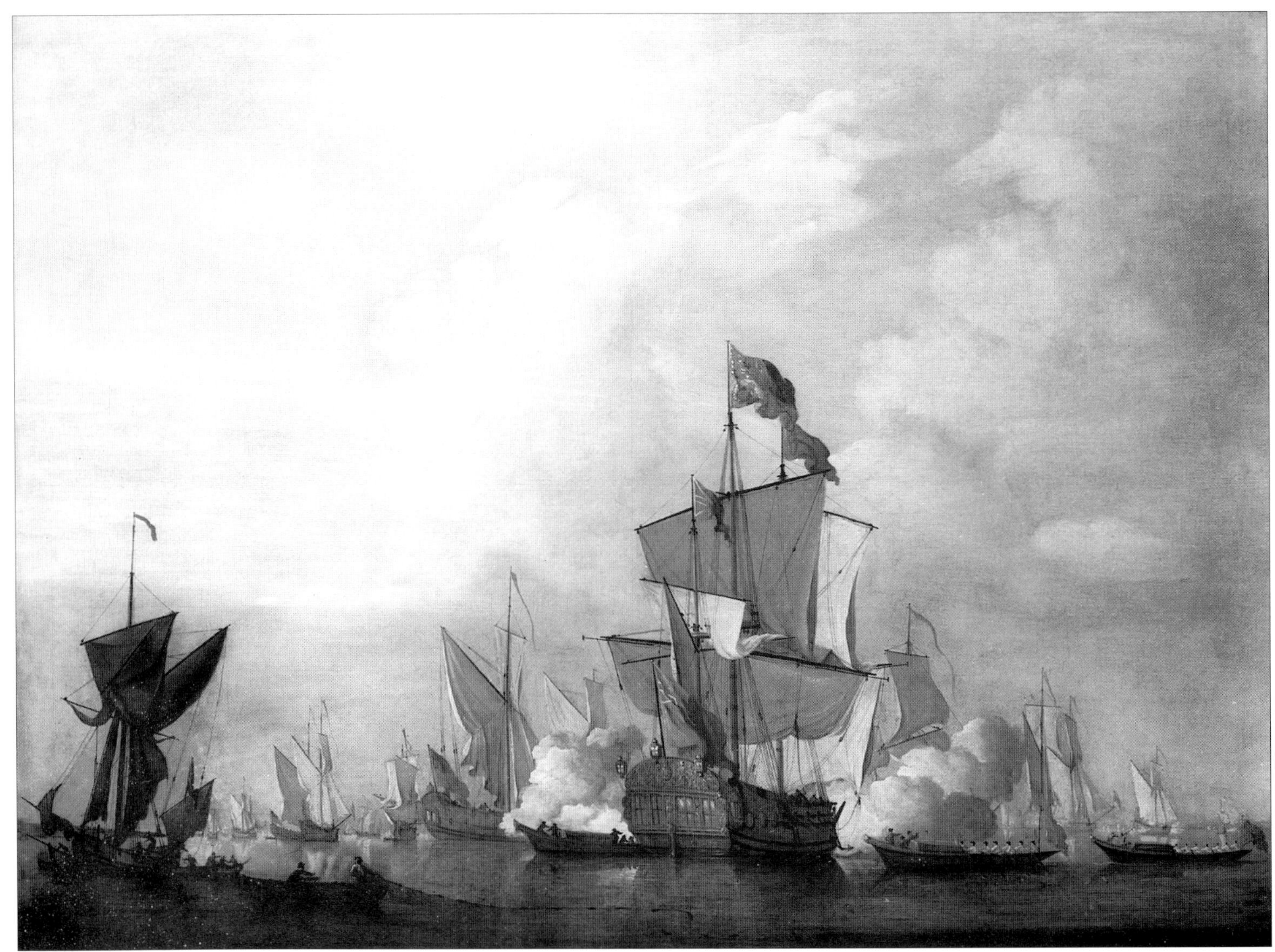

Plate 11. *Arrival of George II in England after a visit to Hanover. 40in. x 50in. Signed P. Monamy pinxit.*   ROYAL COLLECTION
The disembarkation of the King from the royal yacht Royal Caroline *is shown. This is one of a large number of pictures by Monamy (and others) showing the arrival and disembarkation of either George I or George II. Both of them made many cross Channel voyages to visit Hanover.* (Category 1E)

reputation developed. Numerous calm estuary scenes, with large and small ships of war, and small very attractive pictures of ships at sea flowed from his studio. In addition he did pictures of notable marine events, such as the arrival of George I from Hanover and voyages to and from the continent by both George I and George II, usually in the favourite and much used royal yacht called the *Royal Caroline* (Plate 11).[6] When the yachts were endangered by great storms (such as those of 1703 and 1726) this was usually thought worthy of some pictures. The completion of both the first and the second Eddystone Lighthouses (in 1698 and in 1709) were illustrated by appropriate paintings (Plate 12 and Colour Plate 7).

The War of Jenkins' Ear and the Austrian Succession

The colonial gains which had made Britain a dominant naval world power after the war of the Spanish Succession brought with it greatly increased trade opportunities in the Caribbean, Pacific and Indian Oceans. It was not long before this sparked off fighting and quarrels with our old trade rivals, the French and the Spanish. It was the rough handling of one of our sea captains, Captain Jenkins, by Spanish coastguard officials in 1739 that aroused a public outcry, and which forced Sir Robert Walpole to declare war against Spain. This was the so-called 'War of Jenkins' Ear' (his ear was badly mutilated and was shown off to Parliament!) which was declared in 1739 and soon merged into the greater conflict known as the War of the Austrian Succession. This war went on until 1748, when it was terminated by the Treaty of Aix la Chapelle.[7]

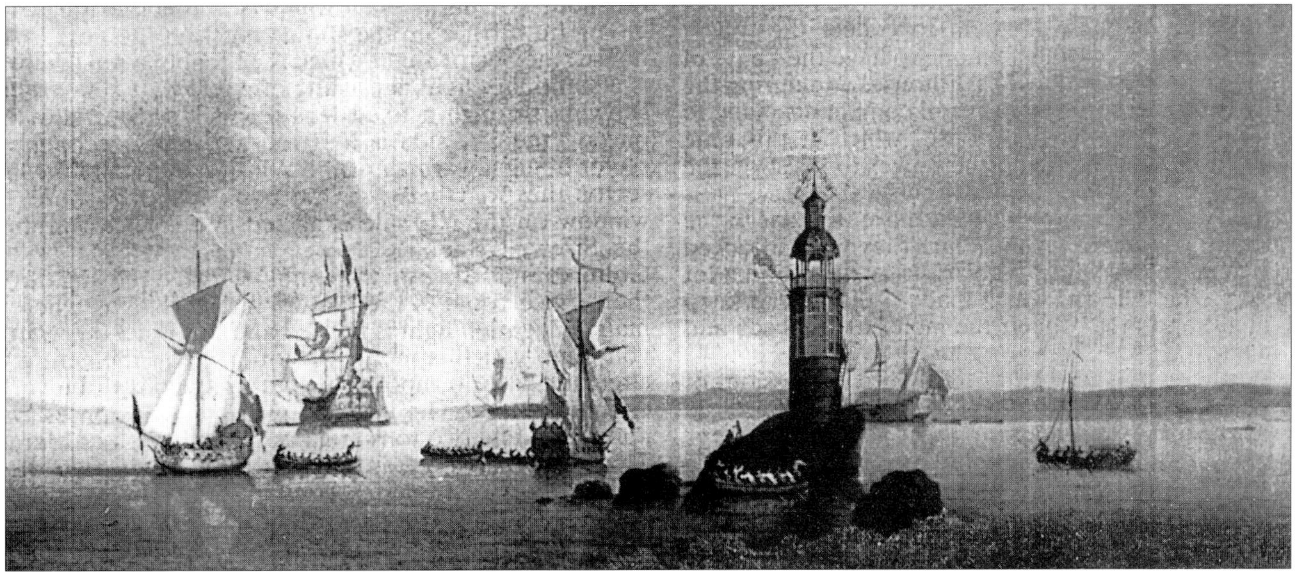

Plate 12. *This is Monamy's picture of the opening of the first Eddystone Lighthouse in 1698. 24in. x 54in. Signed.*
Known as Winstanley's Tower after its designer and builder, it was demolished by the great storm of November 1703 and Winstanley, who was in it at the time, was drowned. The original picture is in the Yale Center (U.S.A.) and is said to have been based on an original print.

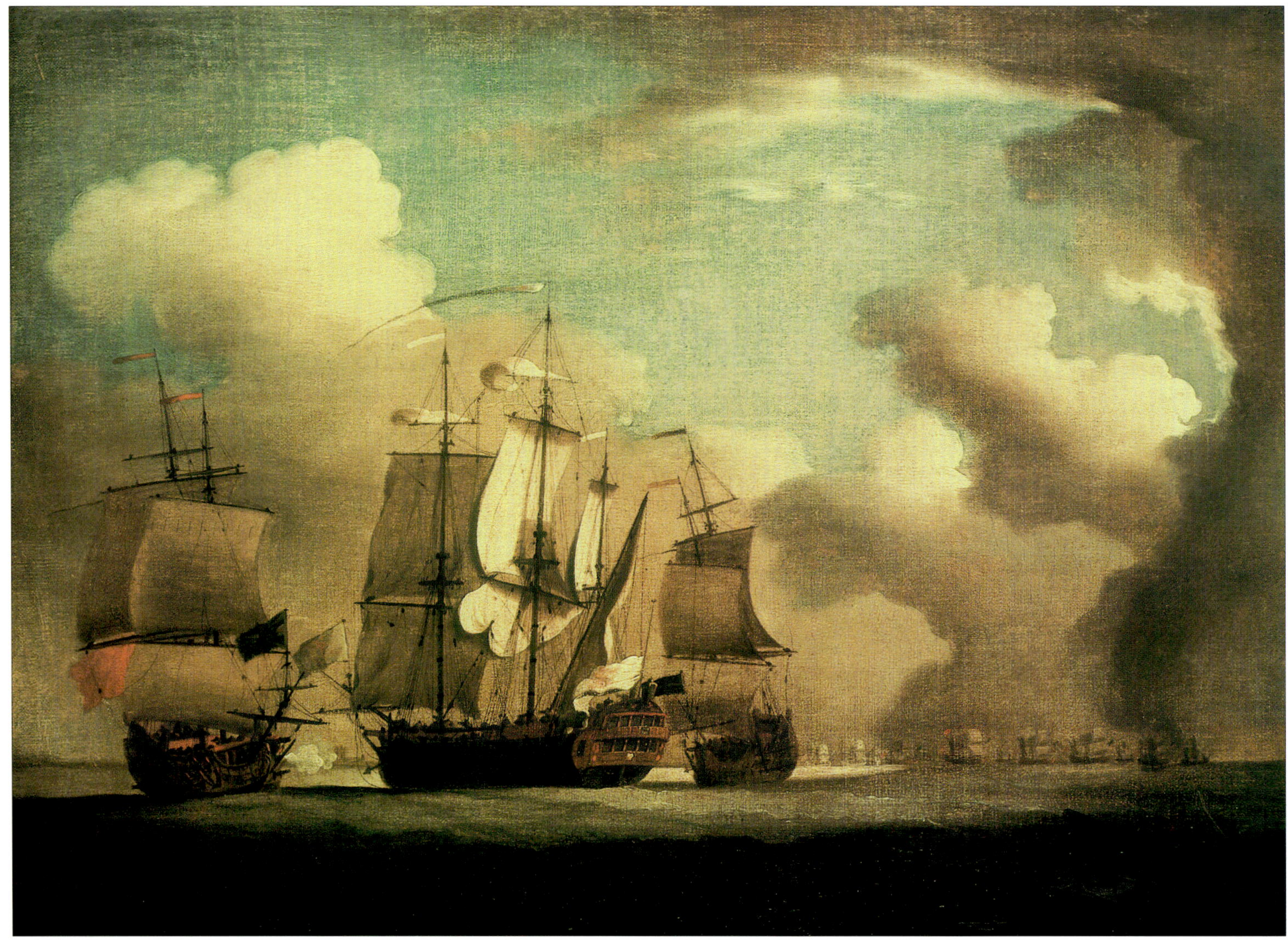

Colour Plate 9. *The Capture of the* San Joseph, *September, 1739. 15in. x 19½in. Signed P. Monamy.* NATIONAL MARITIME MUSEUM
The San Joseph, *a Spanish caracca, surrendered to the British ships* Chester *and* Canterbury *on 23 September 1739. (Category 1C)*

Colour Plate 10 *(Opposite). The Capture of Louisbourg, 1745. 21in. x 38½in. Signed P. Monamy.* NATIONAL MARITIME MUSEUM
Commodore Sir Peter Warren's squadron arrived, landed troops and blockaded the harbour. Louisbourg surrendered just before a joint attack by land and sea was made. With Louisbourg fell the whole of Cape Breton, thus destroying a nest of French privateers and relieving the British fishermen of Newfoundland. (Category 1F)

The various naval actions of this war took place when Monamy was at the height of his fame and so they were nearly all illustrated by him, as various commissions. The first action of the war was the sending of Admiral Vernon with six ships to the West Indies to chastise the Spanish. He arrived at his base, Port Royal in Jamaica, and decided to attack Porto Bello in Panama, one of the main Spanish bases. This he did with his six ships, bringing off a brilliant victory, capturing Porto Bello, and it stirred the public imagination in England in quite a big way. It was illustrated by several paintings by Monamy based on information and drawings brought back by one of his Channel Island relations, Captain Durell (Colour Plate 8). Samuel Scott also made paintings of this episode.

Further operations in 1741 to capture Cartagena were not so successful, although one or two illustrations of this effort also appeared.

In 1739 and 1740 Monamy did two paintings of notable small ship actions – 'Capture of the *San Joseph*' (Colour Plate 9) and 'Capture of the *Princesa*' (see Colour Plate 3). Captain Durell, was involved in the *Princesa* action.

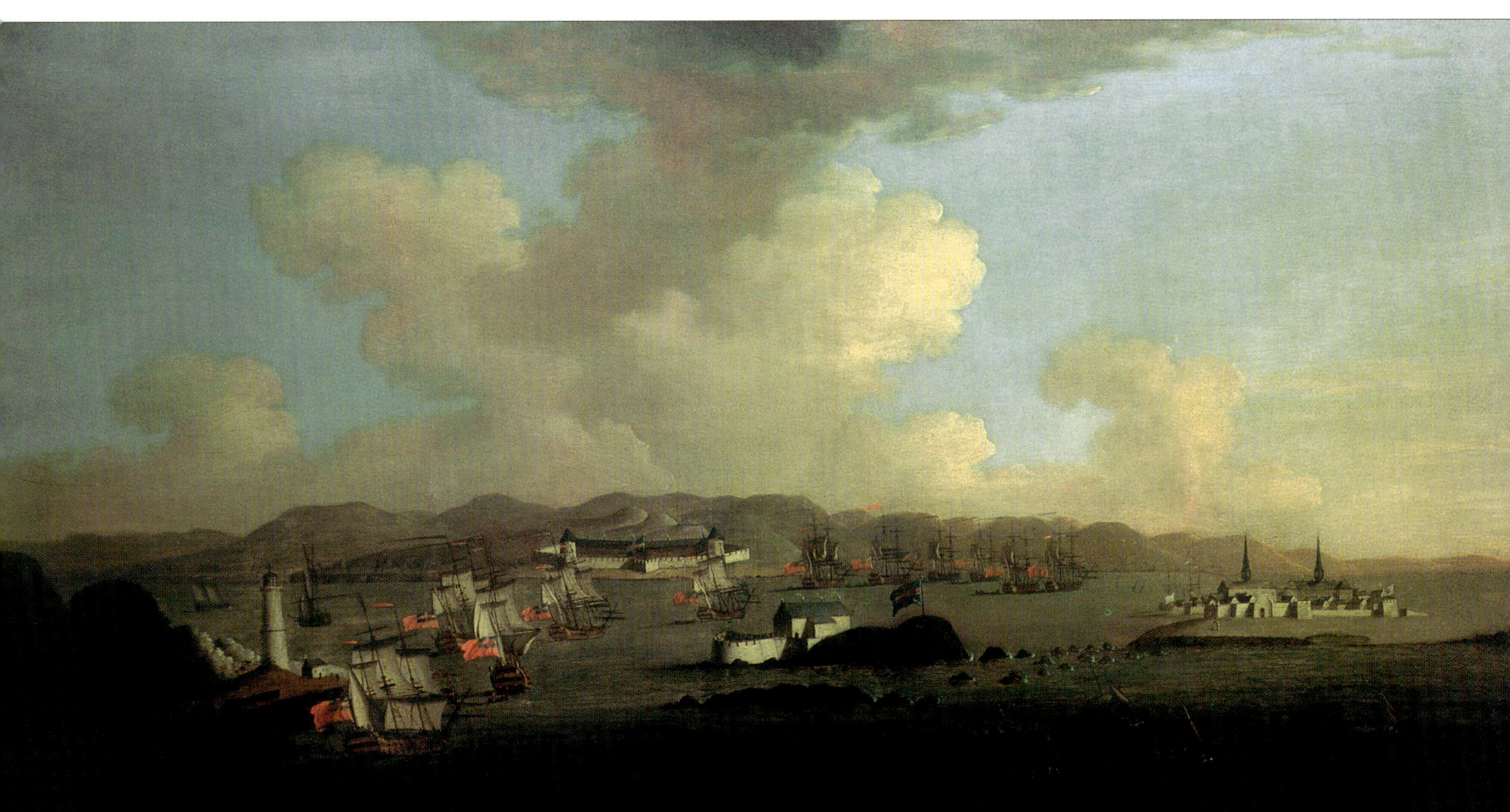

Chronology

A short chronological table of the main events of Monamy's life in the context of the reigns of the various monarchs and the main events of history makes it easier to envisage his life and times.

REIGNING MONARCH	PETER MONAMY	HISTORICAL EVENTS
CHARLES II 1660–1685	1681 Monamy born	
JAMES II 1685–1688		
WILLIAM AND MARY 1689–1702	1696 apprenticed to William Clarke for seven years	1688 Landing of William of Orange at Torbay 1692 Battles of Barfleur and La Hogue
QUEEN ANNE 1702–1714	1704 'made free' from his apprenticeship 1705 first marriage 1707 second marriage to Hannah	1702–1713 War of Spanish Succession 1704–1706 Marlborough's Campaigns **Naval Events** 1702 Battle of Vigo Bay 1704 Gibraltar taken and Battle of Malaga 1705 Barcelona taken 1706 Relief of Barcelona 1707 Admiral Cloudesley Shovel wrecked on Scillies while returning home (longitude navigation error) 1708 Vice-Admiral Leake captures Minorca 1713 Treaty of Utrecht
GEORGE I 1714–1727	1723.Living in Fish Yard, Westminster 1725 Does the 'Byng' paintings at Southill Park 1726 Made a Liveryman of Painter-Stainers Company	1718 Battle of Cape Passaro (Admiral Sir George Byng) 1724 Robert Walpole Prime Minister
GEORGE II 1727–1760	1731 His portrait by Thomas Stubley 1732 Hogarth's Portrait of P. Monamy and client (Mr. Walker) 1749 Monamy dies	1739–1748 War of 'Jenkins' Ear' and Austrian Succession 1739 Capture of Porto Bello 1739 Foundling Hospital set up by Captain Coram 1741 Anson sets off round the world 1745 Capture of Louisbourg 1748 War ends with Treaty of Aix la Chapelle

The last notable action of this campaign was the capture of the fortress of Louisbourg in the island of Nova Scotia by Admiral Warren in 1745. This meant the loss by the French of the whole of Cape Breton Island, the key to the St. Lawrence River leading to Canada. This again was commemorated by some excellent paintings by Monamy (Colour Plate 10).

By this time Monamy's powers were failing at the age of sixty-five, but he did produce at least one more painting of a single ship action of this war in 1746. This was the engagement of H.M.S. *Nottingham* (commanded by his Guernsey friend and distant relation Captain Saumarez) and the French ship *Mars* (see Colour Plate 4 and Plate 6).

At the time of Monamy's death in 1749, Britain was on the brink of a series of mainly naval wars which would keep marine artists busy for the next half century. Samuel Scott (1701-1772) and Charles Brooking (1723-1759) were already in their prime when Monamy died, to be followed by Francis Swaine (1715-1782), Richard Paton (1717-1791) and Dominic Serres (1722-1793), all of whom were going to have ample opportunity to exercise their talents.

Peter Monamy, as well as recording current naval events, did of course also paint pictures of recent famous naval episodes which had taken place in his youth or even just before he was born. The Battles of Barfleur and La Hogue (1692) and the landing of William of Orange at Torbay (1688) are examples of these retrospective works.

Other artists of the 1700-1750 period, contemporary with Peter Monamy

Peter Monamy was the first of a new group of artists who were born and trained in England. Marine painting in England really started with the arrival in England of the Van de Veldes, father and son, in 1673, at the invitation of Charles II. They established a studio at Greenwich, under royal patronage, and enjoyed a pre-eminence in marine painting until Van de Velde the Younger's death in 1707. Nearly all the other artists of that period were immigrants, either Flemish or Dutch.[4]

The first half of the eighteenth century saw the appearance and rise of a group of very competent younger English born artists. As we have seen, Monamy was 'made free' on the same day as Thornhill (mainly famous for his decoration of the Painted Hall of Greenwich Naval College). Other contemporary English artists were Francis Hayman (1708-1776), John Wootton (1678-1764, sporting art), Jonathan Richardson (1665-1745, portraits) and, of course, the great Hogarth (1697-1764). These artists paved the way for the explosion of English artists in the later half of the century who firmly established English painting in a position of excellence comparable with the French and Italian Schools, and more vigorous than the Dutch School which went into a decline in the eighteenth century.

Other events and personalities during Monamy's lifetime

The prestigious East India Company was going through a particularly difficult and precarious time during Monamy's active period (1704-1745). They maintained their own dockyards in London, Calcutta (Fort William) and Madras (Fort St. George).[8] There was a small naval squadron in East Indian waters which was continuously active and occasional scenes from this area were painted by Samuel Scott and George Lambert.

In about 1707 the Moghul Empire was beginning to break up and local conditions of trade were increasingly chaotic. In 1747 the struggle between Britain and France in India really began, leading to Clive's successes in the later half of the century.

There was much activity in the field of *architecture* – Christopher Wren (1632-l723) and Hawksmoor were reshaping London after the Great Fire in 1666. In *music* Frederick Handel was the leading personality, and he was given British citizenship in 1726. In *literature* the great names were Daniel Defoe, John Gay, Pope, Addison and Steele. In *science* it was the age of Isaac Newton, codifying the natural laws of nature. The Royal Society, founded in 1663, was very active. The building of Greenwich Observatory took place and the search for an adequate method of calculating longitude at sea was started (initiated by the loss of Cloudesley Shovel's squadron on the Scilly Isles on the way home from the Mediterranean). *Medicine* was still very backward: there were no anaesthetics, the cause of scurvy was still unknown and on long voyages most of the crew died from this cause (as happened with Anson's voyage round the world 1742-1744). Surgery was practically confined to minor operations, amputations and cutting for the stone. William Cheselden, at St. Thomas's Hospital, was the outstanding surgeon of this era. Infant mortality was appalling, as shown by the death of three out of five of Monamy's children in infancy.

⟶═◆═⟵

1. *History of the Royal Navy,* edited by Peter Kemp, Arthur Barker Ltd., 1969.
2. *Fighting Sail,* Oliver Warner, Cassell Ltd., 1979.
3. *The Wooden Fighting Ship,* E.H.H. Archibald, Blandford Press, 1968.
4. *Early Sea Painters,* F.B. Cockett, Antique Collectors Club, 1995.
5. The Whitbread Collection at Southill Park, near Biggleswade, Bedfordshire.
6. *Royal Yachts,* C.M. Gavin, R.N., Rich and Cowan Ltd., London, 1932.
7. *Sovereign of the Seas. The Story of British Sea Power,* David Howarth, Book Club Associates, 1974.
8. *Lords of the East – The East India Company and its ships,* Jean Sutton, Conway Maritime Press, 1981.

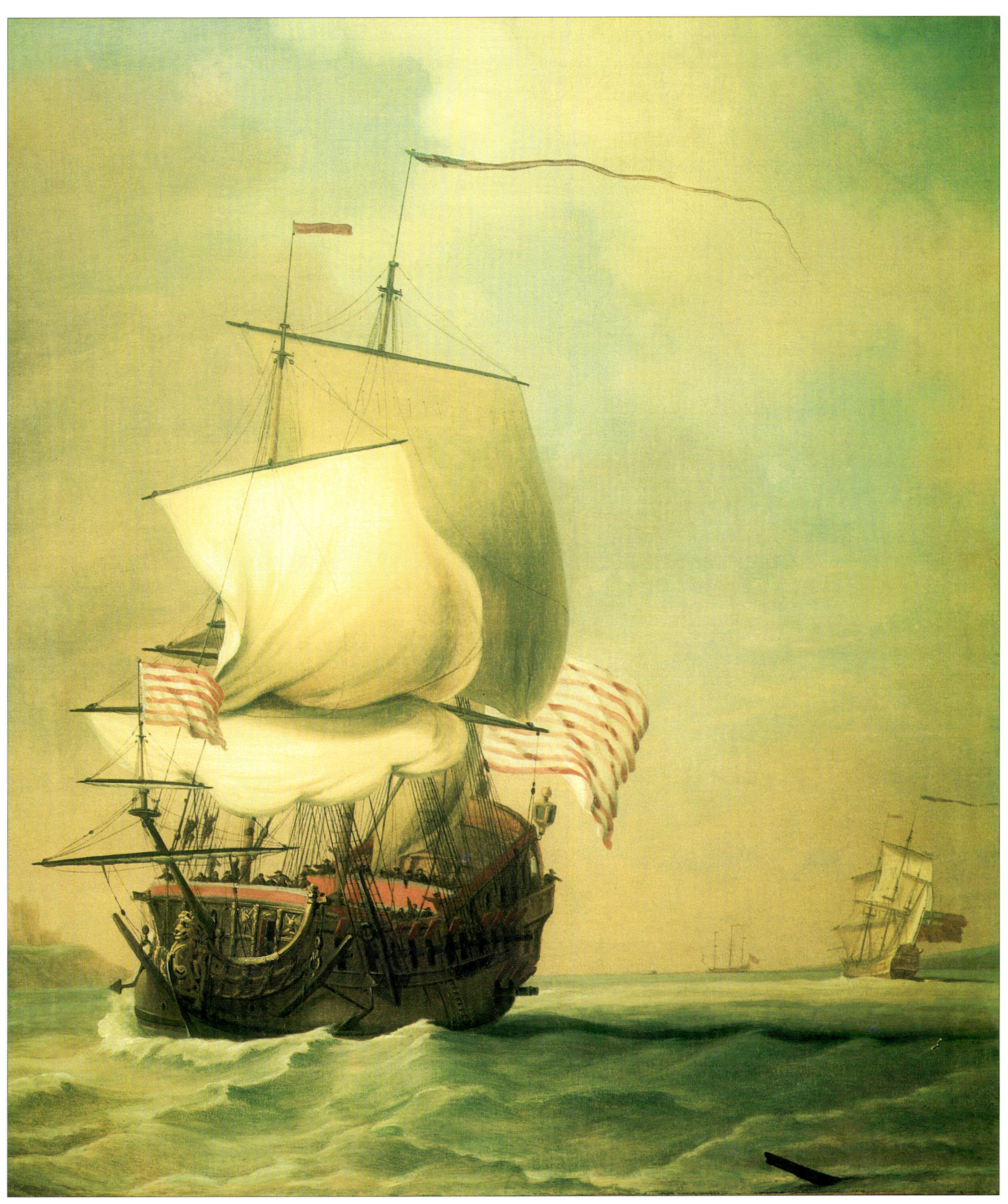

Colour Plate 11. *An English East Indiaman, bow view. 39in. x 32½in. Signed P. Monamy.*

NATIONAL MARITIME MUSEUM

The striped flags are the flags of the East India Company. (Category 4)

CHAPTER 3
The Paintings

Monamy's active painting life spanned the years 1704 to 1749, a period of forty-five years. It is not surprising, therefore, that when one comes to a serious survey of his work, the first thing which strikes one is just how incredibly prolific he was. In the files of the Witt Photographic Library in London there are records of over three hundred pictures either by him or attributable to him. The files at the the National Maritime Museum, Greenwich, contain records of about 250 pictures either by him or attributable. It is quite certain that these two sources do not cover his whole artistic output, as most of his pictures are to be found in private ownership and are consequently lost to accurate or complete record.

The English artists of the first half of the eighteenth century did not have any organised forum in which to display their works and in which their works might be recorded. The first organised exhibition of artists' work in London was at the Society of Arts in 1754, founded by William Shipley. Then by 1761 there were two exhibition societies in London – The Society of Artists and the Free Society. The Royal Academy was not founded until 1768. Marine painting exhibitions were held at the Society of Arts in 1762, 1765, 1766 and 1768.[1]

All this was of course too late for Peter Monamy, which adds to the difficulty of finding and recording his paintings. The main sources for the cataloguing of his works are national museums (particularly the National Maritime Museum),[2] major private collections and, most importantly, the records of the great auction houses such as Bonhams, Christie's, Phillips and Sotheby's.[3] Picture dealers also help in this general search. The founding of well indexed photographic records such as the Witt Library and the research files of the National Maritime Museum have made the task a lot easier in recent years, but it still means that newly discovered unrecorded pictures pop up almost every year even now, so that lists of Monamy's works are by no means final.

In his early years, between about 1704-1720, he must have known about the work of the Van de Velde studio. It is now known from the work of M.S. Robinson[4] that the Van de Velde studio up to 1707 (when Van de Velde died) was working in London with at least two studio assistants

(Cornelis Van de Velde and J. Van der Hagen) to turn out a great number of marine pictures which were sold as 'Van de Veldes'. In fact most of these were 'factory' pictures, usually based on an original by Van de Velde himself, but worked up and finished in the studio to a greater or lesser degree by his two assistants. Even after Van de Velde's death in 1707 the studio continued to turn out 'Van de Velde type' pictures for the public for up to about another ten years. At this period they started also occasionally to sign their pictures or initial them with their own names.

During this early period of his career Peter Monamy could not help but be influenced by these 'Van de Velde' pictures and in his early days he probably turned out a fair number of pictures which were either copies or closely based on Van de Velde originals. In fact the 'valuable sea piece of his own painting' which he presented to the Painter-Stainers Company in 1726 (see Plate 2) is a prime example of this, being based fairly closely on Van de Velde's painting of the first rate *Royal Sovereign*.[5]

Monamy was by no means the only marine artist of his day to start off his career by copying or modelling Van de Velde subjects. Both Samuel Scott and Charles Brooking, and even Dominic Serres later, turned out Van de Velde 'look-alikes', often very attractive and good ones, in the early part of their respective careers.

However, many of these earlier Van de Velde type pictures were unsigned and carried flags of a pre-1707 vintage and showed ships of a design more appropriate to the previous century. This inevitably leads to a certain confusion as to their authorship and origin. Later, from about 1730 onwards, Monamy's own talent and palette are in full command and more signed pictures begin to appear. The pictures are lighter, brighter and full of their own character and charm and there is much less trouble in identifying them, even if unsigned.

As this particular period (1707-1720 or so) was also characterised by some changes in the flags used by the Navy, which are usually prominently shown in these marine paintings, it may be appropriate at this stage to describe the flags shown in many Monamy paintings. There were also some striking changes in ship and sail design during this period.

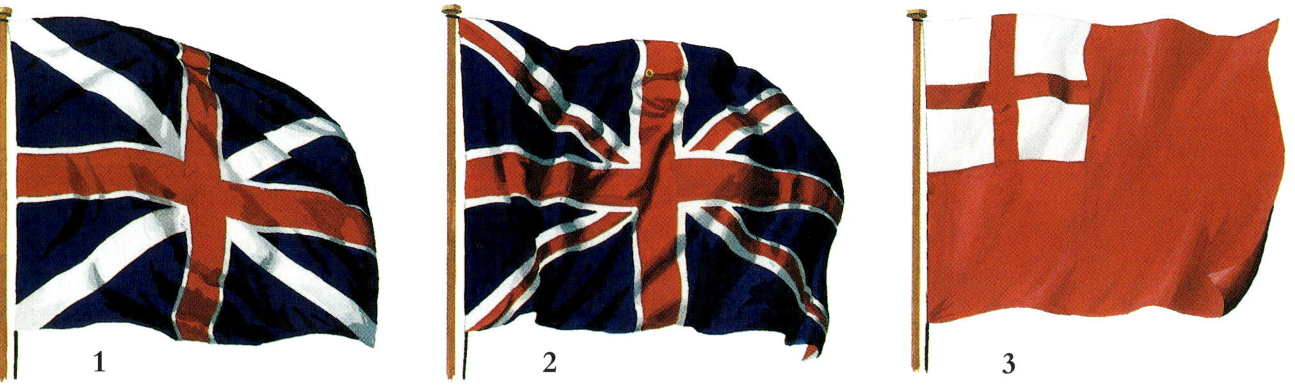

Flags shown in Monamy's Paintings

1. The 'Union flag' or 'Jack'. 1606 –1801. This flag first appeared in 1606, when James VI of Scotland succeeded Elizabeth I to become James I of Great Britain. It was usually flown either at the mast head or on a jackstaff mounted on the bowsprit.

2. This flag, the *modern* 'Union Jack', with the addition of the red St. Patrick's saltire to represent Ireland, replaced the old union flag in 1801 to the present day. *It should not be seen in any paintings prior to 1801.*

3. The Ensigns. These flags were usually flown on the stern jackstaff and they were always very large flags, easily identifiable from a distance.

This was the ensign in use prior to 1707 – simply with a red cross (St. George's) on a white background in the canton (i.e. upper left-hand corner). The red ensign was the normal flag flown by all naval ships and any large English merchant ship.

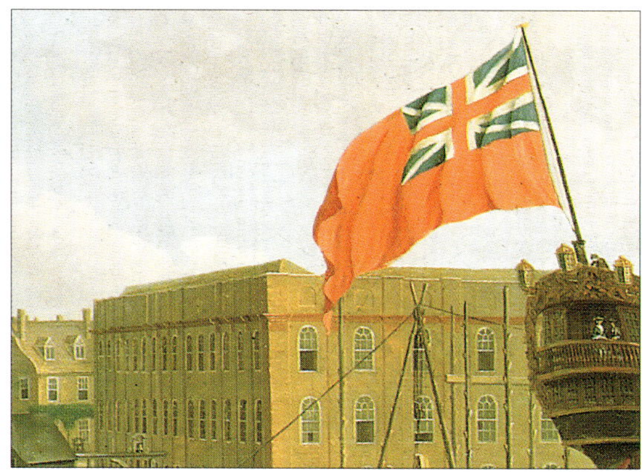

4. From 1707 onwards the *union* flag was introduced into the canton of the red ensign instead of the plain red cross. If this flag is shown in a painting, then *it must have been painted in 1707 or later.* On the other hand pictures showing ensigns of an earlier date *need not necessarily* have been painted before 1707.

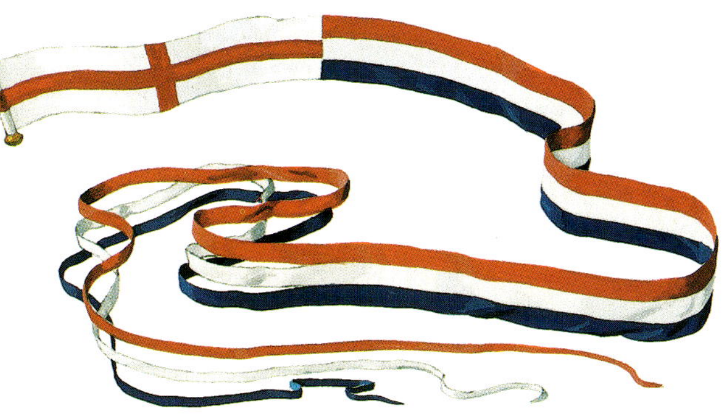

5. Masthead Pennants. Masthead pennants (or streamers) were usually flown at the masthead by all naval ships (not by merchantmen). The colours followed that of the ensigns.

As well as showing that the ship was British, ensigns and pennants were used to denote which squadron in a fleet the ship belonged to.

6. Royal Standards
These were the personal standards of the reigning monarch, and were flown at the main masthead when the monarch was on board. They were also sometimes used as signal flags by a Commander in Chief. When hoisted on the stern jackstaff or mast head, it signified 'All commanding officers come aboard for a conference' (see Colour Plate 5).

The following three royal standards sometimes appear in Monamy pictures and are important in dating a particular painting.

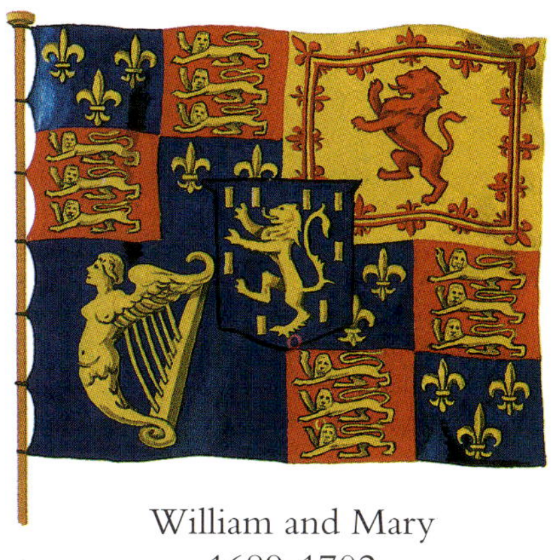

William and Mary
1689–1702

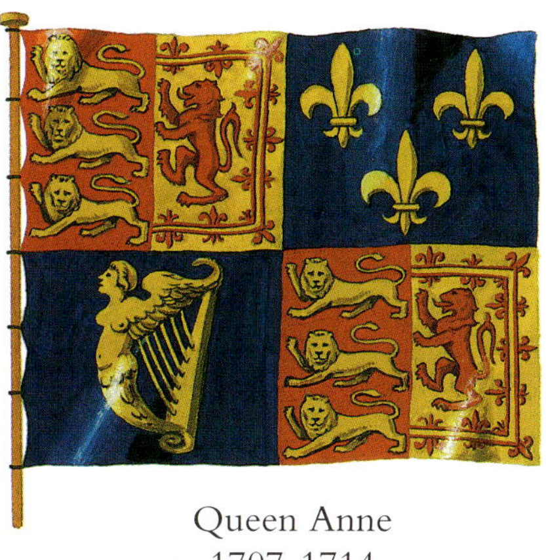

Queen Anne
1707–1714

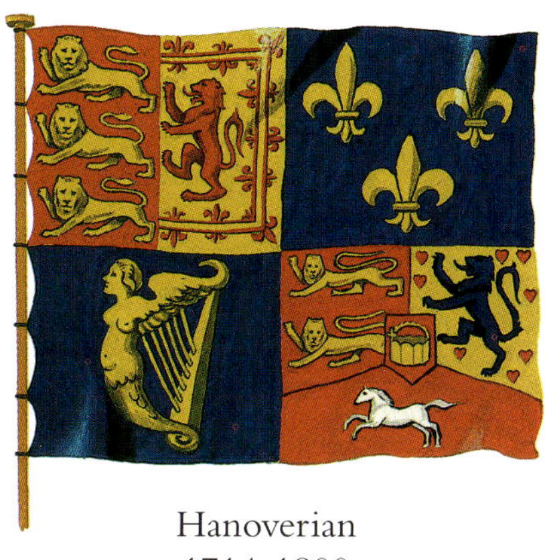

Hanoverian
1714–1800

7. The Admiralty Flag
This flag was often carried at the main in any ship which was either in the Navy or was temporarily on official Admiralty business.

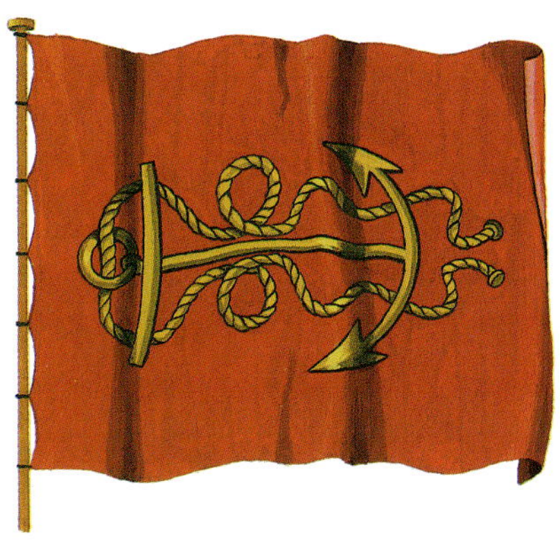

These were the main flags worn by English ships in the first half of the eighteenth century, apart from one or two special signal flags such as the large black and white striped flag (shown in Colour Plate 25) which means 'prepare to anchor'.

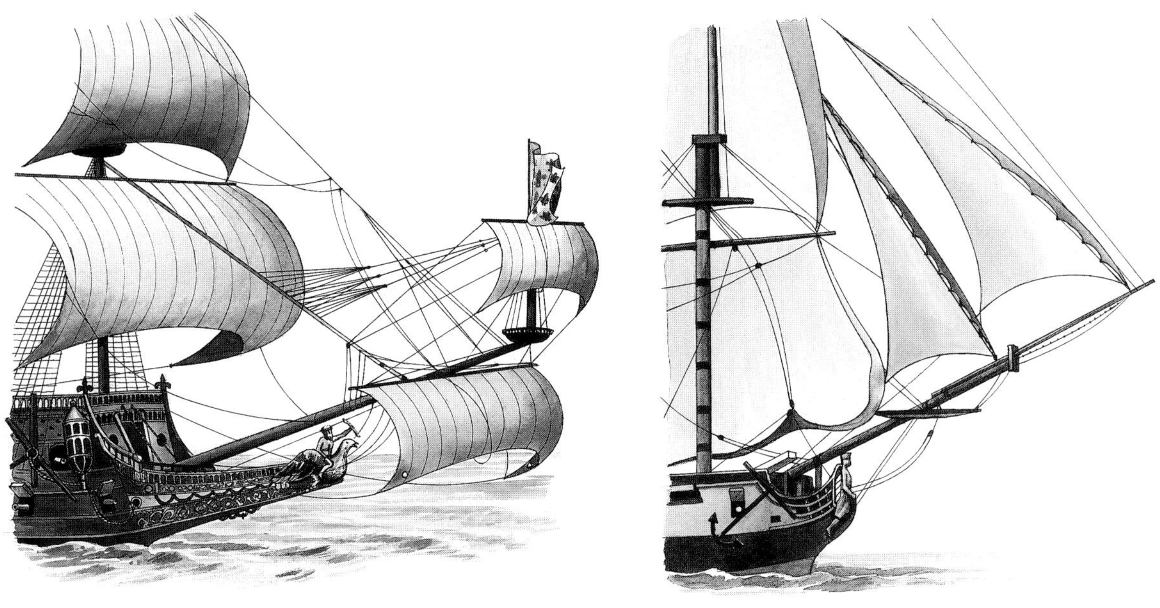

The first general instructions for signalling at sea were issued to the Navy on the authority of James, Duke of York, in 1673 when he was Lord High Admiral. There were just the five flags which have been mentioned here, and the meaning of a signal depended on on which part of the ship the flag was hoisted. The hoisting of a signal was usually accompanied by the firing of a gun – to draw attention to it. Many of Monamy's paintings of ships in a calm, or at sea, are in the act of firing a 'signal gun'.

These signalling arrangements were by no means universal and were often altered to suit a particular commander or a particular campaign. The signalling arrangements of the first half of the eighteenth century were indeed somewhat chaotic, particularly from the point of view of the art historian! Proper codes of signals and signal flags only appeared later in the century.

Changes in Ship Design

There were certain changes in ship design from the late seventeenth century (when Van de Velde and his studio were active) to the early eighteenth century (Peter Monamy). The two most obvious charges were:

1. The disappearance of the small spritsail top mast on which a small square sail was set in all large warships up to about 1700. After about 1710 this was replaced by a jib boom and small jackstaff which carried a flag.

2. The disappearance of most of the carved and gilded stern decorations and carved wreaths round the gun ports. The eighteenth century ships had much plainer sterns, often with open stern galleries and lines of undecorated gun ports. (Compare Colour Plate 38 with Colour Plates 39 and 33.)

From the artist's point of view, both these changes led to an obvious difference in appearance of the eighteenth century ships which Monamy

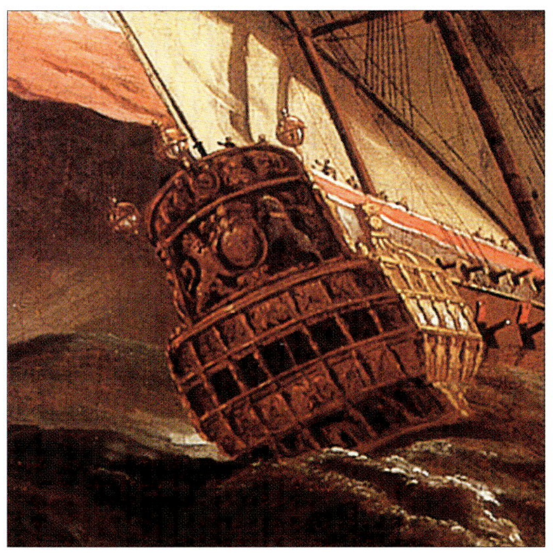

17th century stern

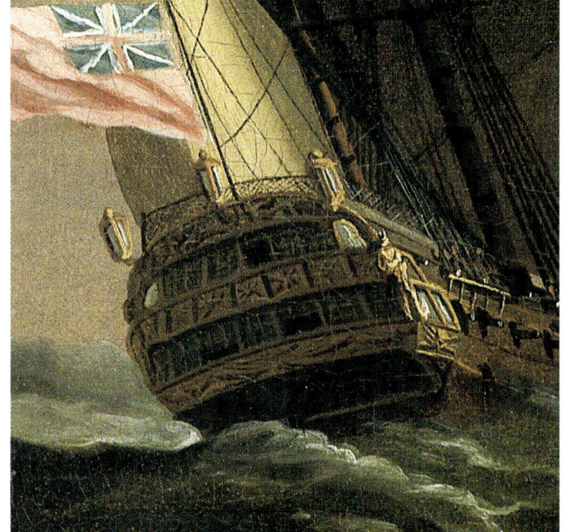

Early 18th century stern

painted, particularly in the later part of his painting career, from about 1720 onwards.

When a Monamy painting shows a large three-decker warship, with spritsail topmast rigged and perhaps flying the earlier pre-1707 ensign on the stern, then it is likely that this painting is based on an older Van de Velde composition.

These considerations are quite important in dating eighteenth century marine pictures by any artist, particularly unsigned or 'attributed' pictures. For instance a picture showing a red ensign with the union flag in the canton (upper corner) must have been painted after 1707. Monamy was painting particularly in this period, and his own paintings of contemporary ships very frequently show this post 1707 ensign somewhere.

The Monamy 'Studio'

As we have seen, the output of paintings attributed to Monamy is very large. On looking through them a certain variation in quality is apparent. Also there are certain paintings which were repeated as several copies or versions, often of different sizes. This inevitably leads to the question of whether he had studio assistants who helped in the finishing of a picture or even in certain cases produced one or more 'studio copies'. It seems more than likely that he had skilled assistants working with him from time to time. It is not unlikely that the young Brooking may have spent a little time in this way. It is even more likely that artists such as Francis Swaine, T. Leemans and Thomas Allen (see Chapters 5 and 6) may have worked with him in this capacity.

It is also quite possible that Monamy himself may have turned out versions 2, 3 and 4 of a particularly successful picture. Unfortunately we have no documentary evidence that he worked in this way, but we do know that other well-known artists of this period did so. For instance, we have unequivocal documentary evidence that Jonathan Richardson repeated his famous portrait of William Cheselden (the surgeon) at least five times for members of the family and other institutions. Allan Ramsay, at the height of his fame at this time, employed an assistant who regularly did the clothes and background of his subjects (J. Van Haeken).

So it seems possible that some of the less competent seascapes and ship portraits which appear from this period may be wholly or partly from his assistants, who may also have done some of the routine furniture for many of his calm scenes (such as the little beached 'hoy' or yacht which appears almost routinely in many of his calms, as in Colour Plates 34, 35 and 36).

It must also be remembered that the two brothers Richard and Humphrey Vale were about in London at this period (up to 1727 at least) producing seascapes and ship portraits which were often unsigned.[6]

Also in the early part of his career there must have been a certain trade in sign painting, which would have been a good outlet for his apprentice or any assistant he may have taken on.

Signatures on paintings

The practice of signing a painting was not universal in the first half of the eighteenth century. In Holland the generally accepted practice was that an artist did not sign his painting until after his apprenticeship was over and he had become a full member of his guild. This rule was followed fairly rigorously by the Dutch sea and river painters of the seventeenth century. They often signed in unusual places, such as on one of the flags, or on the lee-boards of a barge, or on a piece of driftwood in the water. Moreover they sometimes adopted special monograms, or nicknames. (For instance the great Renier Nooms always signed himself Zeeman!) Hunting for the signature in a seventeenth century seascape or ship portrait can on occasion be quite a skilful pastime.

Van de Velde in his later days, when he was running the studio in Greenwich, is known to have signed works coming from his workshop on the back of the canvas with his big bold flowing signature. This did not mean that he had painted every detail himself, but that he approved the work as a worthy product of his studio.

In England the early seascape painters only rarely signed their works. No signed work by Isaac Sailmaker has yet been discovered. Jacob Knyff never signed his seascapes, which were often large and impressive.[6]

Peter Monamy seems to have gradually formed the habit of signing his seascapes, particularly in his later years after 1725 or so when he was becoming well known. His signature never varied and was always P. Monamy, usually with an embellished P. Sometimes he added 'pinx' after his signature and, even more rarely, a date.

On the whole, a mature well-drawn and well-painted picture which is signed can be reliably assigned to him. It does seem likely, however, that many of his earlier efforts (pre-1726 or so) may have been unsigned.

Usually his signature is somewhere along the lower margin of the picture, or right- or left-hand corner, or sometimes on a piece of driftwood. He never signed with initials (or almost never! – one picture is known with a P.M. monogram) or on a flag.

The Paintings

Peter Monamy was the first English sea painter. He developed a style which was technically very advanced, but was also brighter, more colourful and somehow more decorative and immediately attractive than the routine output of the Van de Velde studio. They were immensely more competent and realistic than those of Isaac Sailmaker (who was the only regular seascape artist painting at the same time). Sailmaker died in 1721 and this left Peter Monamy as the undisputed master in this field for a short period of five to ten years until the competition and expertise of Samuel Scott and Charles Brooking gradually became recognised.

Most of Monamy's paintings were on canvas, and of medium size – so-called 'cabinet' size – suitable for display and decoration of a small or moderate sized room. Occasionally, however, there are examples of very large size, up to six or seven feet in length (Colour Plate 17, for example). Very occasionally his paintings were on an oak panel, specially if the painting was for decorating a box or carriage door or for over a mirror. The author has only seen one true Monamy on a copper panel (unlike the paintings of Francis Swaine, q.v. Chapter 5).

Although the range of his subjects was immense, they are all concerned with ships and the sea, rivers and estuaries and a few large seaports. There are no pure landscape paintings. Peter Monamy was a true specialist marine painter.

In describing and illustrating his work it is best to consider it in several sections or categories which may be listed as follows:

1. Works which commemorate definite events.
2. Views from the sea of certain landmarks or seaports.
3. Formal ship portraits.
4. Attractive small or medium size seascapes, showing ships in a light breeze or ships in a calm.
5. Storm scenes.

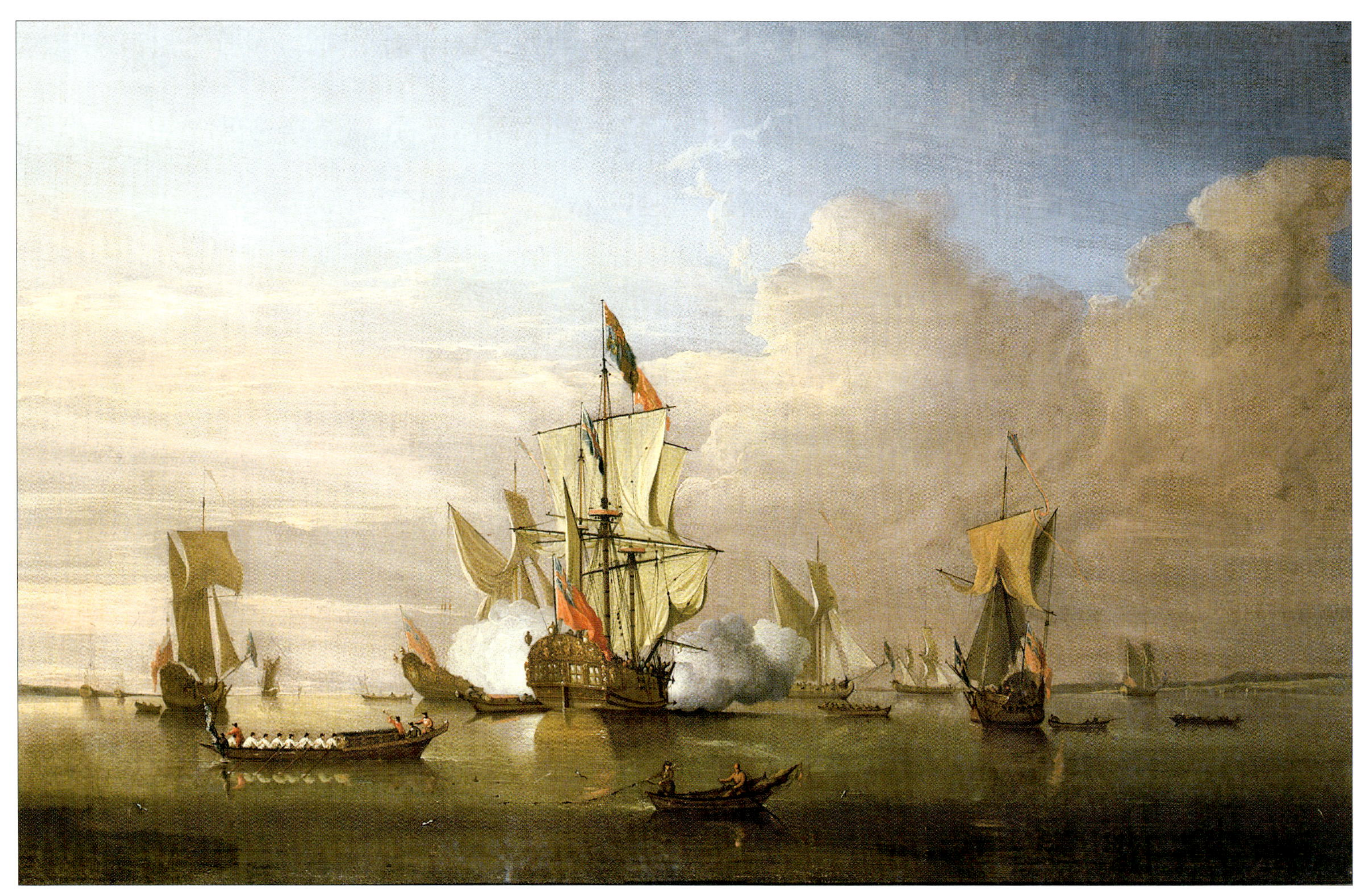

Colour Plate 12. *The royal yacht* Peregrine *arriving in the Thames estuary with King George I aboard in September 1714. 39in. x 60in. Signed P. Monamy and dated 1724.*

CHRISTIE'S

This painting was exhibited in Chichester at Pallant House in August 1983, No. 15. There are up to seven or eight known variations on this theme, all slightly different, but all purporting to show the arrival in England of either King George I or II from a cross Channel voyage. Plate 11 and Colour Plate 52 show two other versions. (Category 1E)

Colour Plate 13 *(Opposite below). The royal yacht* Royal Caroline *in a storm. 14½in. x 33¼in. Signed P. Monamy. pinx.* SOTHEBY'S LOT 10, 20.11.85
The storm depicted probably occurred in January 1726, when George I was returning from a visit to Hanover. It continued for three days before the royal party was able to make a landfall at Rye.

The picture shows well Monamy's ability to show with great realism a Force 8 gale at sea with the tops being blown off the waves. (Category 1E)

Colour Plate 14 *(Opposite above). British ships in Lisbon Harbour. 51½in. x 70in. Signed P. Monamy. 1735. (Category 2)* ACKERMANN AND JOHNSON LTD., LONDON, UK/BRIDGEMAN ART LIBRARY

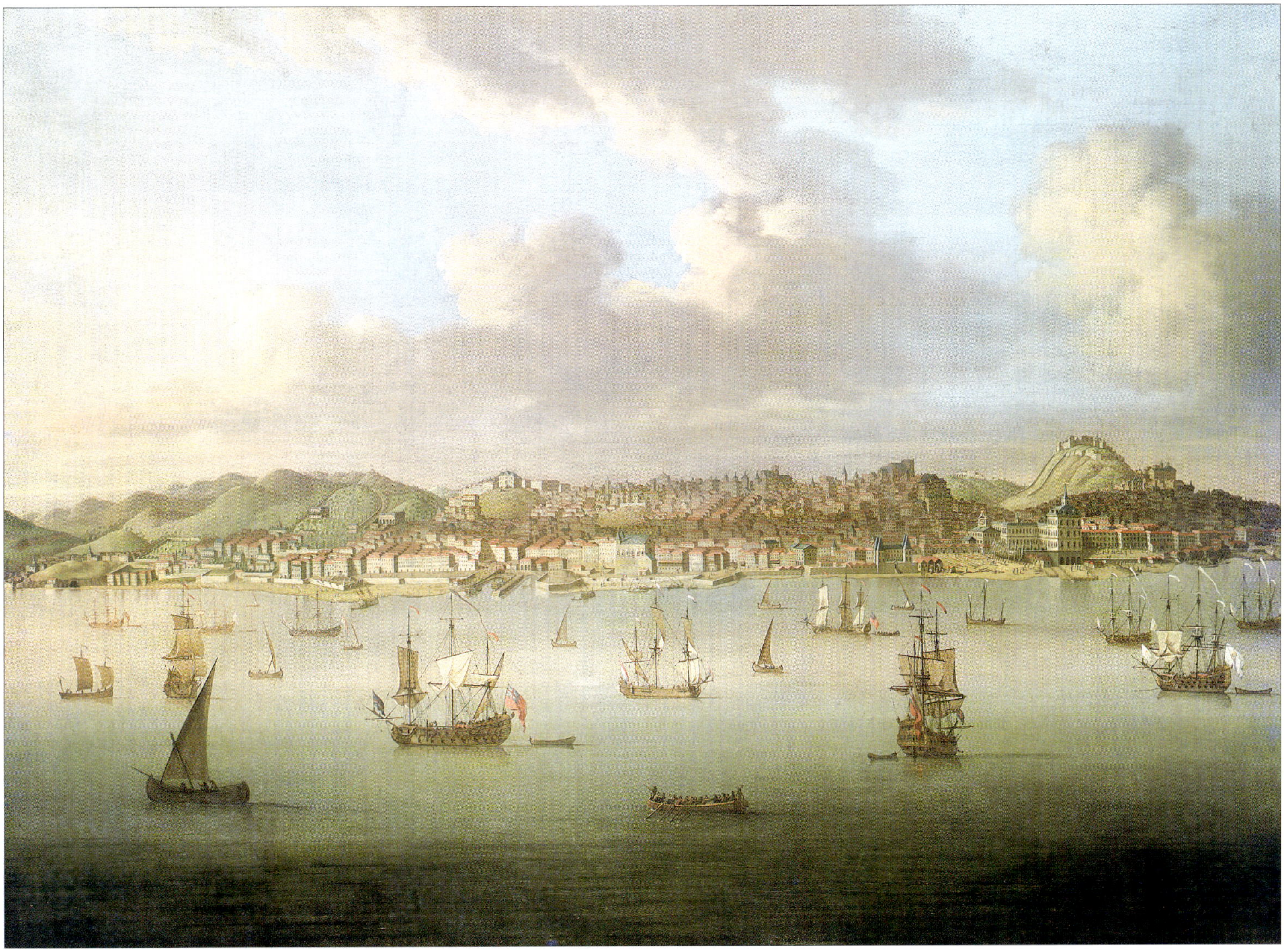

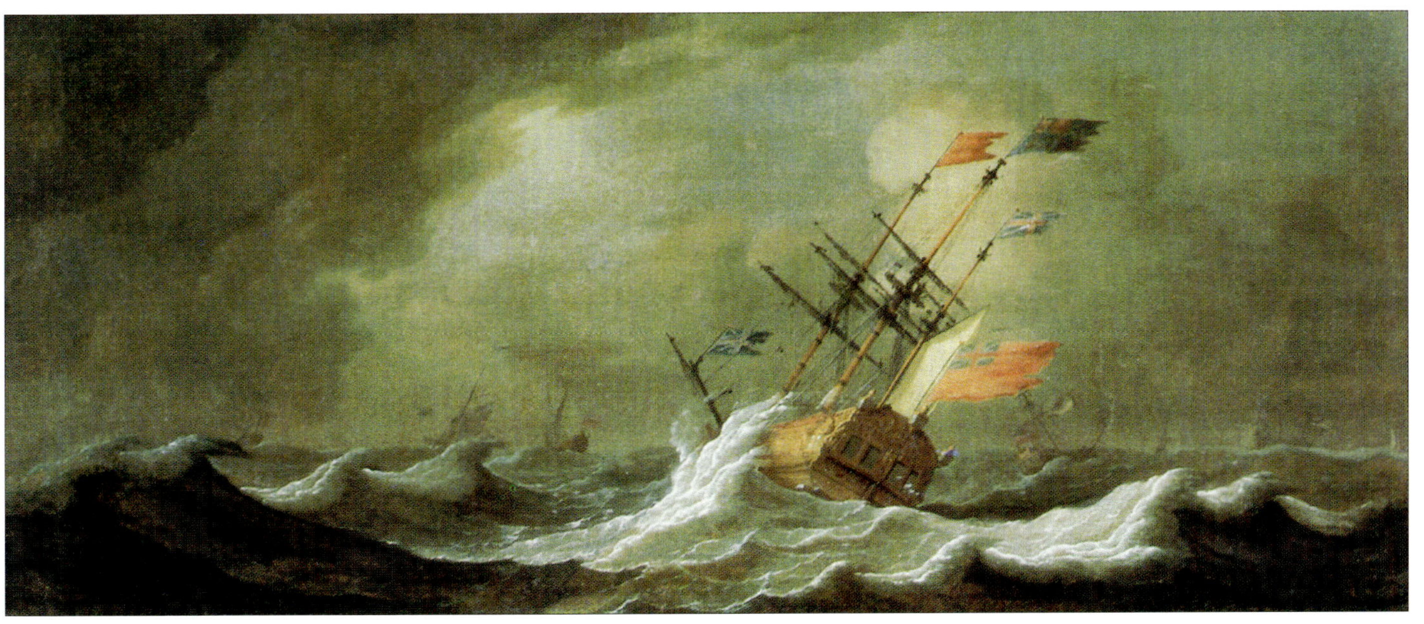

6. Moonlight scenes.
7. Ships on fire.
8. Copies of Van de Velde subjects, or pictures closely based on Van de Velde pictures or drawings.

Before examining these categories in more detail there are two further points to consider. First is the fact that during his mature years, when his paintings were at their best and his reputation and fame at its height (roughly 1720-1745 or so), there was a long period of relative peace. The war of the Spanish Succession ended with the Treaty of Utrecht in 1713 and the next major war, the War of the Austrian Succession, did not start until 1739. This meant that for a period of twenty-six years there were no major actions at sea (with the sole exception of the action off Cape Passaro in 1718). This was really very bad luck for a professional marine artist as there were no great naval actions to commemorate in pictures and major commissions were therefore a little thin on the ground. It is for this reason that so much of his mature output consists of the attractive little seascapes and calm scenes which were in demand from the picture buying public.

Second is the problem of putting the paintings in chronological order. Unfortunately it is not until fairly late in his career that occasional paintings are signed *and dated* (after 1720). Many of his commemorative paintings can of course be roughly dated by the date of the event depicted. For instance there are quite a number of his paintings depicting the arrival of George I in England on board the royal yacht *Peregrine*. These, therefore, must have been done after 1714 (George I's accession). In the same way there are a number of paintings of the royal yacht (now called the *Royal Caroline*) at sea with George I aboard in a terrible storm. These must have been done after the well documented great gale of 1726. Using such events (see the 'Chronology of events' at the end of Chapter 2), an approximate dating of many of his paintings can be achieved.

The Subjects of Monamy Paintings
As we have seen, it is best to consider these in various definite categories.

Category 1 – Commemorative Paintings
These commemorate certain definite events or places and can be classified into six sub-groups.

Category 1A
Waterman in a wherry. The first winner of Doggett's Coat and Badge Race on 1 August 1715 on the River Thames (Colour Plate 1). This picture is still in the

possession of the Company of Watermen and Lightermen of the River Thames. It is the earliest signed painting by Monamy that we know of. The Doggett's trophy is still raced for on the Thames.

Category 1B   Sea Battles – *Current*. Battle of Cape Passaro (1718)
There are two versions at least of this.
One is in the Whitbread Collection at Southill Park,
and the other is in the Royal Collection.
Sea Battles – *Past* (i.e. battles which took place before Monamy was actively painting – before 1704).
Mary Rose Action - two versions (Plate 20)
Battle of La Hogue and Battle of Barfleur (at least five versions)
Battle of Sole Bay (at least five versions)
Most of these last four actions are based on pictures by Van de Velde.

Category 1C – Small or Single Ship Actions
The taking of the *San Joseph* (three versions) (Colour Plate 9)
The taking of the *Princesa* (at least three versions) (Colour Plate 3)
The taking of the *Mars* by *Nottingham* (two versions) (Colour Plate 4)

Category 1D – Eddystone Lighthouse Pictures
The first Eddystone Light of 1699 (Plate 12)
The Second Eddystone Light of 1705 (Rudyard's Tower) (Colour Plate 7)

Category 1E – Voyages and Landings of King George I and II
Arrival of King George I in royal yacht *(Peregrine* - later called *Royal Caroline)*. At least five different versions of this scene (all by Monamy) are known (Plate 11 and Colour Plate 12)
The royal yacht *(Royal Caroline)* at sea in a violent storm (three versions of this by Monamy are known) (Colour Plate 13).

Category 1F – Capture or Attacks on Various Enemy Sea Ports
The Relief of Barcelona
The Bombardment of Alicante
The Blockade of Dunkirk
An Action at Gibraltar

These four paintings (Plates 7 to 10) were commissioned by Admiral George Byng, for his house at Southill Park, being actions in the War of the Spanish Succession in which he took part.

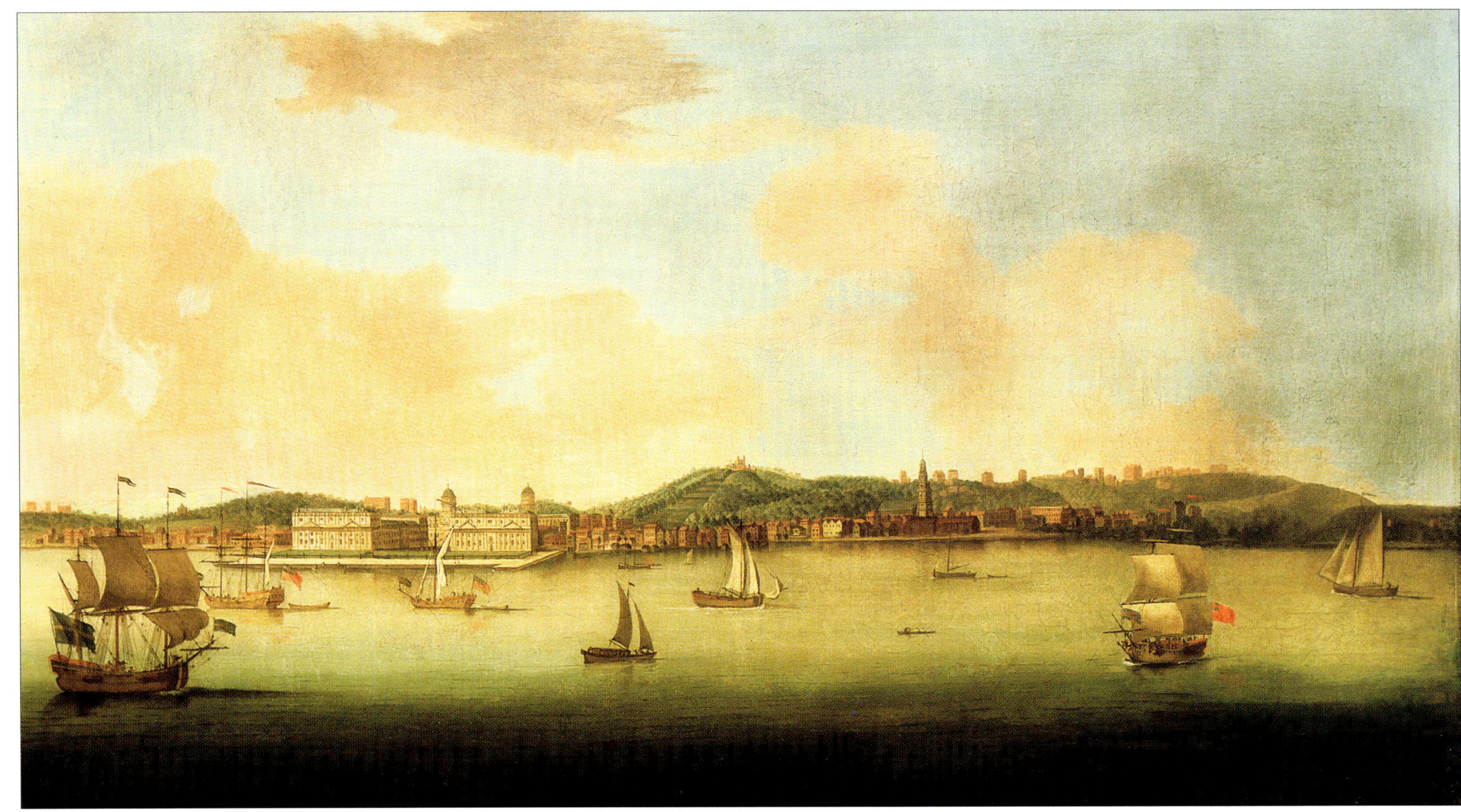

Colour Plate 15. *Greenwich from the North bank of the Thames. Signed P. Monamy.*
SOTHEBY'S LOT 5, 10.4.91
The two Wren domes of the Royal Naval College and the Royal Observatory on the hill can be clearly seen. This dates the painting to about 1740 as the building was not complete until then. (Category 2)

Later, during the War of the Austrian Succession, Monamy did two more series of paintings:
The Capture of Porto Bello by Admiral Vernon (Colour Plate 8). (Five different versions of this painting are known.)
The Capture of Louisbourg in Nova Scotia in 1745 (Colour Plate 10). At least four different versions of this are known. (Samuel Scott did paintings of these last two events which are sometimes confused with Monamy.)

Category 2 – Views from the sea of various landmarks or seaports
View of Greenwich (Colour Plate 15)
View of Gibraltar (Plate 10)
View of Lisbon (Colour Plate 14)
View of Constantinople (Colour Plate 17)
View of Cartagena
There is no evidence that Monamy ever visited Lisbon, Gibraltar, or Istanbul, or Cartagena, so these views must have been executed from drawings or prints by some other hand.

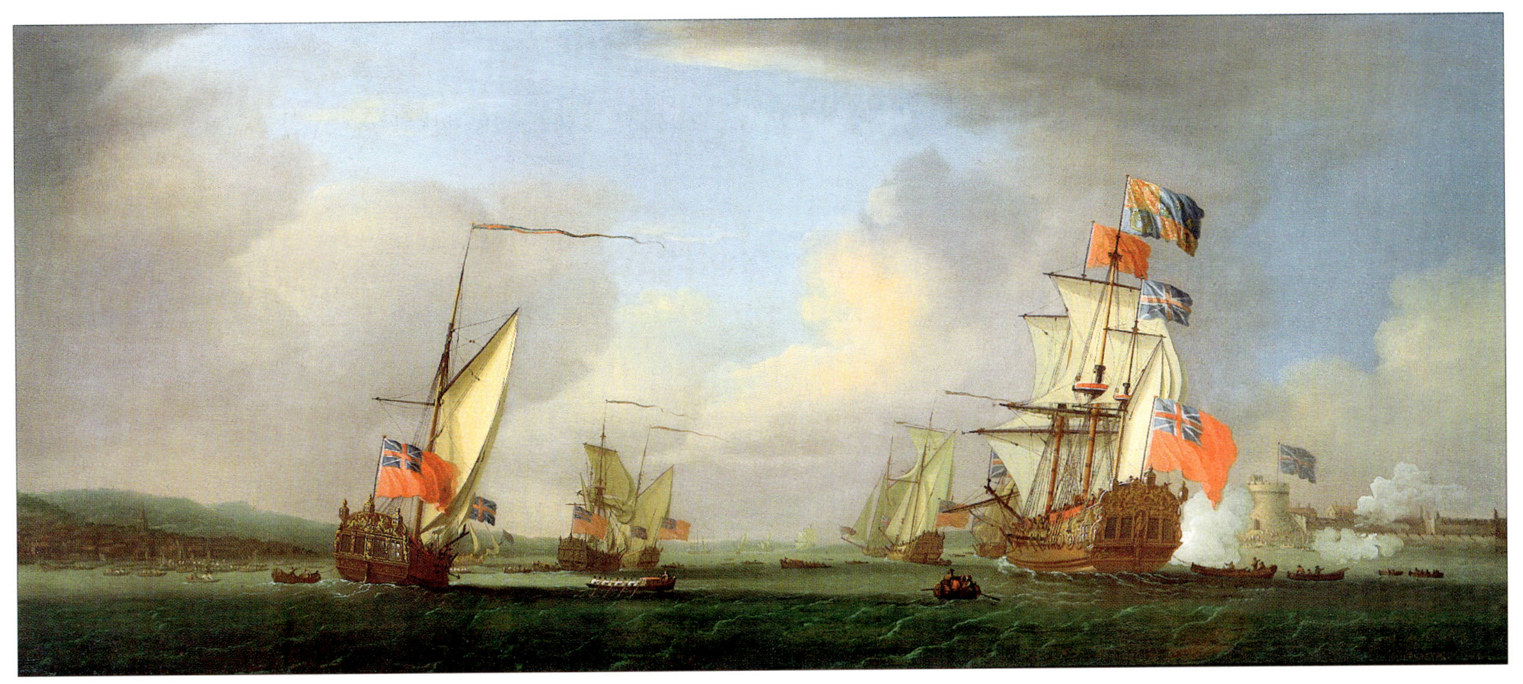

Colour Plate 16. *The royal yacht* Peregrine *and another yacht in the Medway off Gillingham, Kent, passing Upnor Castle. 26¼in. x 61in. Signed P. Monamy. Pinxit.*
RICHARD GREEN GALLERY
After 1716 Peregrine *was renamed the* Royal Carolina *until 1730 when she became the* Royal Caroline. *In this picture the yacht bears the royal standard of Queen Anne. (Category 2)*

Colour Plate 17 *(Below). A panorama of the Bosporus at Constantinople, the City spread along the European western shore, the Asian eastern shore guarded by Leander's Tower, with Dutch, English, and Turkish ships and galleys in the roadstead. 27in. x 85in. Signed P. Monamy. pinx.*
CHRISTIE'S LOT 473, 15.11.96.
The arrival of an English ship in Constantinople in the 1740s must have been a rare event and this painting therefore may record a specific event or voyage. (Category 2)

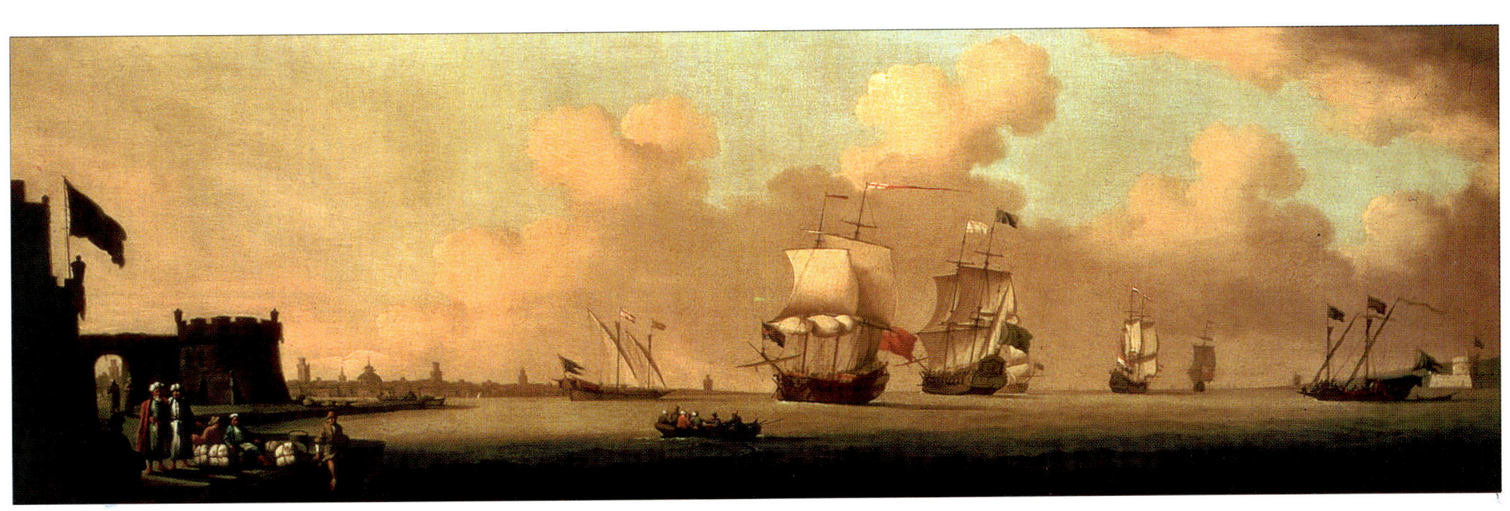

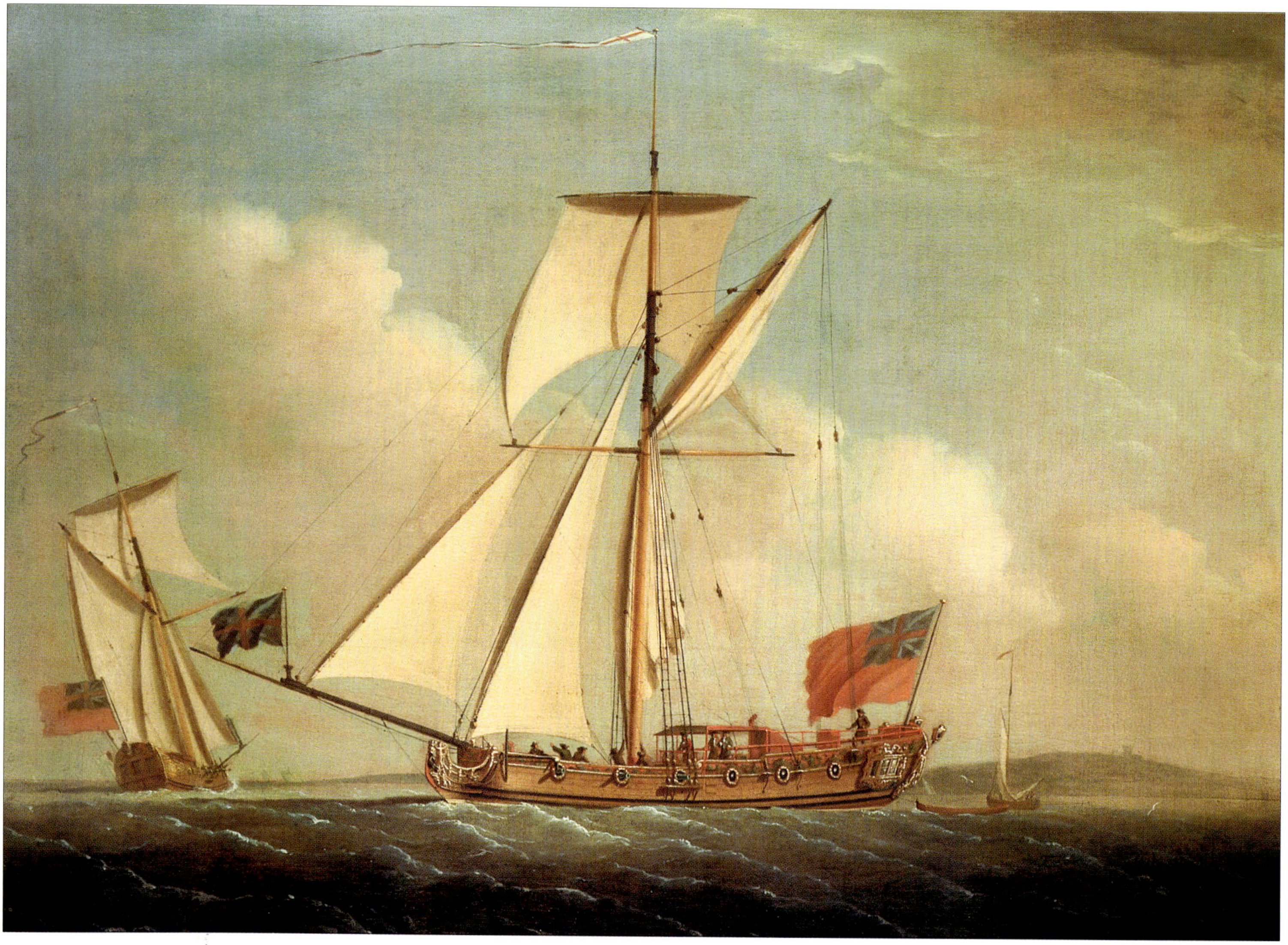

Colour Plate 18. *An English cutter-rigged yacht in two positions. 29in. x 36in. Signed P. Monamy.* PHILLIPS, 18.6.96 *Traditionally believed to be the royal yacht* Mary. (Category 3)

Colour Plate 19. *An English privateer in three positions. 23¾in. x 29¼in. Signed and dated P. Monamy. 1734.* (Category 3) SOTHEBY'S LOT 9, 20.11.85

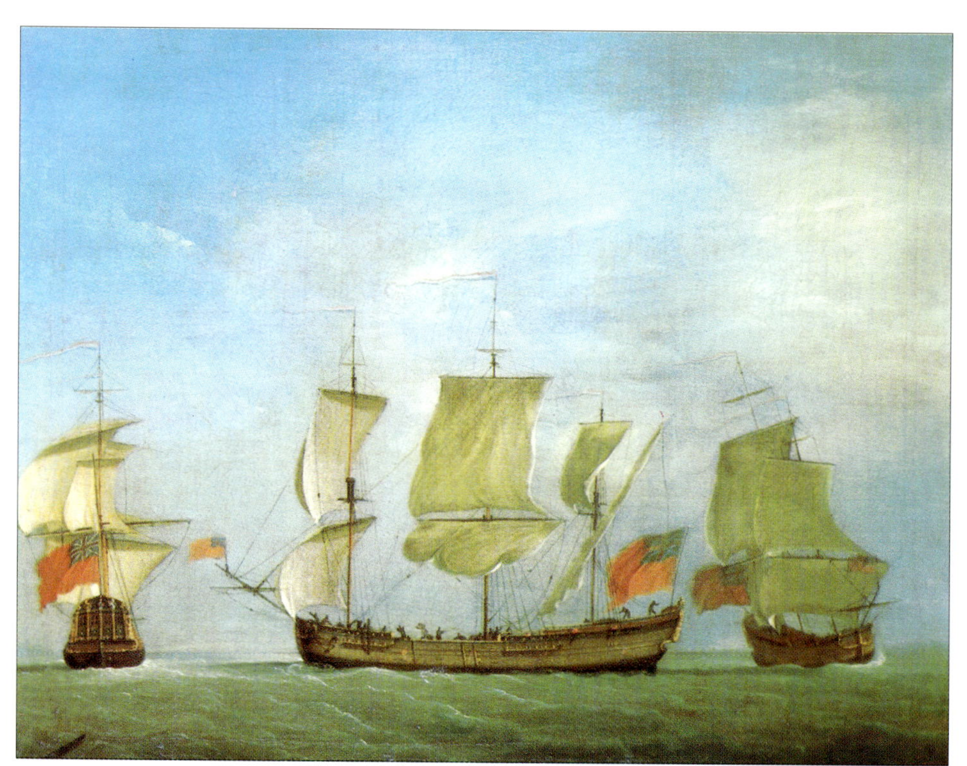

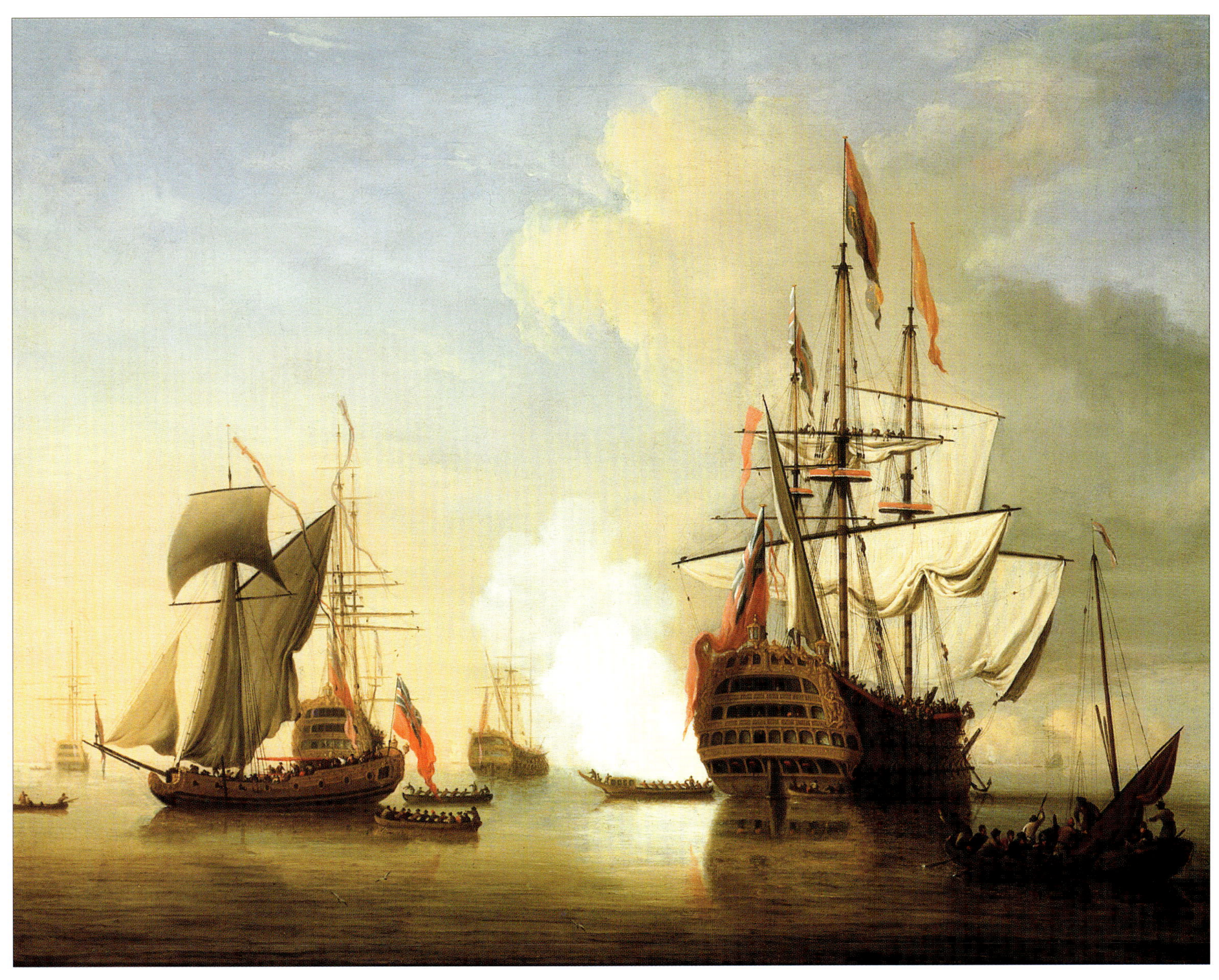

Colour Plate 20. *Stern view of the* Royal William *firing a salute. Signed P. Monamy.*

Note the typical Monamy 'edge' to the white clouds, and the same in the 'layers' of white gunsmoke. (Category 3)

Category 3 – Ship Portraits
Formal ship portraits, with the ship shown in three positions (broadside on, from bows and from stern) are remarkably rare in Monamy's *oeuvre*. Two examples are:

> A privateer in three positions (Colour Plate 19)
> A third rate in four positions, possibly the *Monmouth*

However, formal views of large important ships either from bow or stern, half turned to starboard or port, are more common (Colour Plates 20 and 23).

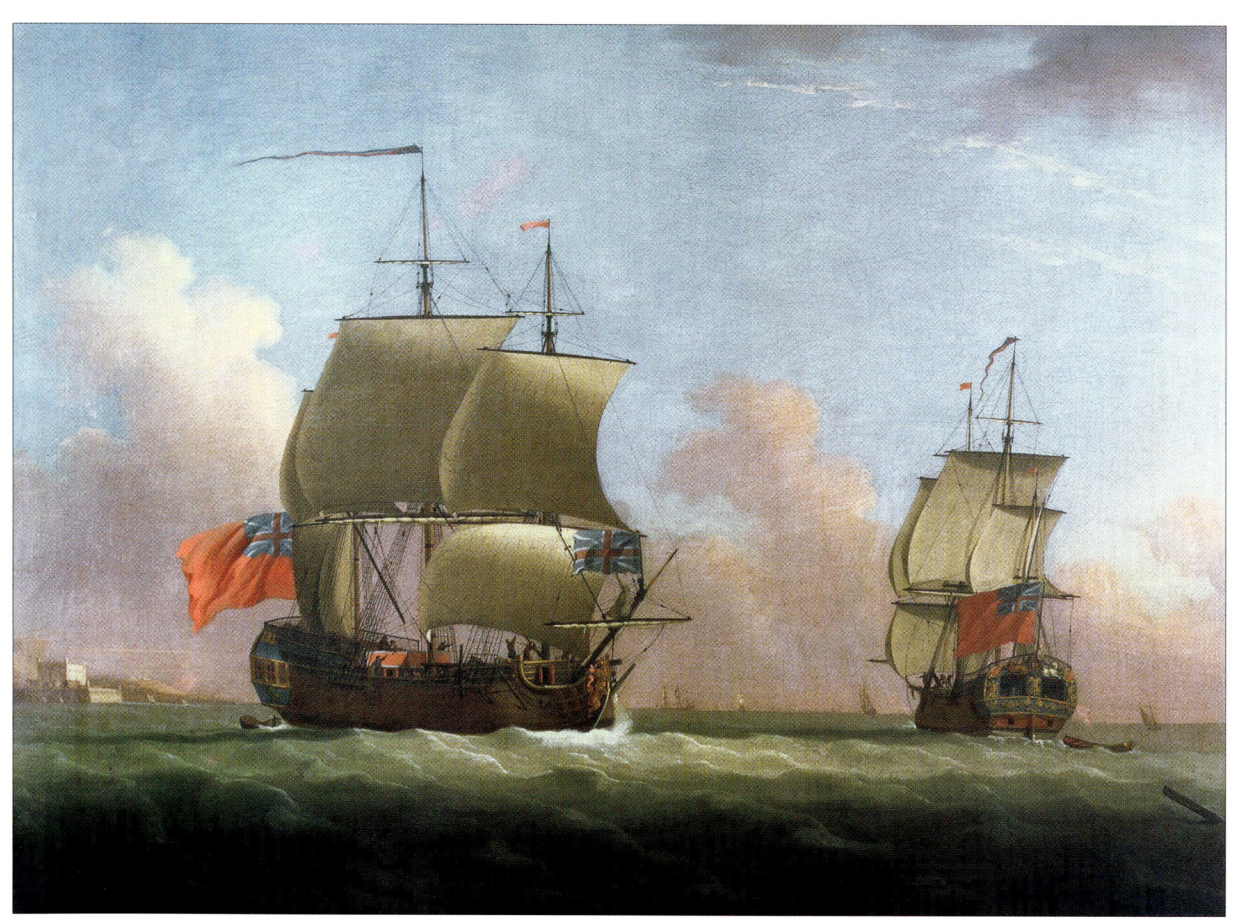

Colour Plate 21. *The 'ship-rigged' royal yacht* Dublin *in two positions. 43in. x 55½in.*
Signed P. Monamy. BONHAMS, LONDON, UK/BRIDGEMAN ART LIBRARY
This yacht was in service to the Viceroy of Ireland until 1753. (Category 3)

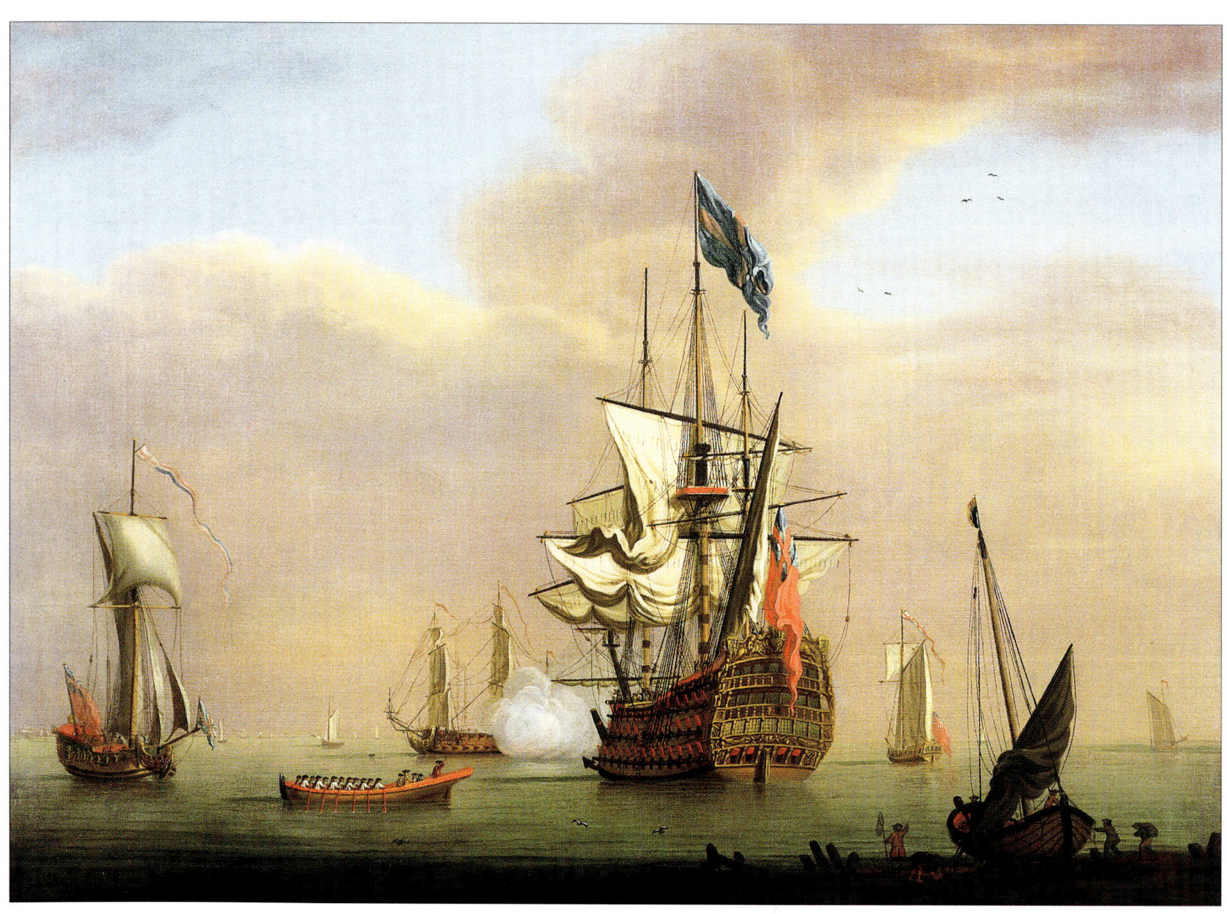

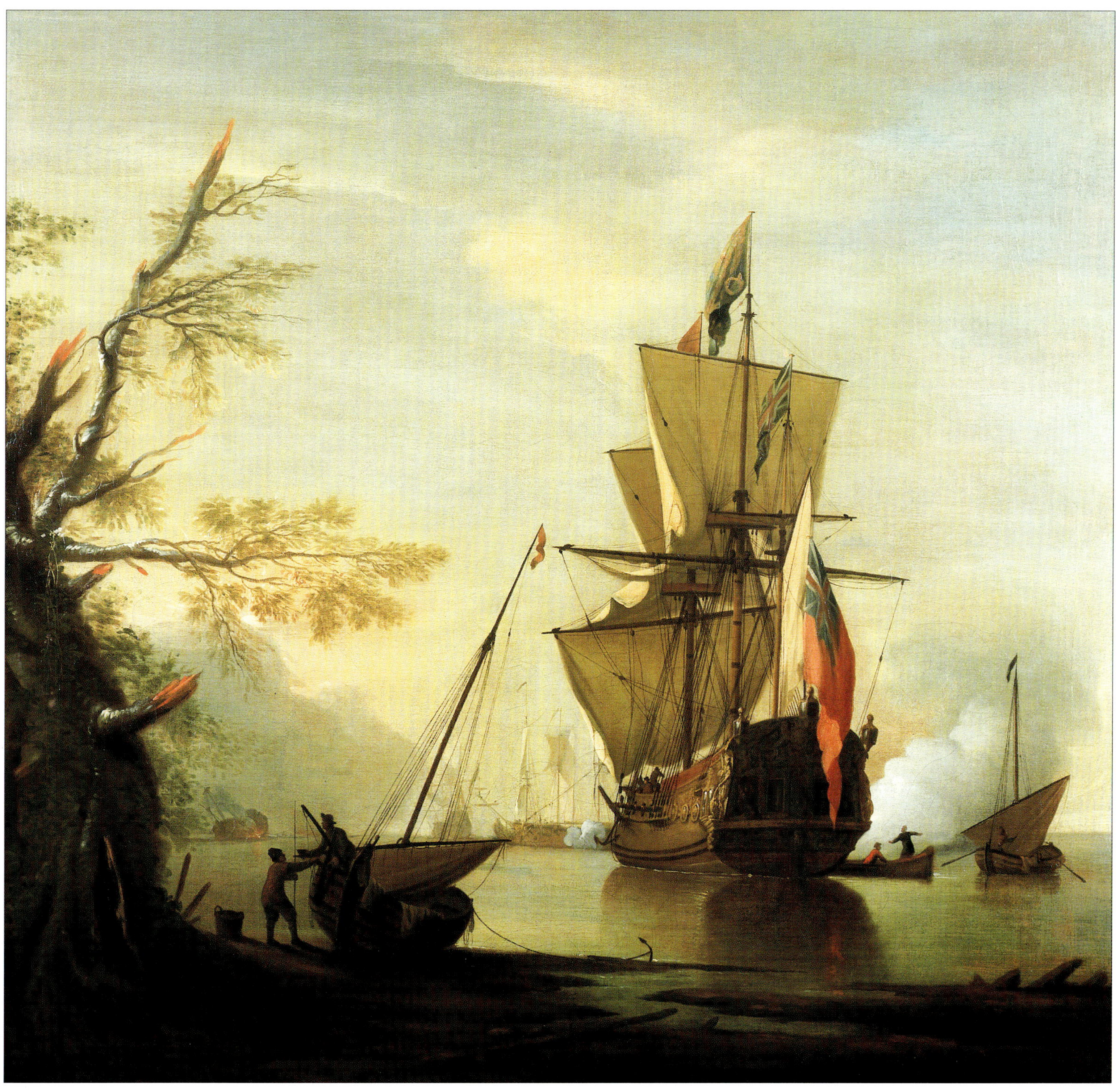

Colour Plate 22. *Stern view of the* Royal Caroline. *38in. x 39in. Indistinctly signed.*   AGNEWS
Note the typical wind vane pennants at the masthead of the small boats, also the white impasto edge to some of the clouds. (Category 3)

Colour Plate 23 (*Opposite). Stern view of the first-rate* Britannia. *28in. x 36in. Not signed.*   HAHN
This picture is included to show just how difficult it can sometimes be to differentiate between a Monamy and a Swaine. The cloud effects here and the preciseness of the outlines and general formality of the composition are like Swaine, but the layered white smoke from the cannon shot is very Monamy. On balance it is more likely to be the hand of Swaine. (Category 3)

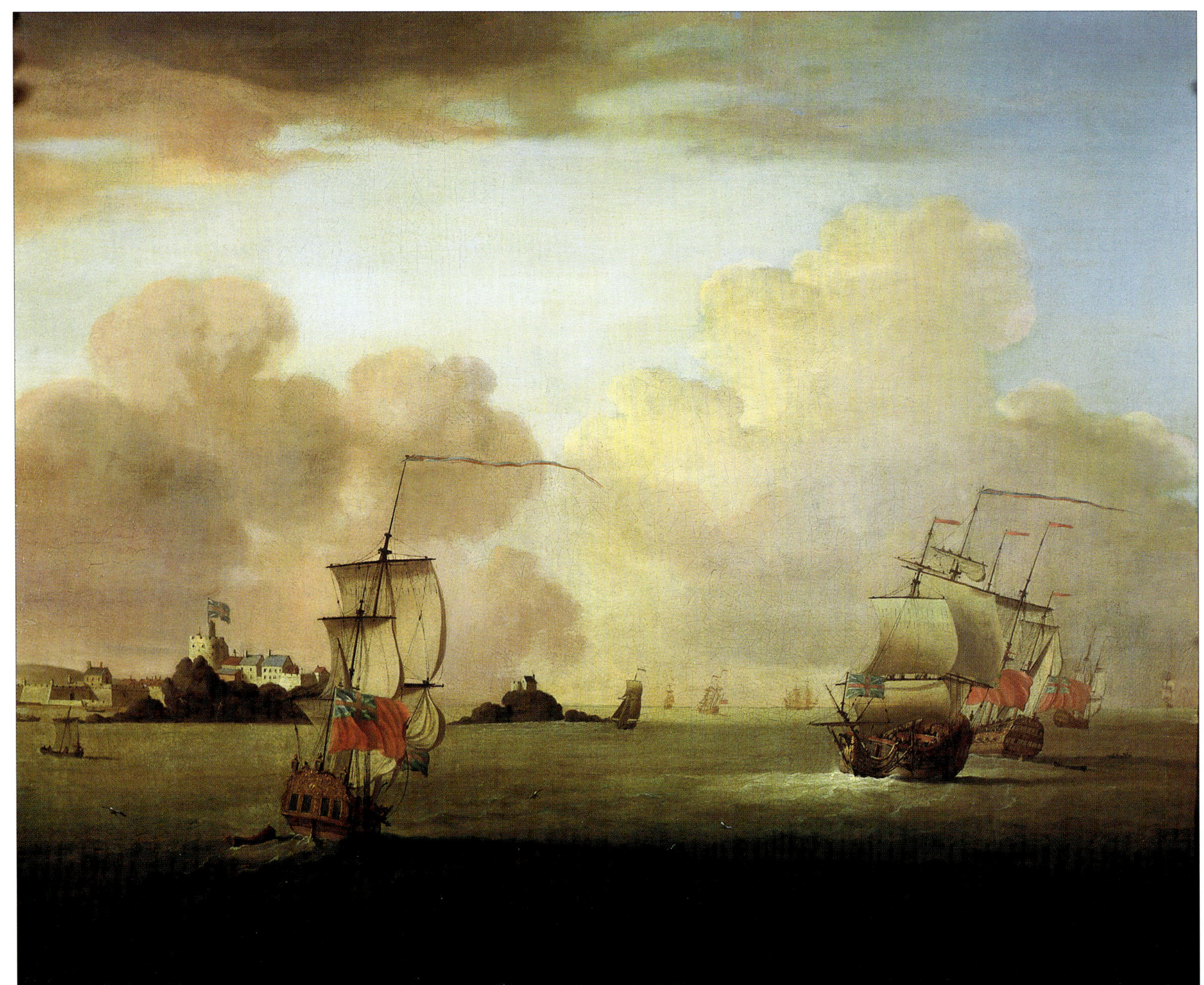

Colour Plate 24. *British men-o'-war and a merchantman off Elizabeth Castle, Jersey. Signed P. Monamy. 1740.*   JERSEY MUSEUM
One of his few little general seascapes which shows a specific recognisable location. (Category 4)

Colour Plate 25 *(Opposite above). A fleet coming to anchor. 36in. x 51in. Signed P. Monamy pinx.*   NATIONAL MARITIME MUSEUM
This large and important picture shows the arrival of the Queen of Portugal at Spithead in September 1708. In the centre a port quarter view of Sir George Byng's flagship, the Royal Anne. *On her starboard bow is Rear Admiral Baker's* Revenge *which escorted the yachts bringing the Queen from Holland. The striped flag on the stern jackstaff of the* Royal Anne *is the signal for the fleet to anchor.* (Category 4)

Colour Plate 26 *(Opposite below). A small sailing boat and a merchantman at sea in a rising wind. 19in. x 23½in. Signed P. Monamy.*   BONHAMS, LONDON, UK/BRIDGEMAN
                                                                                                   ART LIBRARY
This small typical sea piece shows Monamy at his very best. The composition and painting of the sea and sky are very realistic and the picture is most attractive. (Category 4)

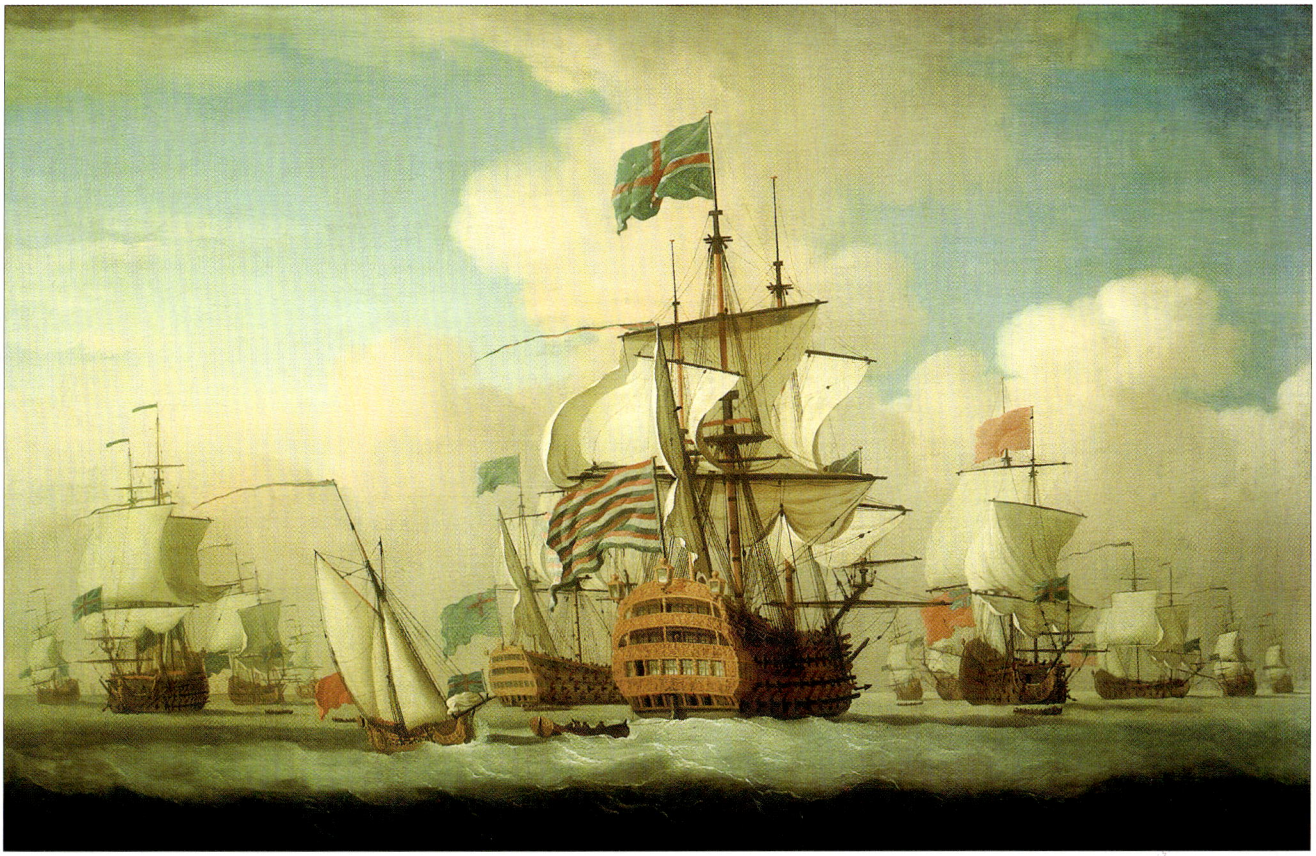

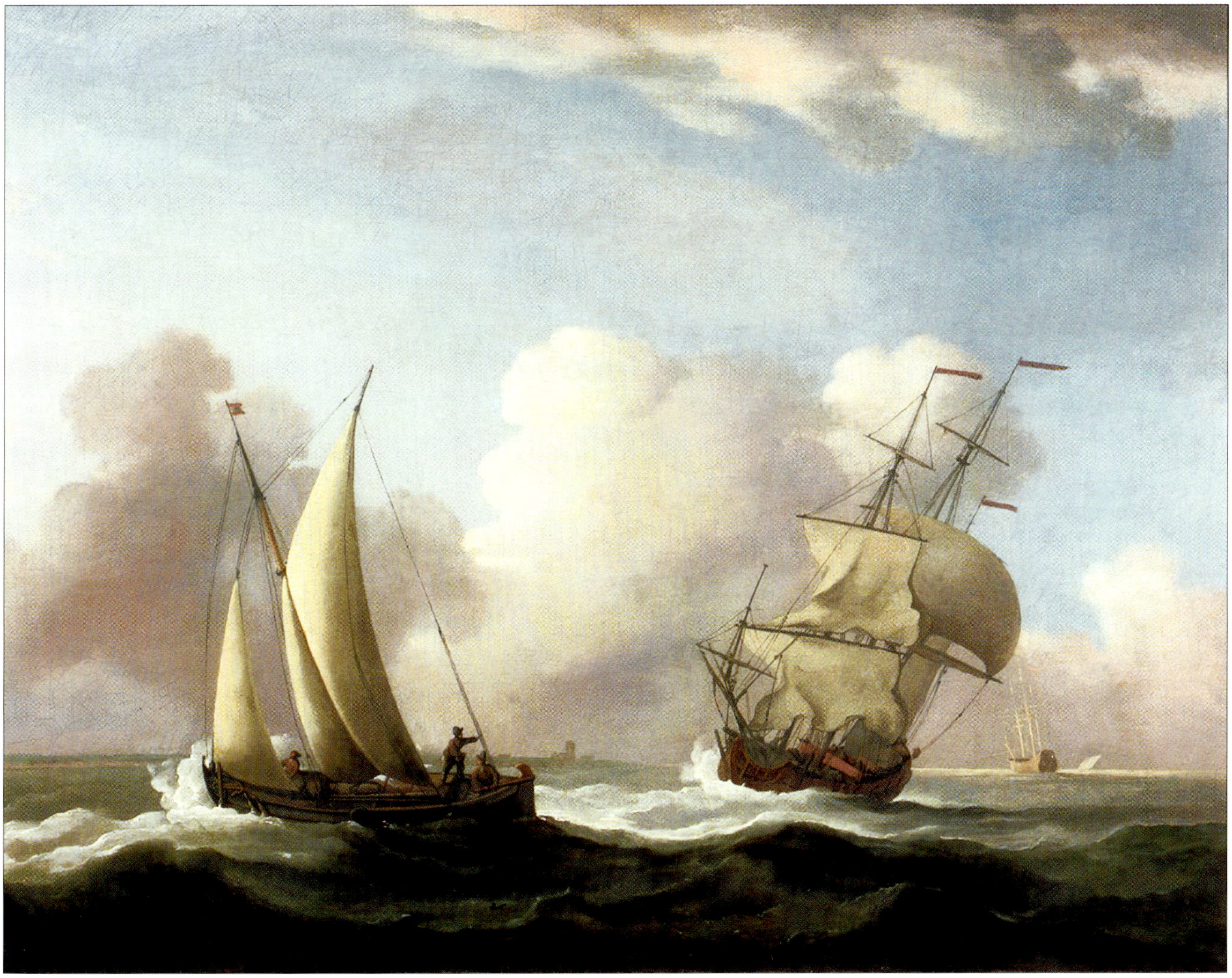

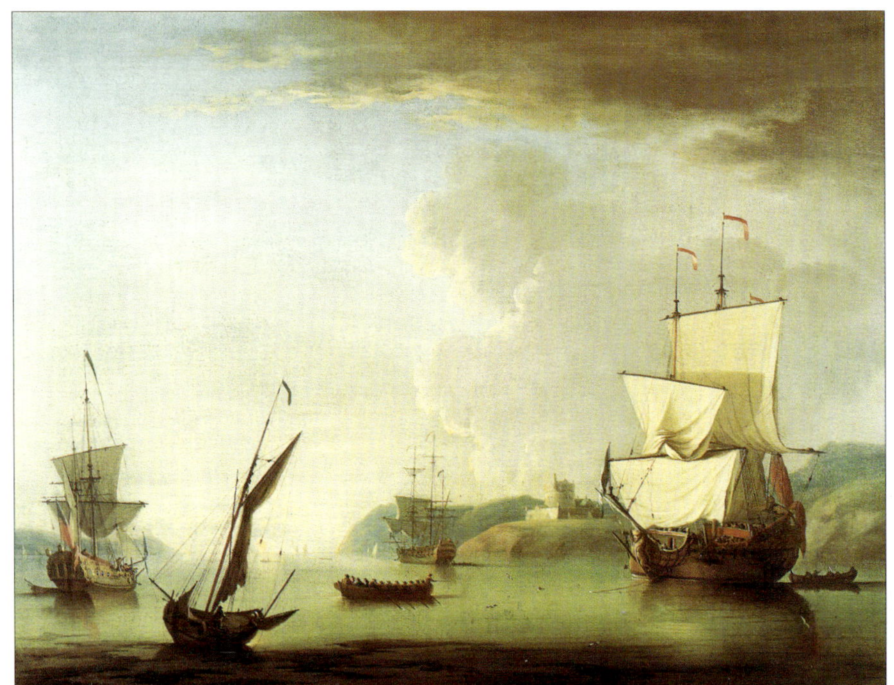

Colour Plate 27. *A calm estuary scene. 27in. x 35in. Signed.*

AGNEW

The composition, with ships at anchor on each side and the scene fading into the distance with typical Monamy billowing clouds, was much used by him. It is very calm, attractive, decorative and 'easy to live with'. (Category 4)

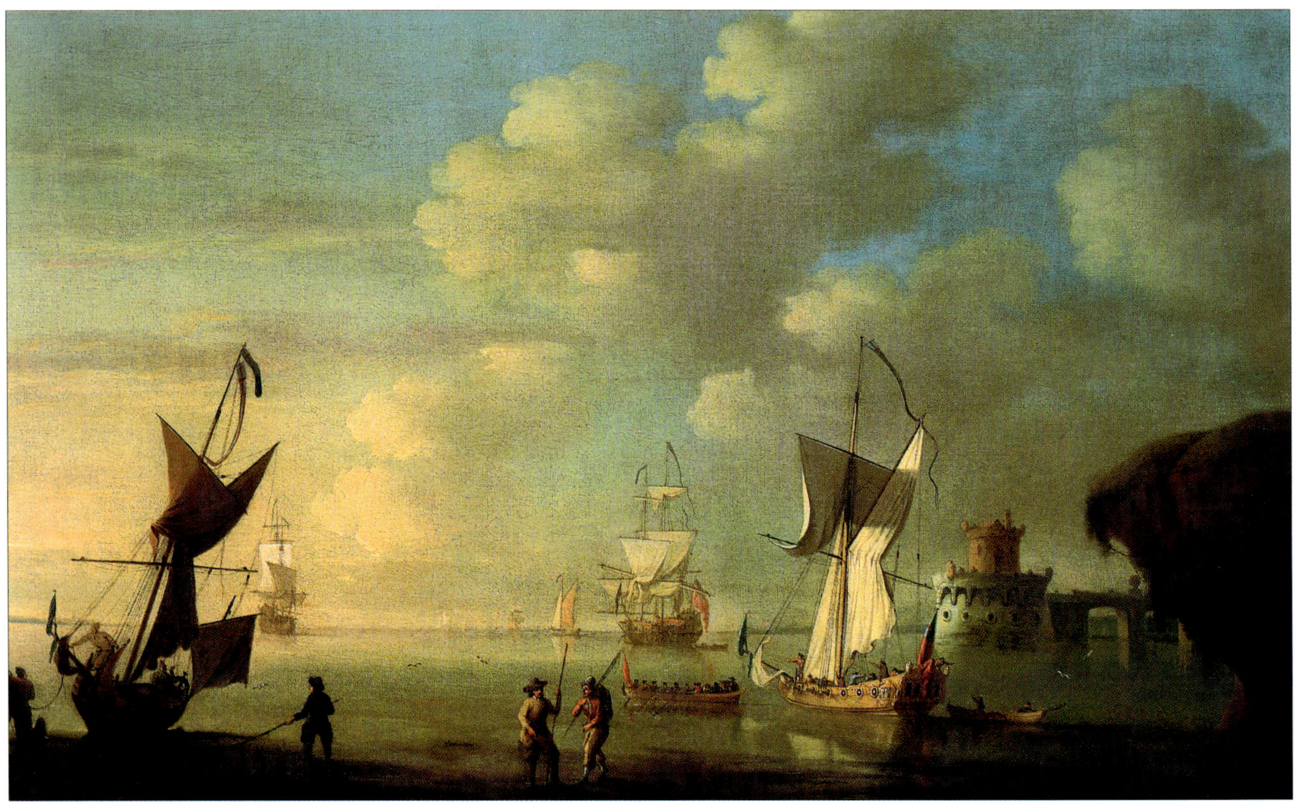

Colour Plate 28. *A royal yacht and other shipping off the coast. 25in. x 39in. Signed P. Monamy.*

O'MELL GALLERY

Again a classic calm Monamy composition with the little beached 'hoy' and seashore figures in the foreground. A little castle by the shore and plenty of wonderful Monamy clouds. All very attractive and restful. (Category 4)

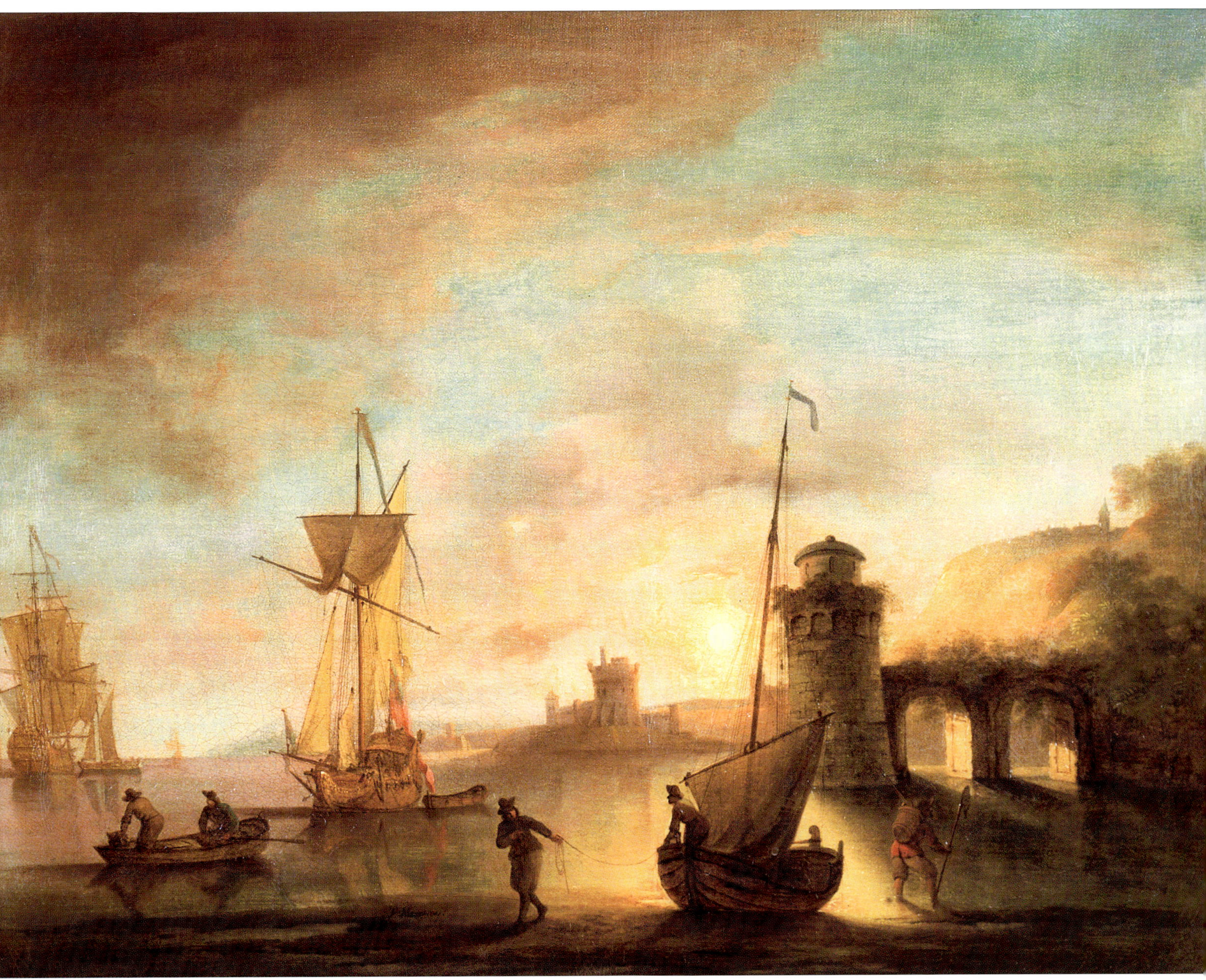

Colour Plate 29. *A calm sunset scene. 19¼in. x 25in. Signed P. Monamy.*
CHRISTIE'S LOT 63, 26.4.85

A typical Monamy calm scene. Monamy was very interested in the handling of light effects in his pictures (for example firelight, evening, sunset, moonlight, etc.). (Category 4)

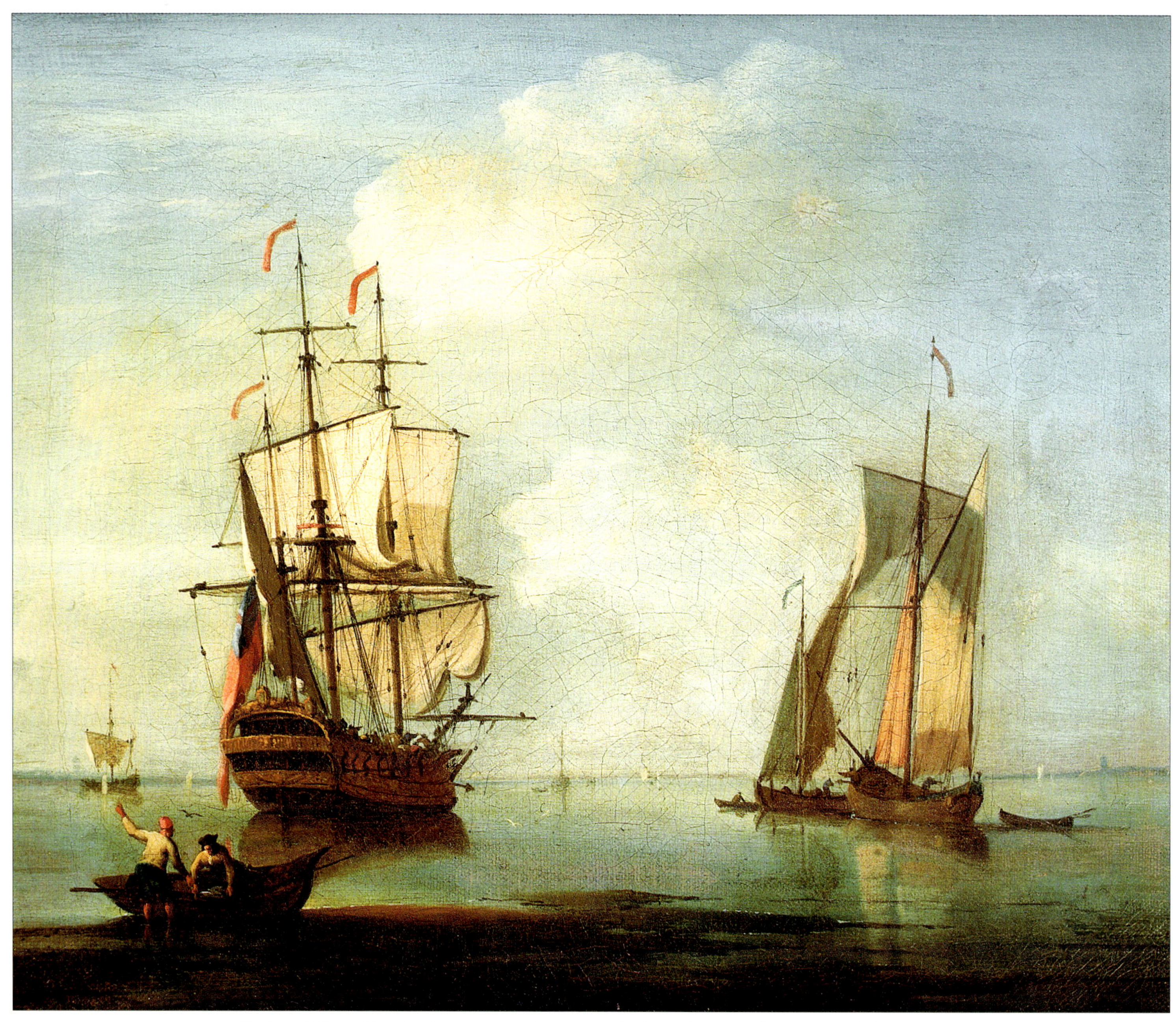

Colour Plate 30. *A calm scene, with two small ships drying sails. 11in. x 13½in. Signed P. Monamy.*
(Category 4)   PRIVATE COLLECTION

Colour Plate 31 *(Opposite above). A fleet lying at anchor in an estuary. Signed P. Monamy.*
                                                                                                 PRIVATE COLLECTION
This picture was formerly part of the Ingram Collection. The light effects are particularly sophisticated,
as the scene is late evening just before dusk. Once again Monamy clouds much in evidence.
(Category 4)

Colour Plate 32 *(Opposite below). An English fleet at anchor, with the Admiral's ship signalling.*
33in. x 61in. Signed P. Monamy.   LANE FINE ART
This large painting shows the royal standard flying from the stern jackstaff. In this position it was used
as a signalling flag for all commanders to come aboard for a conference. The barges on either side of the
flagship are the Admiral of the White and Admiral of the Red Squadrons coming aboard. (See
page 47.) (Category 4)

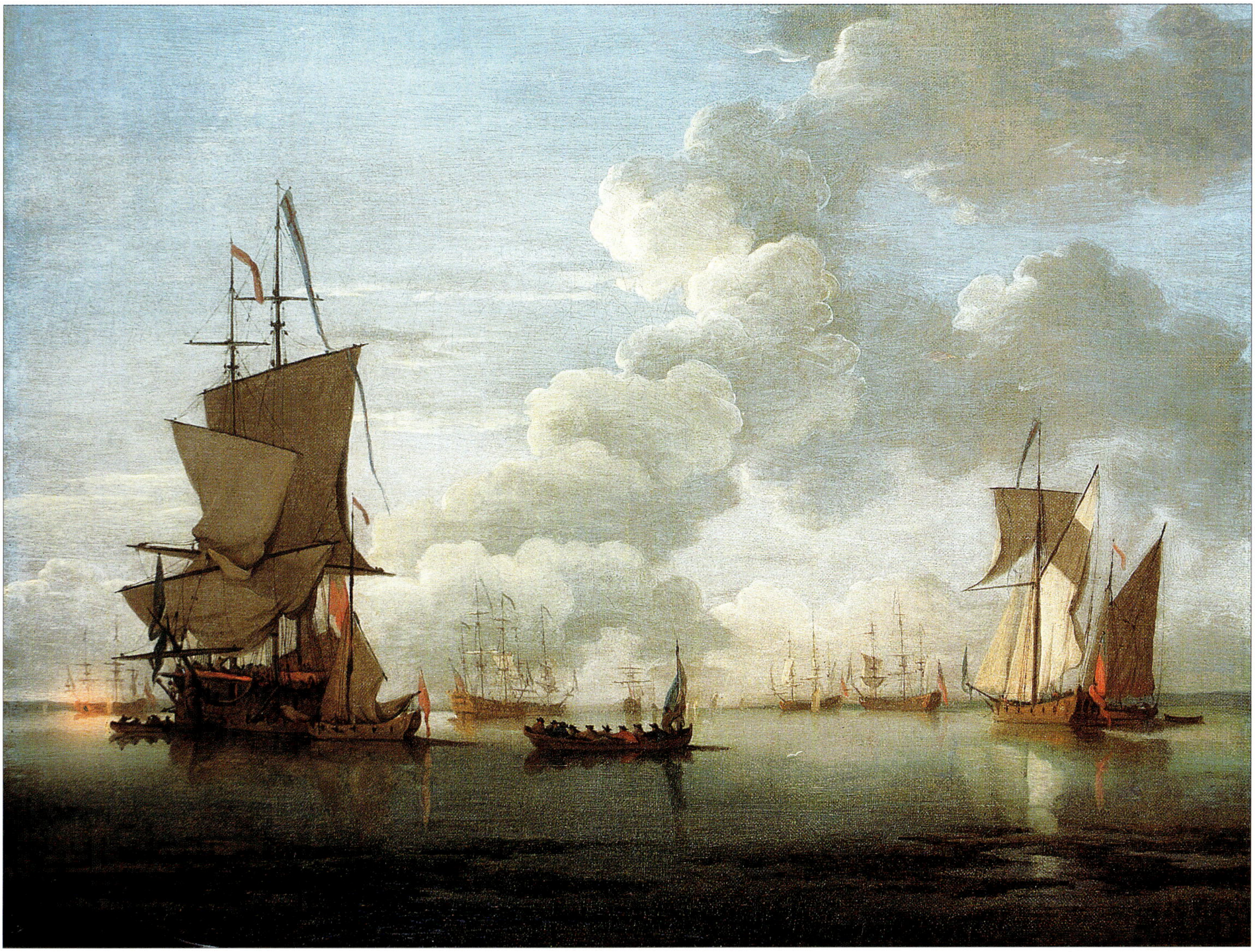

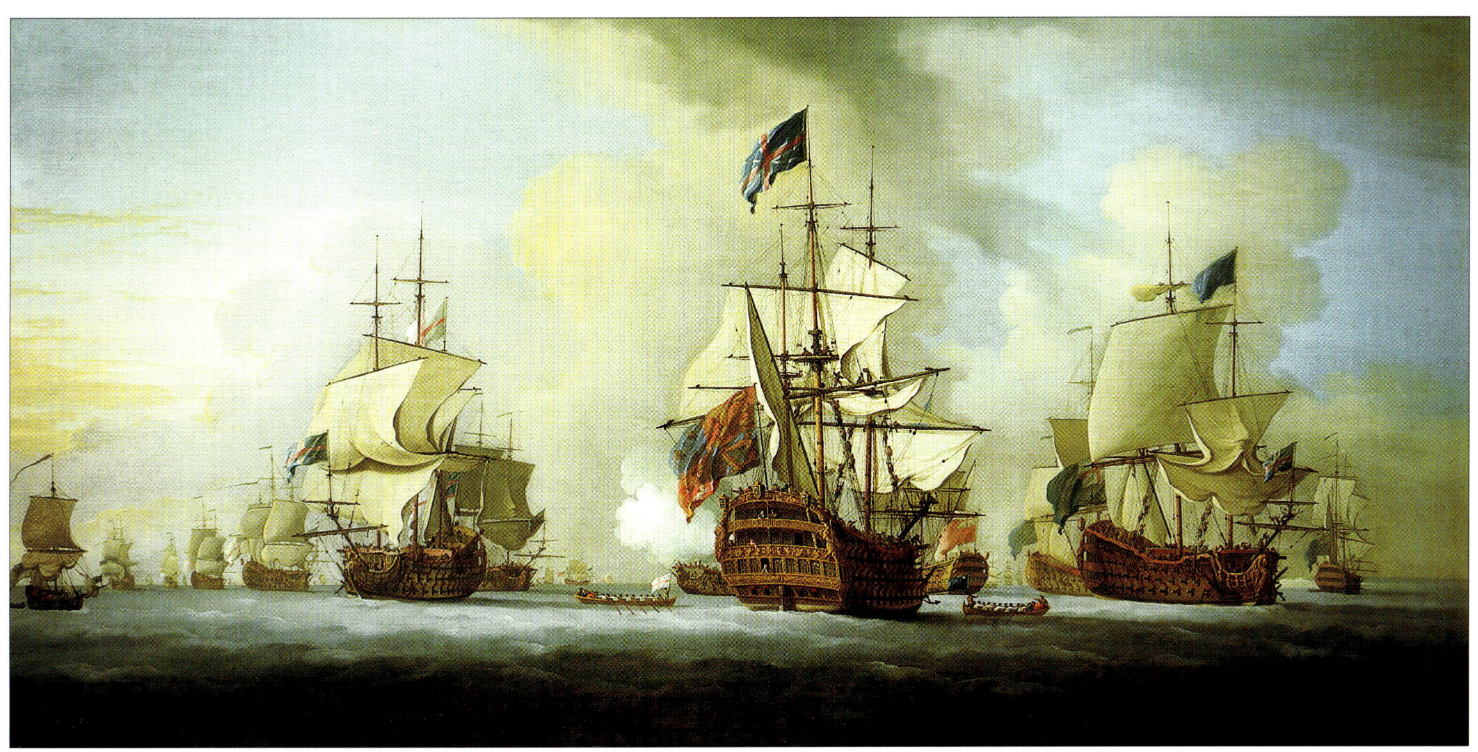

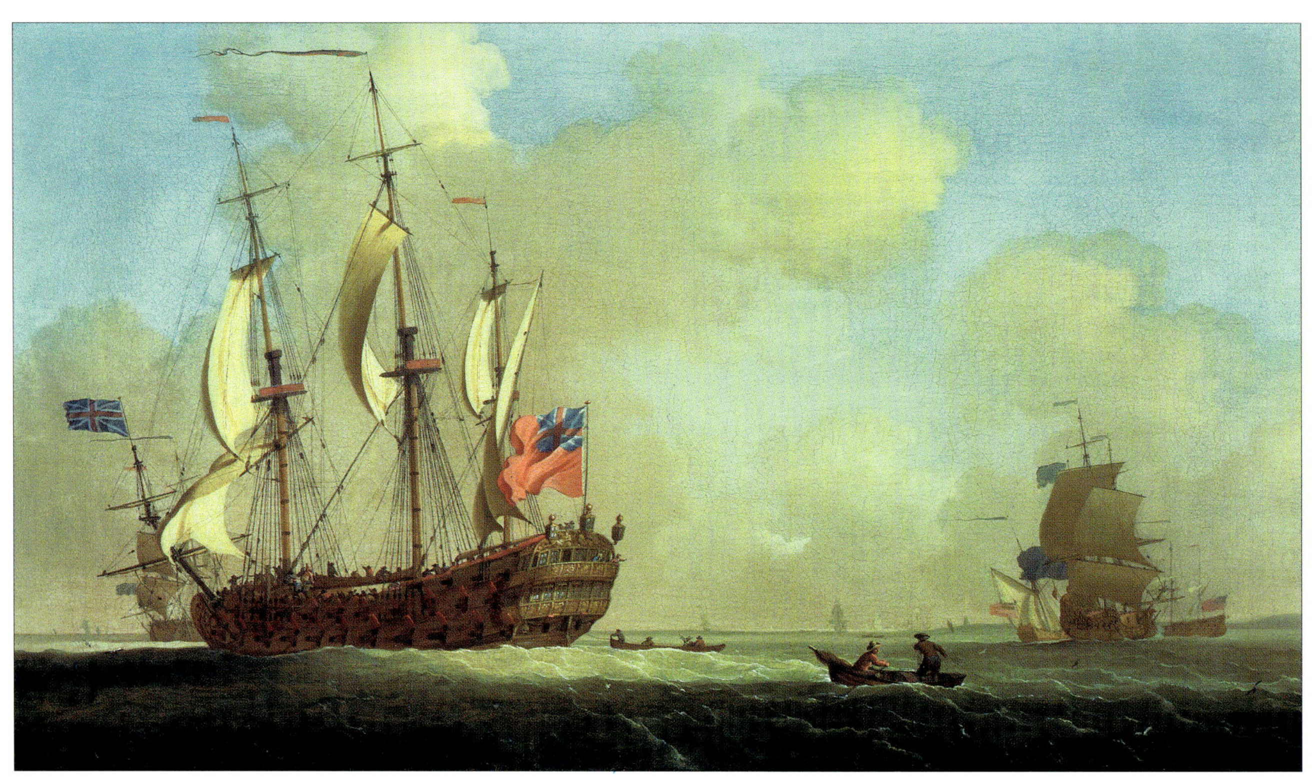

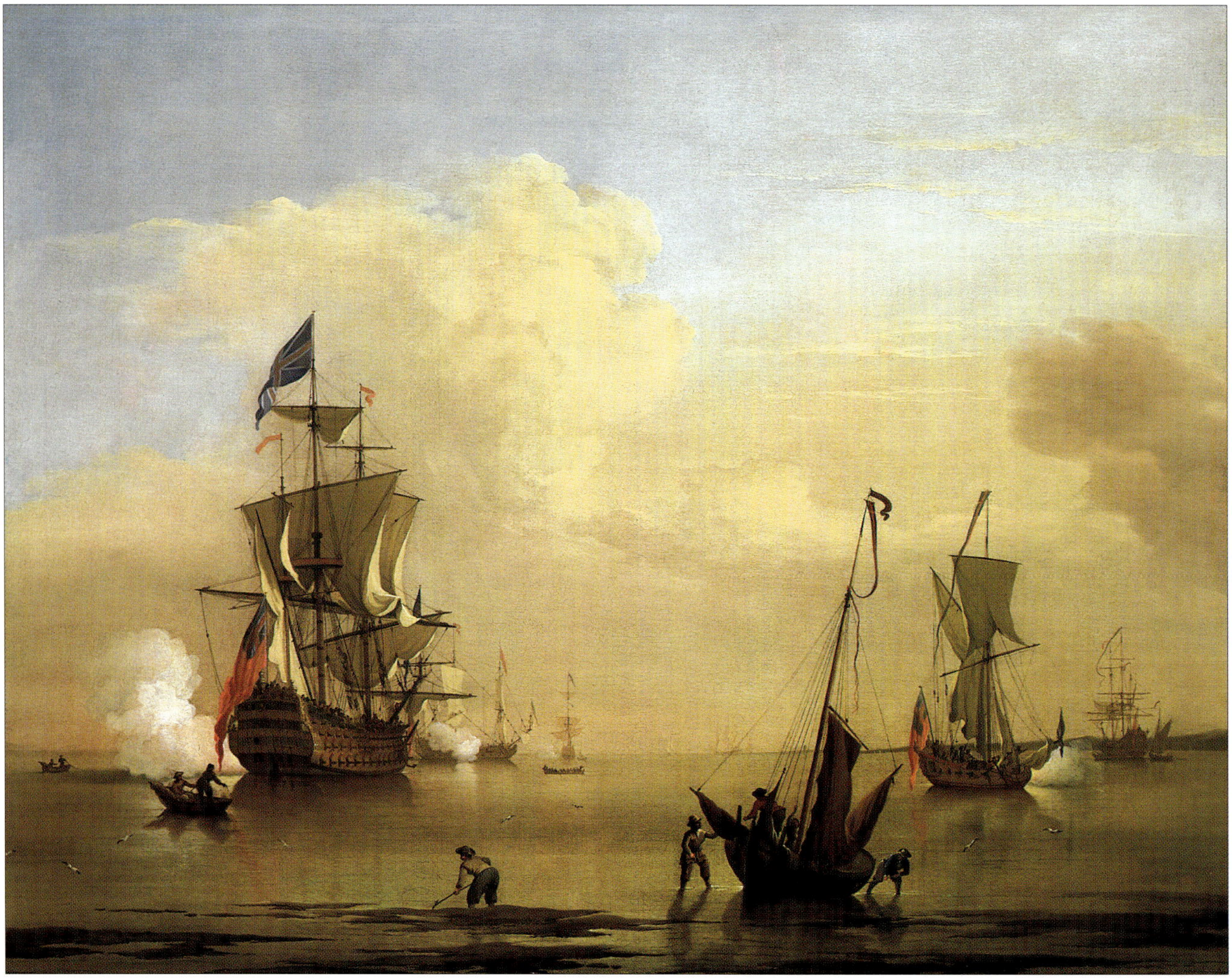

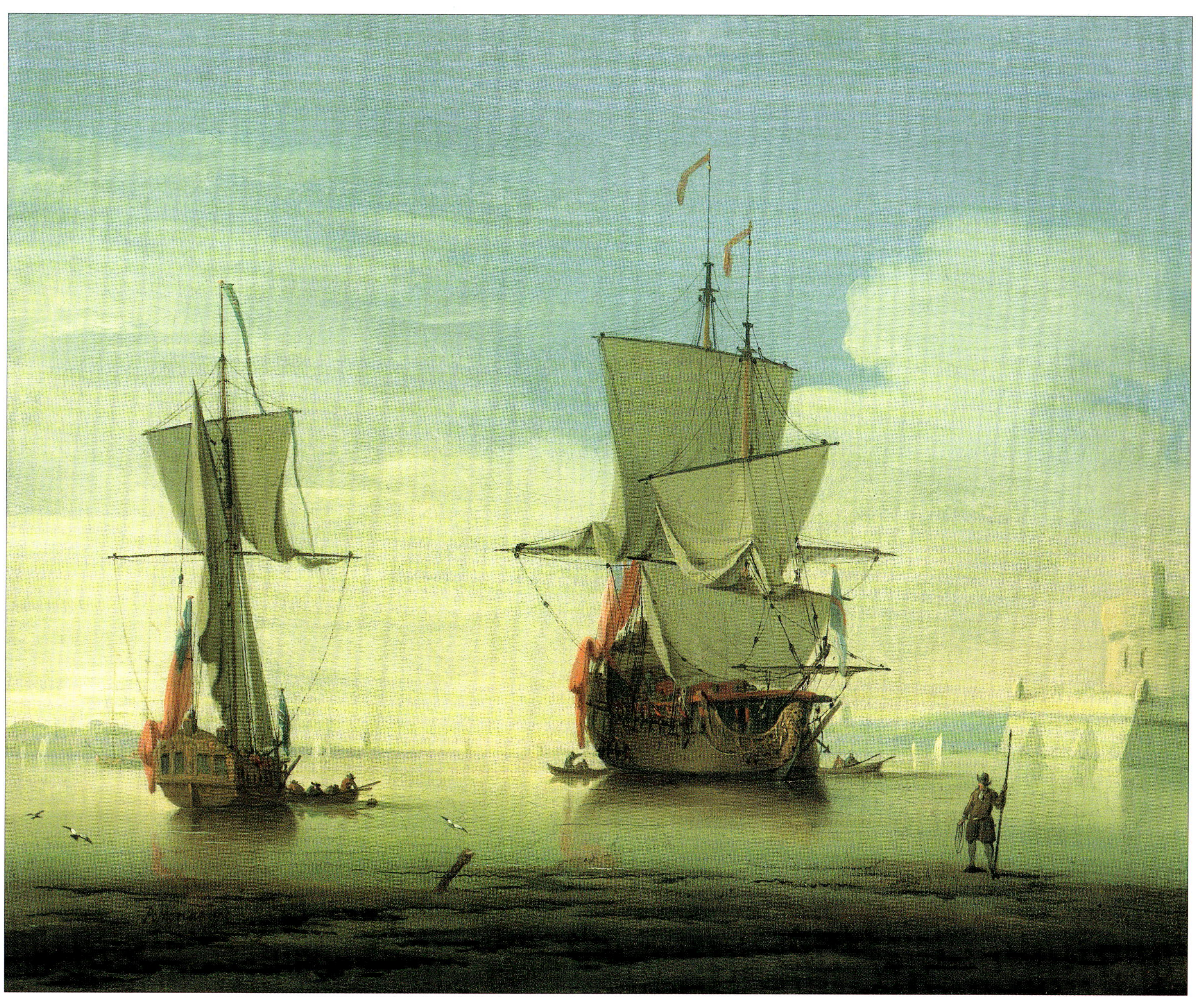

Colour Plate 35. *A two-decker and a yacht anchored near a tower. 11¾in. x 13¾in. Signed P. Monamy.*   RICHARD GREEN GALLERY
A small picture for a small intimate room. Very restful and relaxing. (Category 4)

Colour Plate 33 *(Opposite above). A fifty gun, two-decker, at sea near a coast. 16½in. x 28½in. Signed P. Monamy.*   RICHARD GREEN GALLERY
This picture, like Colour Plate 26, shows Monamy at his best, with a typical naval ship of the 1730-1740 vintage, at sea, and drawn with wonderful accuracy and feeling. This picture rivals the best that Van de Velde could ever produce – which is high praise indeed. (Category 4)

Colour Plate 34 *(Opposite below). Calm estuary scene with a large two-decker firing a signal gun. 35in. x 58in. Signed P. Monamy.*   RICHARD GREEN GALLERY
This and the next picture are examples of his so-called 'commercial' calm scenes, but they are painted with skill and accuracy and are very easy to live with. (Category 4)

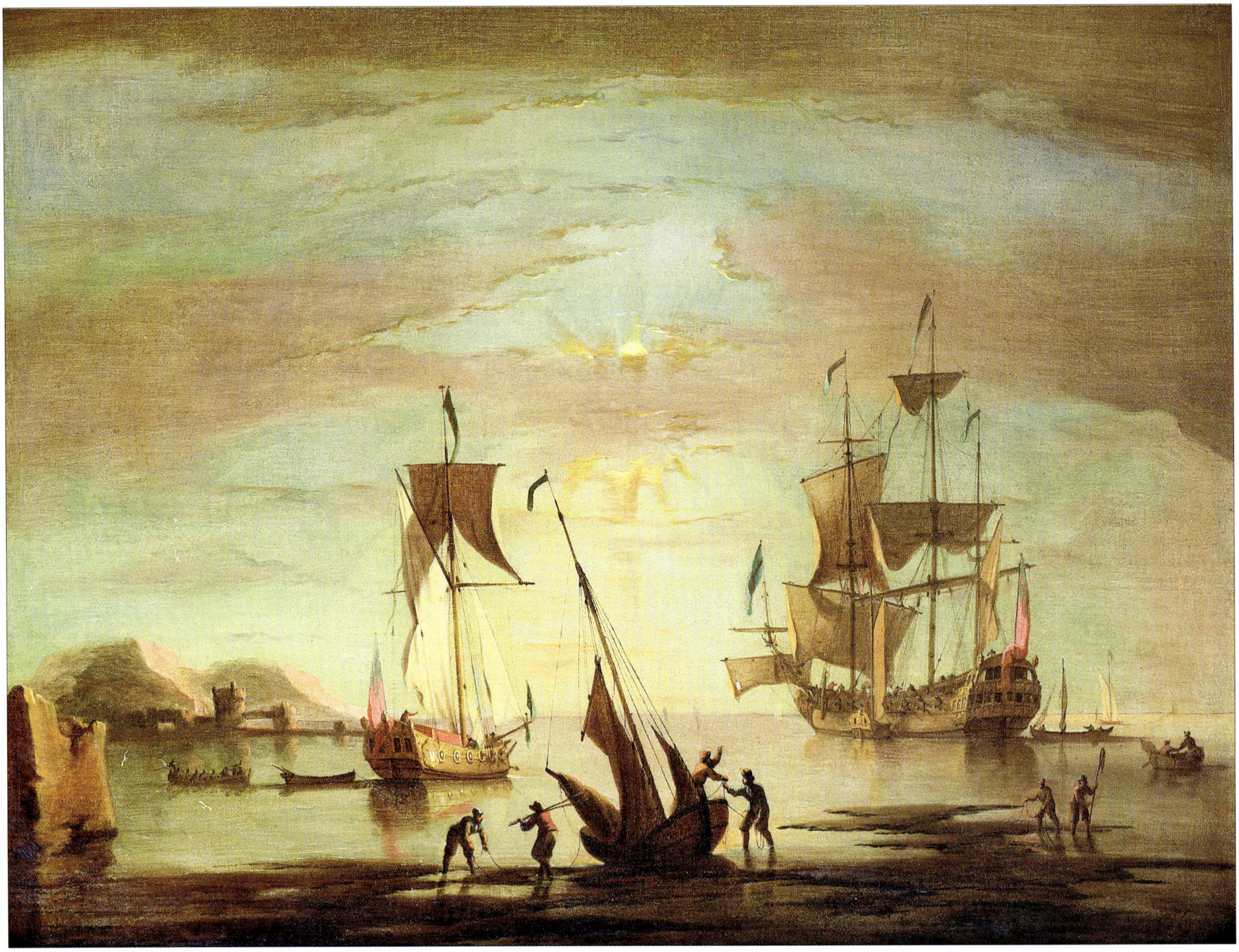

Colour Plate 36. *Shipping becalmed offshore at sunset. 21¼in. x 26½in. Signed.*

CHRISTIE'S LOT 64, 26.4.85

A rather dramatically lit little calm picture with quite a lot of activity in the foreground, including the usual little beached 'hoy'. The unusual sky is painted looking right into the sun. (Category 4)

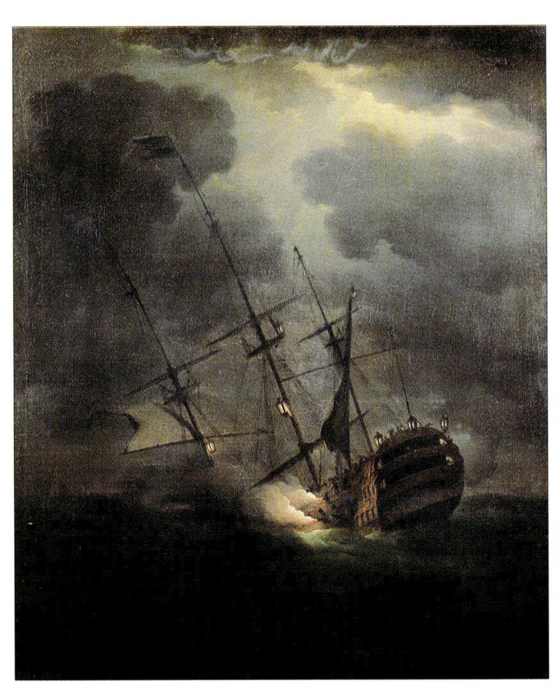

Colour Plate 37. *The loss of H.M.S.* Victory *in a gale on 4 October 1744. 30in. x 24in. Not signed.*

NATIONAL MARITIME MUSEUM

This Victory *was the fourth ship of the Royal Navy to bear the name. She was a first-rate of 100 guns and was wrecked on the Casquets, near the island of Alderney, in 1744 with the loss of all hands. Nelson's* Victory *was laid down and built at Chatham in 1759. (Category 5)*

70

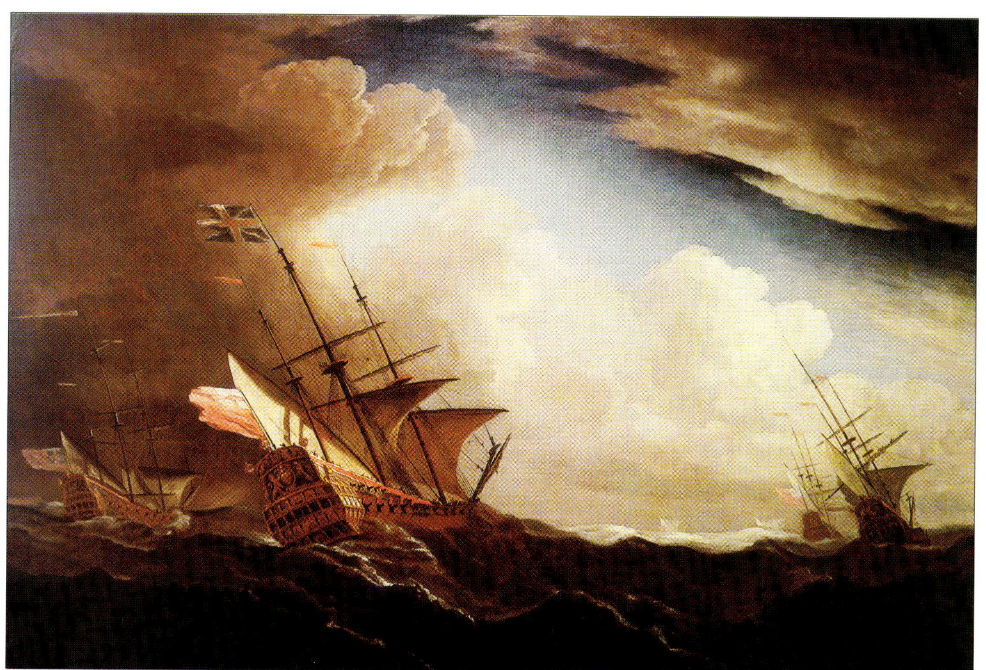

Colour Plate 38. *English ships beating to windward in a gale. 34in. x 48in. Signed W.V. Velde J.*   NATIONAL MARITIME MUSEUM
This is a famous and much copied original picture by Van de Velde the younger, now in the National Maritime Museum collection, painted some time between 1680 and 1690. (Category 8)

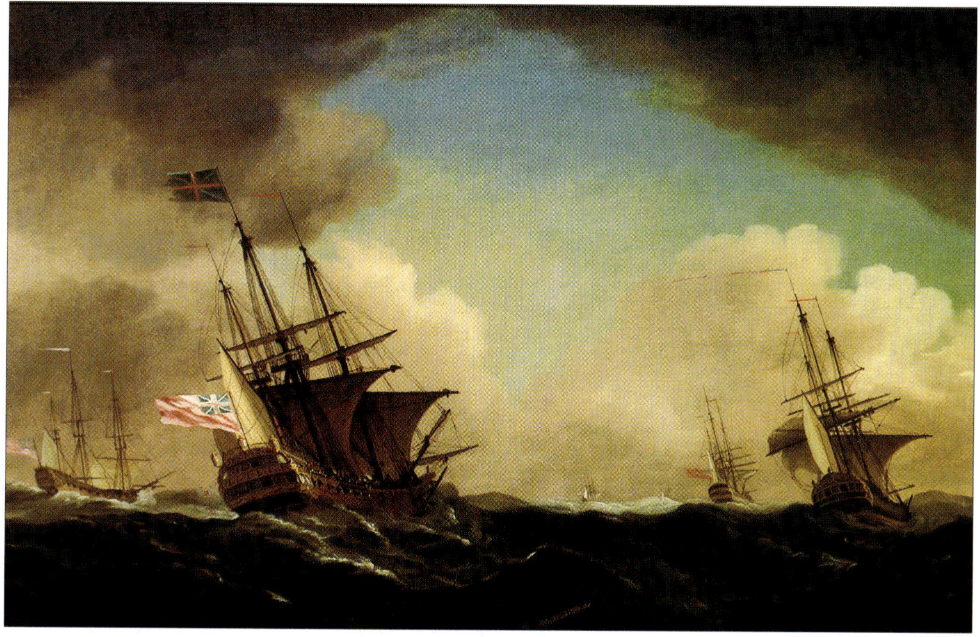

Colour Plate 39. *A squadron of English ships beating to windward in a gale. 12in. x 15¼in. Signed P. Monamy.*   SOTHEBY'S LOT 3, 3.5.95. PRIVATE COLLECTION
This picture is a fairly exact copy of Van de Velde's picture shown above (Colour Plate 38). However, Monamy has updated the flags and he has also updated the sterns of the ships to the more 'open galleried' 1740 style. The clouds too now look much more like typical Monamy clouds. (Category 8)

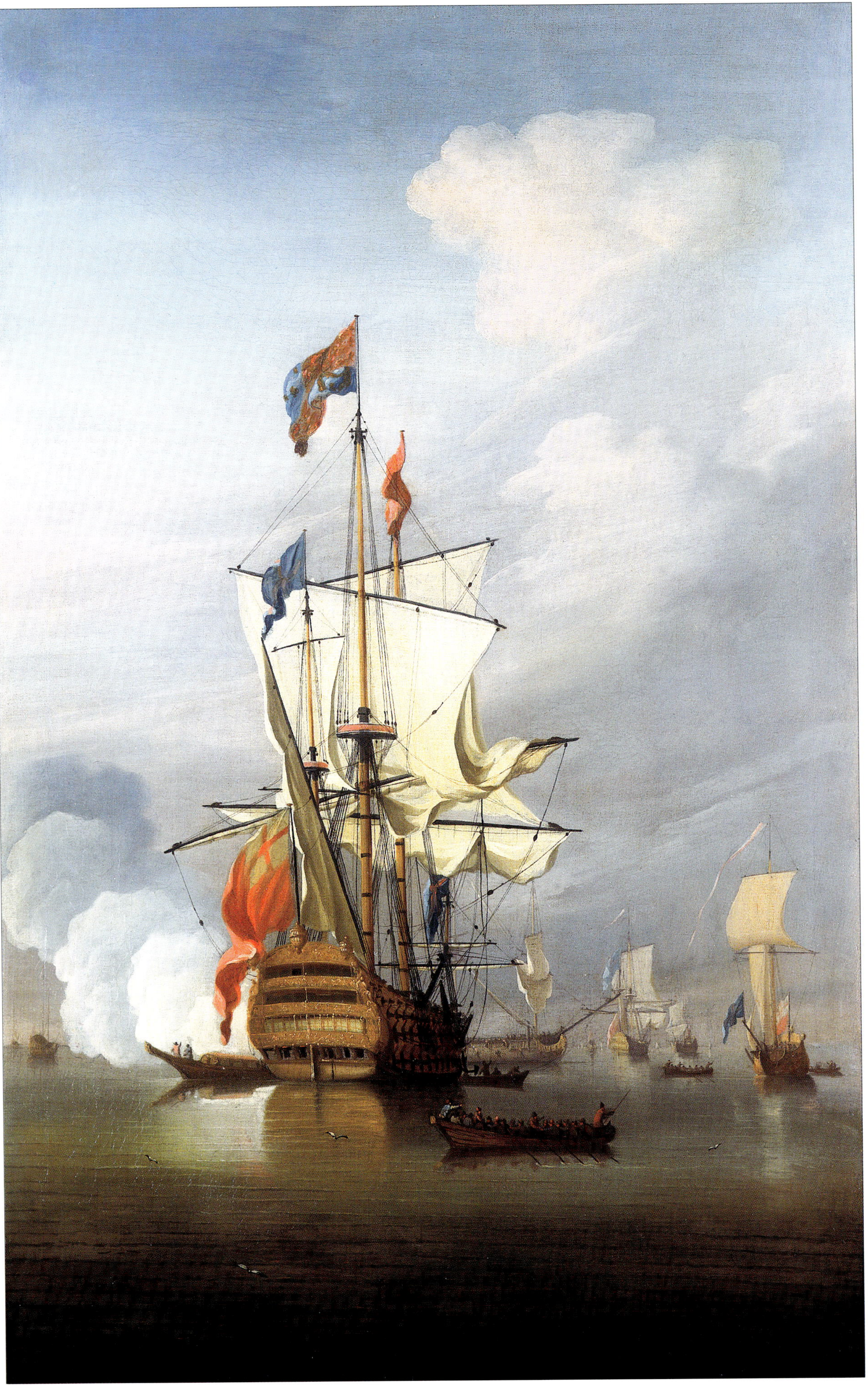

There are numerous views of this type of the *Royal Sovereign* (Colour Plate 40) and the *Britannia*. Most of them are either copies or heavily based on Van de Velde originals. Some are signed by Peter Monamy but some are not signed and are obvious Van de Velde copies, which means that their attribution is open to doubt (see Colour Plate 23).

There are also a number of portraits of the royal yachts of the period. Good portraits of the *Royal Caroline,* the *Mary* and the *Dublin* are recorded (Colour Plates 16, 18 and 21).

Category 4 – General Seascapes and Calm Scenes
This group accounts for by far the greater part of his output. It is difficult to estimate the number in general circulation, but it must be in excess of one hundred and fifty pictures at a conservative estimate. Most of them are medium to small size seascapes, very attractive, light, and well composed, of so-called 'cabinet size' (that is to say suitable for hanging in smaller rooms rather than mansions or palaces). Some, however, are of larger size, and more ambitious, showing larger ships or even a fleet at sea (Colour Plate 25).

His pictures of small ships at sea in a moderate or light breeze are some of his best efforts as he was a master at portraying the sea realistically in all its moods (Colour Plates 26 and 33).

The ships range from large first and second rate warships, through every type and size, to small yachts at sea. There are many attractive and decorative calm scenes, ships at anchor, with their sails drooping, usually set in an estuary with some land visible, often with a fort or castle.

They are very accurately done, and form a wonderful record of the maritime scene of the first half of the eighteenth century. They are bright, realistic, attractive and were readily saleable (still are!) and must have been his best commercial asset, keeping him in reasonable circumstances for most of his life.

***Colour Plate 40** (Opposite). The first-rate ship* Royal Sovereign, *stern quarter view, in a calm. 39¼in. x 24¼in. Signed P. Monamy.*   RICHARD GREEN GALLERY
This beautiful and attractive picture is closely derived from one of the Van de Velde portraits of this ship which was widely copied by a number of artists. Peter Monamy has signed this version and has added a few individual touches of his own. There has been some rearrangement of the background ships, and again the typical layered white smoke of the gunshot is prominent. The clouds are also much more like Monamy than Van de Velde. It flies the pre-1707 ensign on the stern jackstaff. Monamy did several copies or versions of this picture, including the one he presented to the Painter-Stainers Company in 1726. (Category 8)

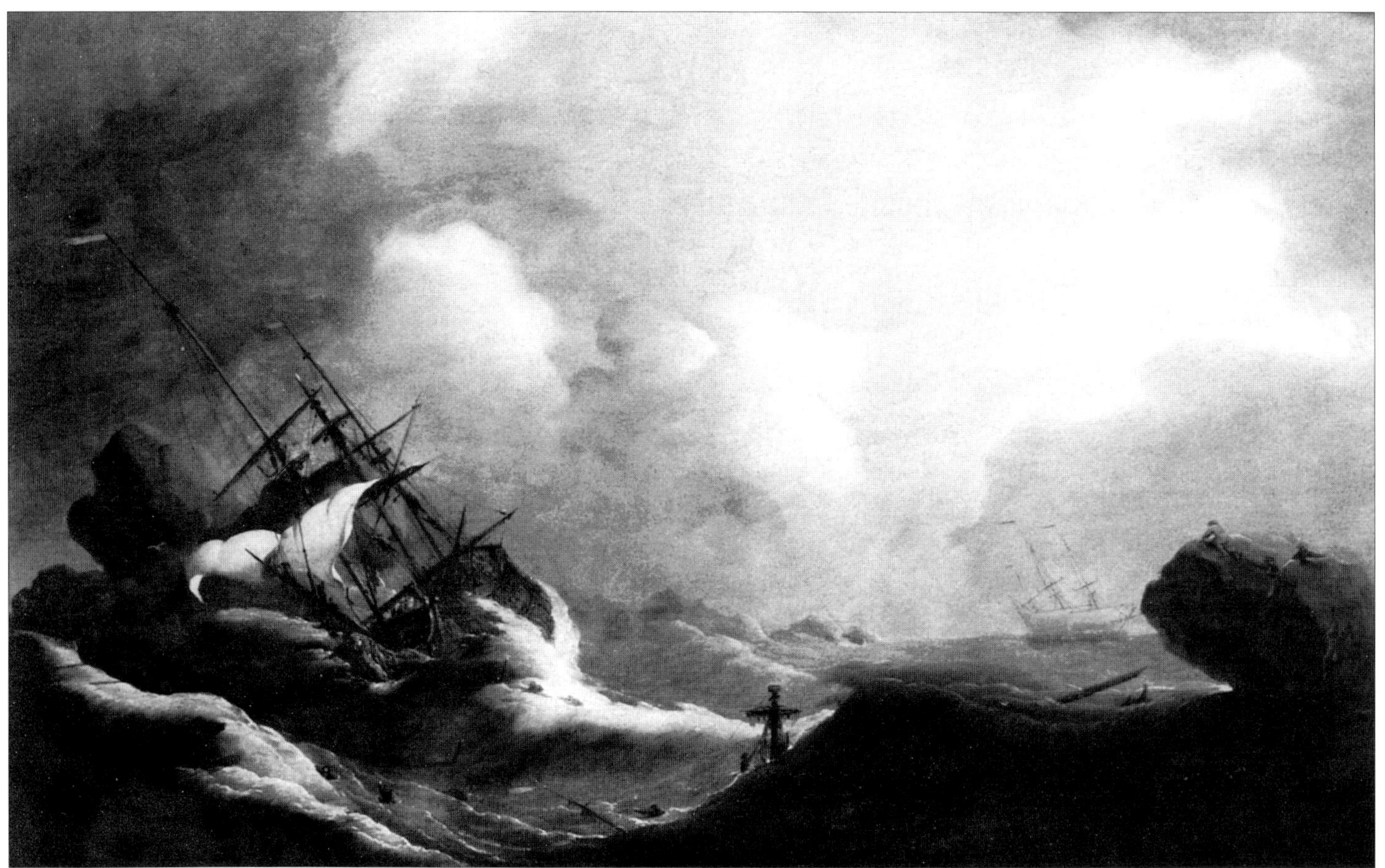

Plate 13. *A ship running on to rocks in a violent storm. Signed P. Monamy.*
CHRISTIE'S LOT 57, NOV. 1974. PRIVATE COLLECTION
This theme, with slight variations, was repeated many times by Monamy. (Category 5)

Most of them were done for dealers, for sale to the general public, although a few may have been special commissions.

Representative examples of this group are shown in this chapter's illustrations.

Category 5 – Storms

Producing scenes of terrible storms and shipwreck has always been a challenge to sea painters. It is a tradition which stems back to the early seventeenth century Dutch sea painters, such as Vroom, Van Artvelt, Porcellis and the Peters family. They all produced terrible storm and shipwreck pictures to illustrate the dangers faced by their brave sailors. Contrary to what one might expect, such pictures were popular and sold well in those early days, although they are now less popular.

Peter Monamy was no exception to this rule. George I was continually travelling back to Hanover and then returning across the North Sea to England during his reign. He usually made the journey in the royal yacht *Peregrine* (later renamed the *Royal Caroline),* accompanied by several other yachts and often a naval escorting ship. Pictures of this journey in severe

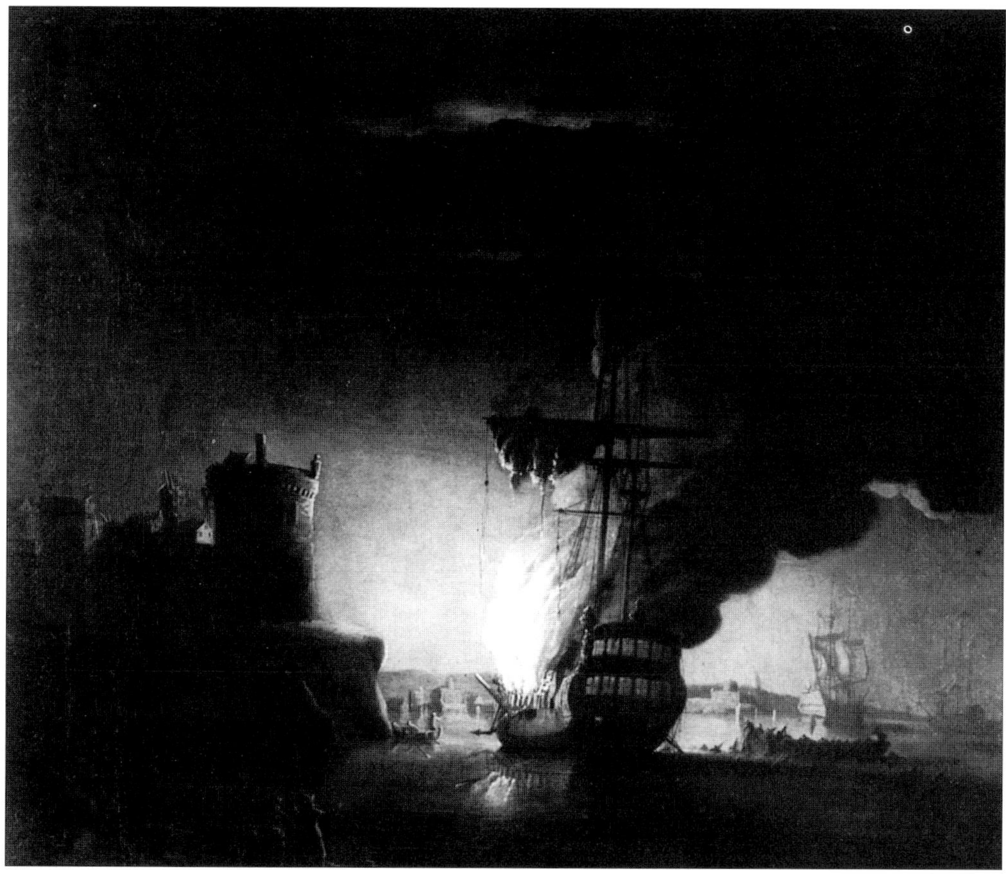

Plate 14. *A ship on fire at night. 25in. x 30in. Signed P. Monamy.*
SOTHEBY'S LOT 62, 19.11.82

A good example of this genre which apparently interested Monamy as he turned out numerous variants of ships on fire. (Category 7)

North Sea gales were popular and Monamy produced about five versions of such scenes, particularly some very good ones of the great gale of 1726 (Colour Plate 13).

He also produced one of the loss of the *Victory* at sea in 1744, which is at the National Maritime Museum (Colour Plate 37).

In addition to these, he painted at least five or six severe gale scenes with ships nearly foundering near rocks. Plate 13 is an example of one of these.

Category 6 – Moonlight Calm Scenes
This and the following category were largely an exercise in the handling of light effects in an oil painting. Several moonlight paintings by Monamy are known, but Francis Swaine and Brooking both indulged in this art form and sometimes it is difficult to attribute unsigned examples.

Category 7 – Ships on Fire
As in Category 6, this was a painting exercise in the handling of light. It was very much a Monamy speciality and he was the first English painter to

be seriously interested in the subject. (He handed on this interest to his son-in-law, Francis Swaine, who also produced a large number.) At least seven examples are recorded and there are probably several more. Some showing a ship on fire at night are particularly dramatic (Plate 14).

Category 8 – Copies or 'Near-versions' of Van de Velde subjects and works closely based on Van de Velde pictures or drawings
This is a somewhat vexed topic because nearly all the budding marine artists of the period made copies (or near versions) of Van de Velde. This was for two reasons – first, simply for practice and second, because Van de Velde copies were in demand. Cornelis Van de Velde, Robert Woodcock, Thomas Mitchell, Monamy, Swaine, Brooking, Scott and Dominic Serres all made excellent copies of varied Van de Velde subjects during this era. Most of these copies are unsigned.

'Stern quarter' portraits of the two large important vessels of that era, the *Royal Sovereign* and *Britannia,* were done by Van de Velde and his studio and these compositions were extensively copied as they were very popular and decorative (and still are!). Mr. Michael Robinson[4] has recorded no fewer than twenty-one copies or 'near versions' of these portraits which he has either seen or has personal knowledge of, and it seems sure that many more exist.

There is no doubt that Peter Monamy painted several versions of these pictures both fairly early in his career (such as his gift to the Painter-Stainers Hall, Plate 2) and also right through his later period when he was well known and beginning to sign his pictures. The example illustrated here (Colour Plate 40) is signed and has the typical Monamy palette and cloud formation.

In the National Maritime Museum files there are at least seven easily recognisable copies of Van de Velde, four of them signed by Peter Monamy.

In general, any composition containing ships wearing the pre-1707 ensign (plain St. George's cross in the corner) and showing ships of older design with spritsail topmasts and seventeenth century-like sterns may be considered likely to be copies or near versions of Van de Velde.

Most such pictures are unsigned and there is a tendency in the salerooms to allocate them to Peter Monamy on rather flimsy evidence. Both Brooking and Samuel Scott did occasionally sign their copies, but many such pictures are probably by either Woodcock, Mitchell, or Cornelis Van de Velde and are quite difficult to sort out as to authorship. A particularly instructive example is shown in Colour Plate 23. Colour Plate 38 is the original Van de Velde studio version of 'A squadron going to windward' – quite a famous and much copied picture. Colour Plate 39 is the signed Monamy version. It will be seen that it is nearly an exact copy, except that Monamy has updated the ensign to the post 1707 type and he has also updated the stern of the main ship to a typical open galleried early eighteenth century type – all quite legitimate and open! (Brooking did almost exactly the same thing!)

However, when doing a signed version of an important Van de Velde ship portrait – as in Colour Plate 40 (Monamy's signed version of the Van de Velde portrait) – no such daring liberties are taken! Some rearrangement of the small craft in the background and the addition of some typical Monamy clouds and layered clouds of smoke from the gunfire are his own personal contribution.

Some typical features of Monamy paintings
There are so many, often unsigned, seascapes and ship portraits from the eighteenth century to be found on the market or in the salerooms that it is worth while studying true Monamys to see if there are any special recognisable idiosyncrasies which may help in identifying his work. Many lesser painters appear on the market under the blanket title of 'Monamy'.

First and foremost is that Monamy was a brilliant draughtsman, comparable with Van de Velde himself in this respect. His ships always look right from any angle, they sit in the water properly and at sea have the right angle of heel. The perspective and composition is usually faultless. If a picture has a ship with too much stern and bow showing, a common fault in broadside views of eighteenth century ships (particularly by T. Mitchell), then it is not Monamy (as in many pictures by Francis Swaine). His painting of the sea itself, in all its moods, is truly realistic. His palette is on the whole a little lighter and more varied and somehow more interesting with more depth of colour, than many of his colleagues.

This general accuracy of his work was originally commented upon by George Vertue (Chapter 1) over two hundred years ago. However, by far the most individual feature of his pictures, particularly in his middle and later periods, is the way he paints his clouds. Nearly always somewhere in the picture will be the billowing white cloud, with rather sharply defined edge pushed out in a series of curved excrescences with often a well-defined impasto on the margin. This typical technique can be observed in Colour Plates 30, 31 and 40.

This technique is observed even more definitely in the clouds of white smoke accompanying the firing of a signal gun (Colour Plate 40). It looks just as though he achieved this effect not with a brush, but with a finger coated in white paint pushed over the surface of the canvas on the edge of the clouds. None of the other painters of the period shows quite this technique which appears to be peculiar to Monamy.

Some unsigned Van de Velde copies attributed to him do not show this technique and are thus probably not by him, whereas some of his signed Van de Velde copies (Colour Plate 40) do show this typical cloud and billowing smoke technique.

The other typical idiosyncrasy of Monamy is seen in the way he paints the drooping short pennant or wind vane at the top of the mast in his calm scenes. Swaine and all other painters show the pennant sticking out at a right-angle from the masthead (as if it has a short length of wire or metal in it, to keep it out at a right-angle). Monamy's pennants droop at an angle of 45° or more. Colour Plates 22 and 34 show typical Monamy pennants. Colour Plate 43 shows a typical Swaine pennant.

Finally the composition of the picture, particularly of a calm scene, may offer some typical clues. Monamy often liked to have a small boat or 'hoy' drawn up on shore in the forefront of calm scenes, attended by two or three figures. Often there is a small castle or fort on the adjacent shore (Colour Plate 36).

Most of Monamy's works are in private collections and at the time of writing they still appear fairly regularly in the major salerooms. 'Proper Monamys' are still recognised as attractive, realistic and decorative works of art of a durable quality. They attract steadily increasing prices and are much in demand, as is right and proper in a sea-faring nation. The National Maritime Museum has a very representative collection of twenty Monamy pictures and this is really the only place where such a collection can be seen by the public. His pictures are surprisingly very thin on the ground in all other national collections.

1. *Marine Painting,* James Taylor, Studio Editions Ltd., 1995.
2. *Concise Catalogue of Oil Paintings in the National Maritime Museum,* Antique Collectors' Club.
3. Special marine art sales catalogues of Bonhams, Christie's and Sotheby's since 1981.
4. *The Paintings of the Willem van de Veldes,* M.S. Robinson, National Maritime Museum, Greenwich, 1990.
5. Ibid., II, p.625
6. *Early Sea Painters,* F.B. Cockett, Antique Collectors' Club, 1995.

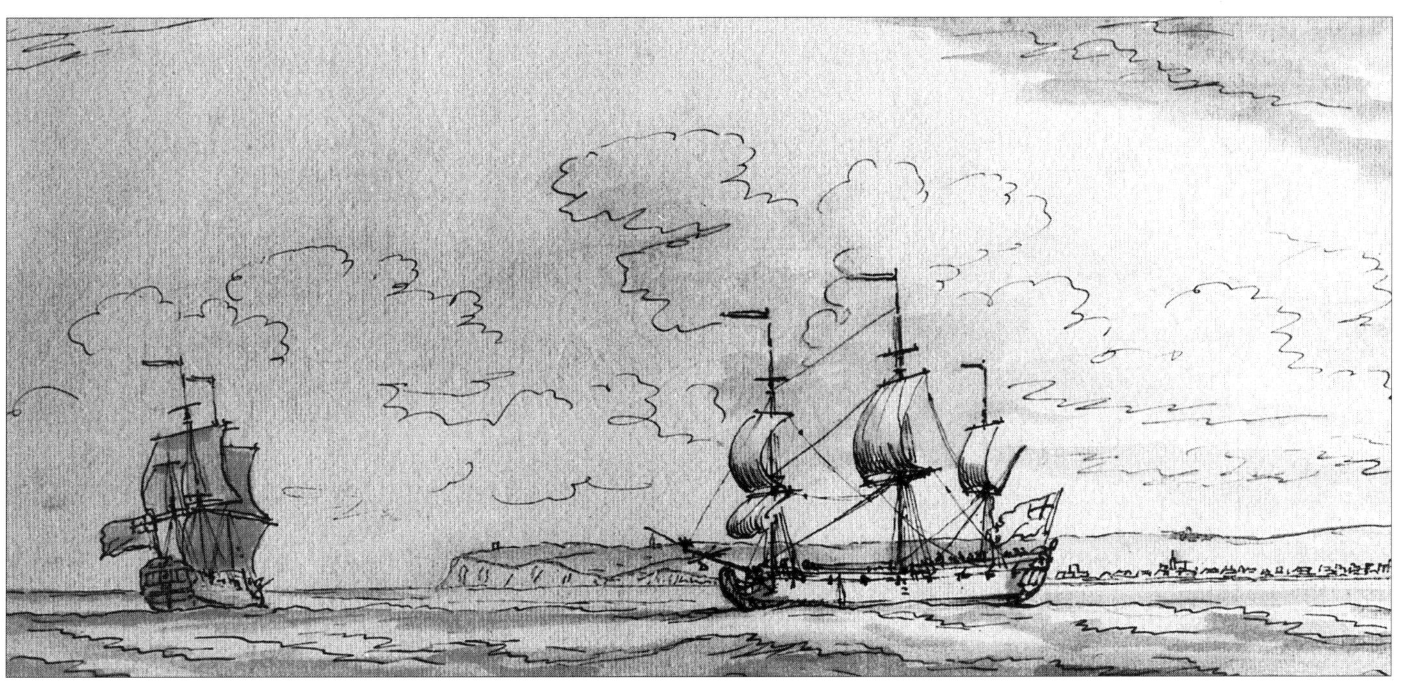

CHAPTER 4
Drawings and Prints

Drawings

Most of the early artists did drawings. Usually these drawings were sketches as a preliminary trial for a formal painting. Many artists, however, became so adept and quick with a drawing that they produced many very finished works which rank as works of art in themselves. The Van de Veldes were of course the supreme exponents of this. Both Van de Veldes, father and son, left a legacy of hundreds of drawings ranging from the quick sketch to the highly finished work of art. These have now become much prized and real collectors' items.

Peter Monamy left few identifiable drawings to posterity. Those that we do know of for certain were very characterful – as shown by the three examples illustrated in Plates 15 to 17 – and it is a great pity that so few remain because he must have done a fair number. Looking at these three one is impressed by his ability as a draughtsman, conjuring up a scene in a few deft strokes of pen or pencil. They were very different from the larger number

Plate 15. A small English man-o'-war proceeding down channel off Deal, the white cliffs in the distance. 8in. x 12in. Not signed. Pen and wash.
Ex Ingram Collection. Private Collection
This bold little drawing is related to a painting by Monamy in the Mellon Collection. It is interesting that even in this quick drawing the shape of the typical Monamy clouds is discernible.

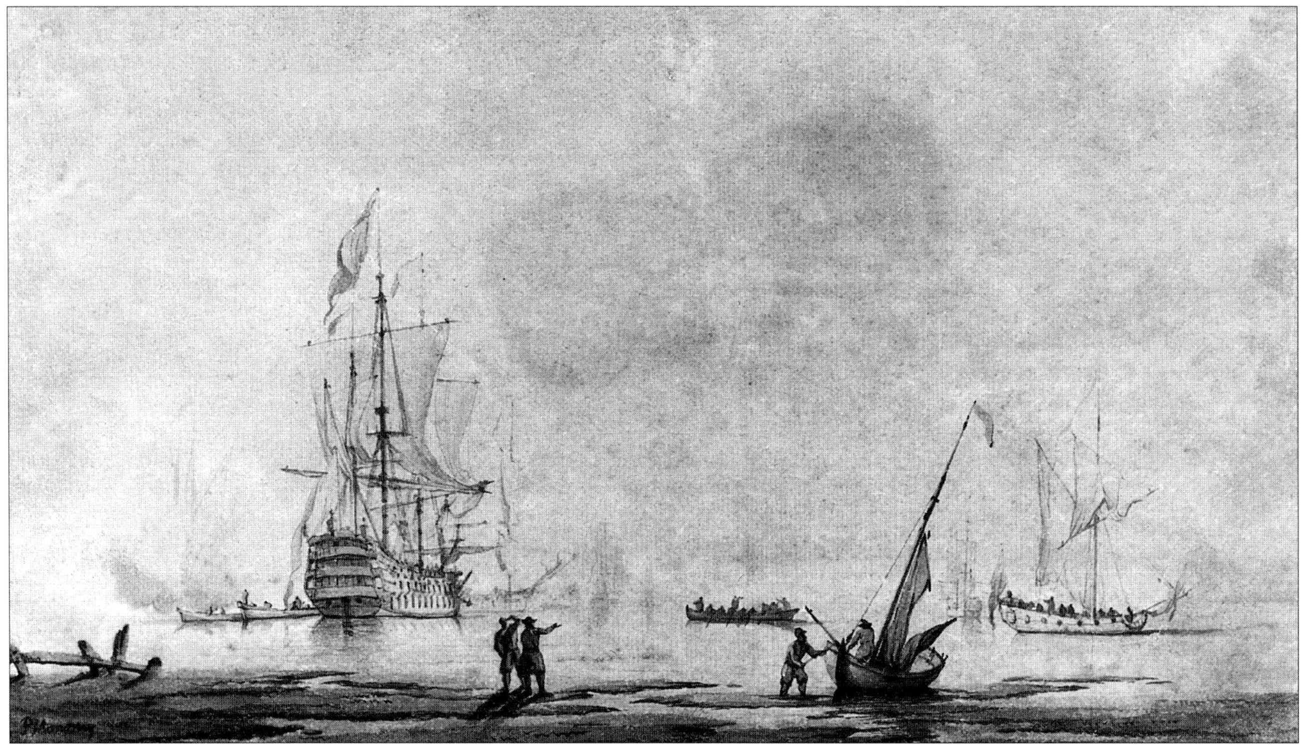

Plate 16 . *A two-decker man-o'-war, stern quarter view, and a yacht in a quiet estuary. 5in. x 7in. Pen and wash. Signed P. Monamy.*

EX INGRAM COLLECTION. SOTHEBY'S LOT 73, 16.7.98

A typical Monamy composition with the little beached 'hoy' and figures in the foreground.

of very carefully finished drawings left by his son-in-law, Francis Swaine. As far as we know, Peter Monamy never became involved in the growing popularity of the watercolour medium which was widely exploited by some of his successors in marine art, particularly Dominic Serres and his son J.T. Serres later in the eighteenth century.

Prints

The eighteenth century in England saw an unprecedented proliferation of prints. The two types of print which were most popular in Monamy's day were line engravings and mezzotints. Line engraving, done by many slightly different techniques but usually on copper plates, was the older and more traditional method. A whole army of professional engravers grew up in the first half of the eighteenth century who were ready to produce good engraved images of any popular painting.

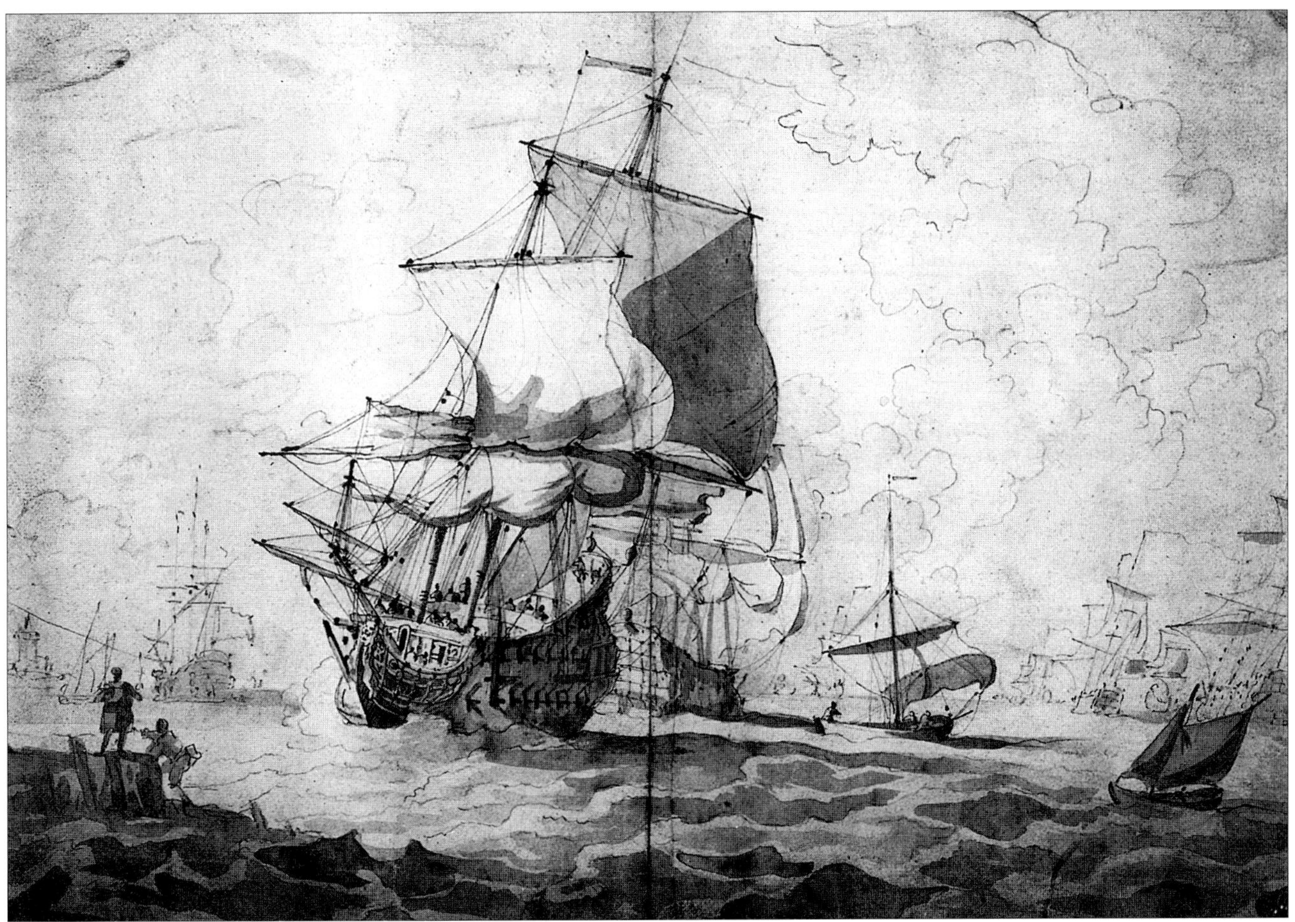

Plate 17. *A two-decker man-o'-war shortening sail, seen from the port bow, other craft lightly pencilled in in the background. Pen, pencil, and wash. 10in. x 14in.*
BRITISH MUSEUM (PRINT ROOM)
A very lively study for possibly a major painting.

Mezzotinting was a newer type of engraving which was a little more difficult but produced a softer image which could then be coloured successfully in various ways. This method had been introduced by no less a person than Prince Rupert himself during his later years when he retired to England in the reign of King Charles II after his turbulent and adventurous early years! Again this method was rapidly taken up by certain professional printmakers and was very successful, particularly with portraits.

Thus the making and selling of prints became a thriving business and the publishers became men of wealth and influence. One of the most famous of them was John Boydell (1719-1804) who was elected an alderman of London and finally became Lord Mayor.

A whole new market for prints emerged in the first half of the century, aimed at a rising bourgeoisie anxious as never before to satisfy a more cultivated taste. Good decorative prints were demanded and for the first

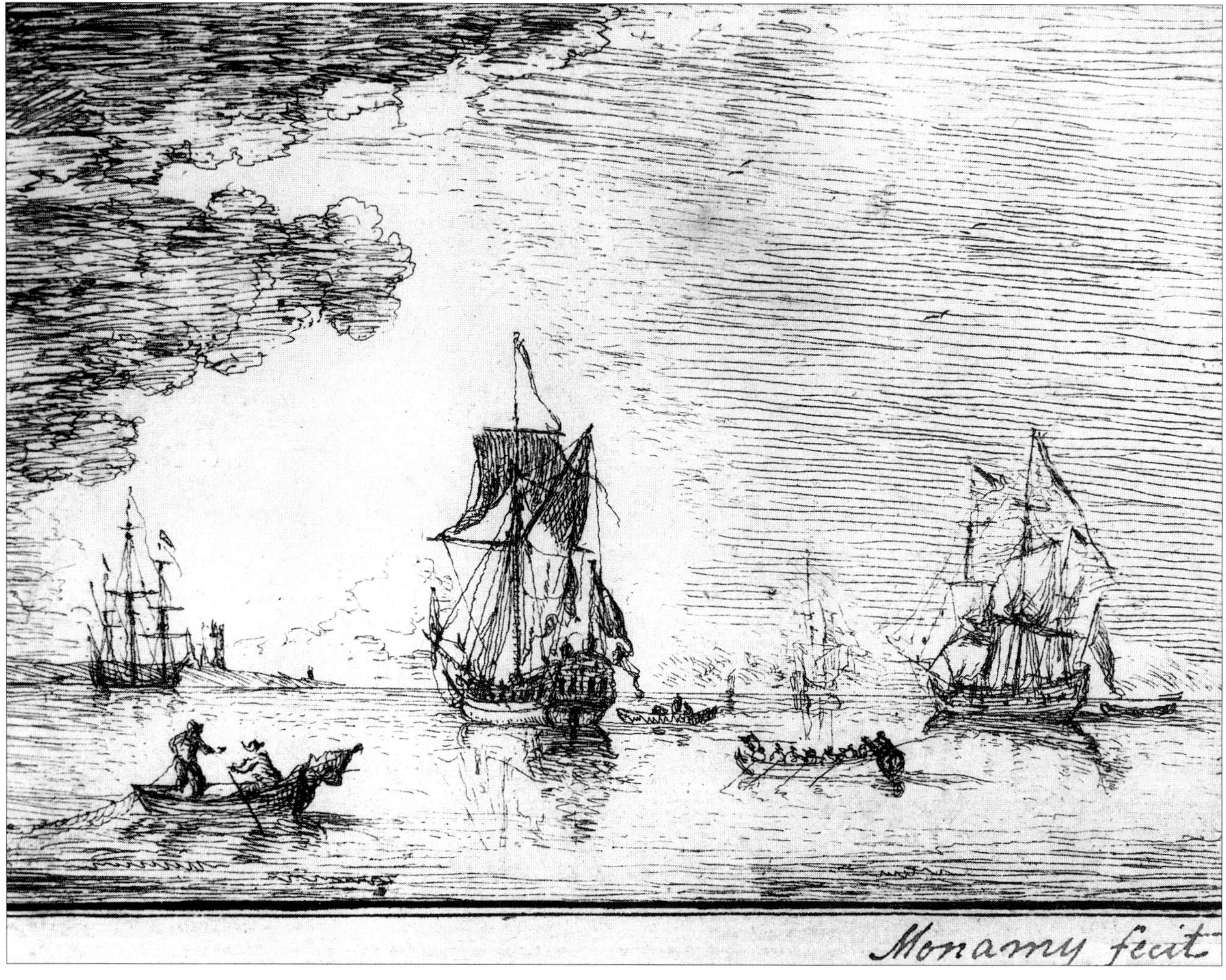

Plate 18. *This and the following plate are the only two line engravings which were executed by Monamy himself. It is prominently (and rather proudly!) signed, bottom right. Obviously not as well finished as the work of a practised professional engraver. Both are quite small pictures.* BRITISH MUSEUM (PRINT ROOM)

Plate 19 *(Opposite above). This is the second of Monamy's personally executed engravings. This time a choppy sea and lots of cloud with, as the centrepiece, the same yacht heeling over to a brisk wind. This also is prominently signed, bottom right.*

BRITISH MUSEUM (PRINT ROOM)

time it became the fashion to frame and display prints on the wall (in 'Hogarth frames').

The rapidly increasing publication of papers and books – which needed prints for illustration (in the same way as we use photographs today) – helped to keep this new army of printmakers busy.

Most of the major artists of the day, such as Hogarth and Jonathan Richardson, for instance, became fairly expert at line engraving for themselves, but the process was so time consuming and repetitive that most of

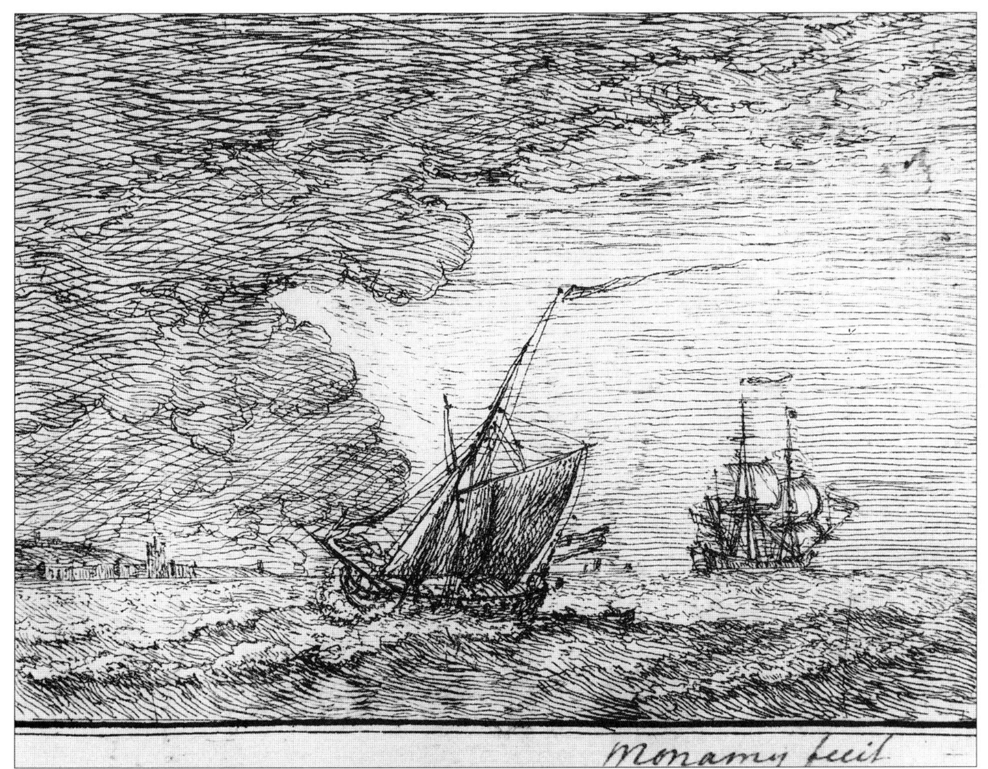

Plate 20 (Below). *A sea engagement between the English and Algerines. Engraved by Fourdrinier after Monamy's original painting in the Vauxhall Gardens. Published in 1743.*
BRITISH MUSEUM (PRINT ROOM)

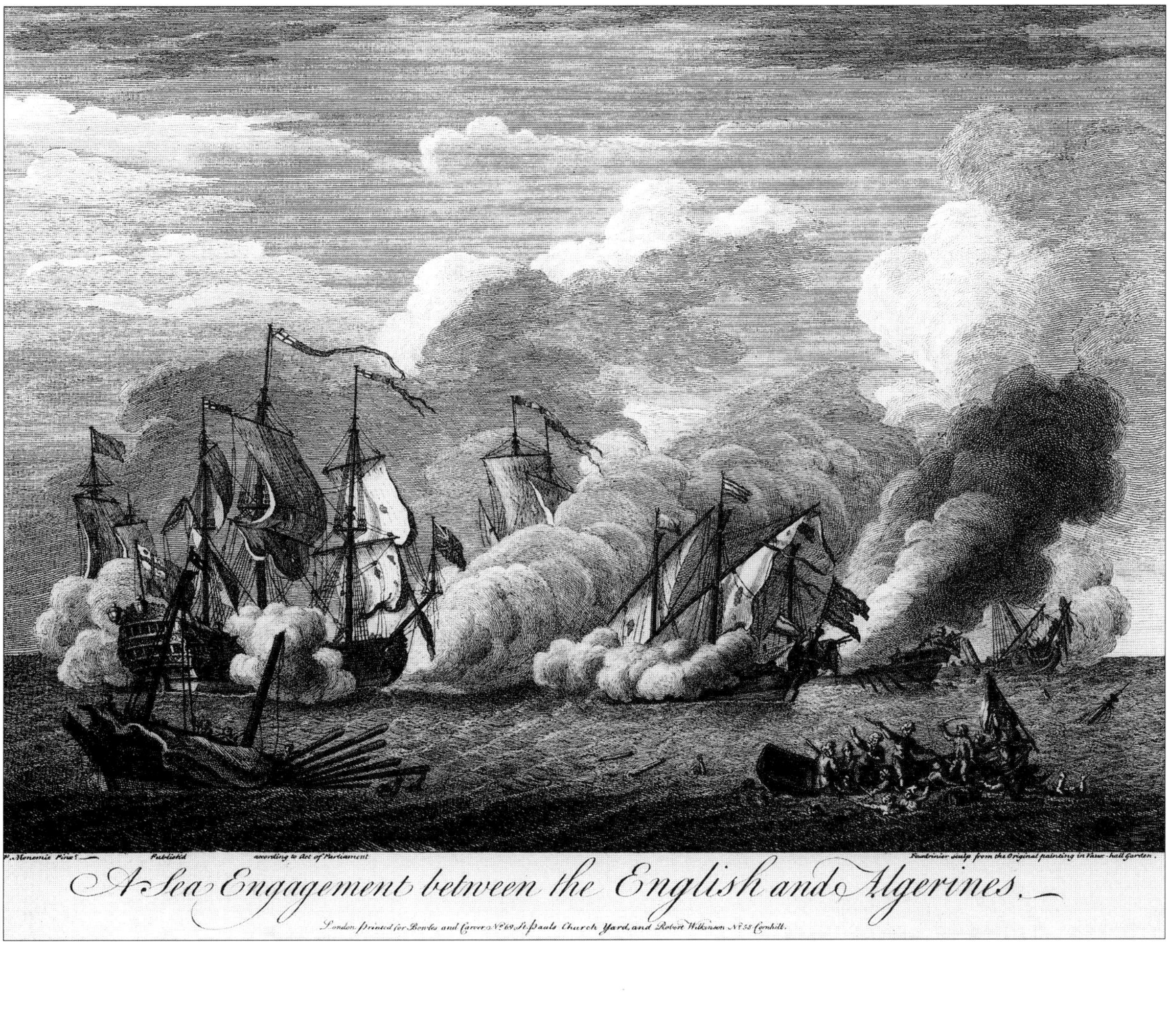

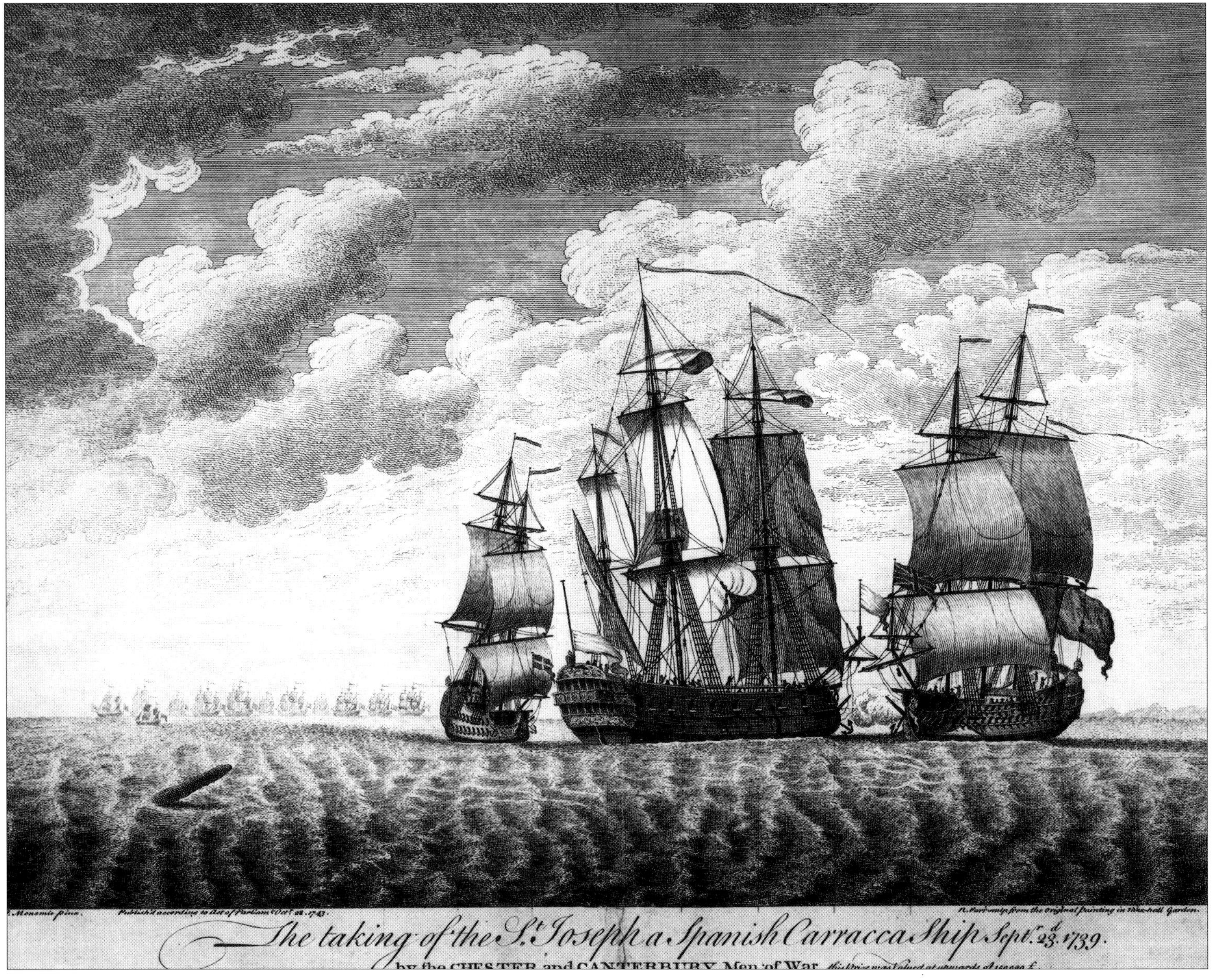

Plate 21. *The taking of the* St. Joseph, *a Spanish caracca Ship, 23 September 1739. Engraved by R. Parr after the original by Peter Monamy in the Vauxhall Gardens. Published in 1743.*   BRITISH MUSEUM (PRINT ROOM)
The two English ships involved were the Chester *and the* Canterbury. *This prize was valued at upwards of £150,000.*

them gave it up as their reputation increased and delegated the process of engraving their pictures to the professionals.

Peter Monamy experimented with making line engravings himself and Plates 18 and 19 illustrate two 'by his own hand' and signed. He rapidly gave this up, however, and entrusted the engraving of his pictures to true professionals of this art, amongst whom were Elisha Kirkall, R. Parr, Fourdrinier and Canot.

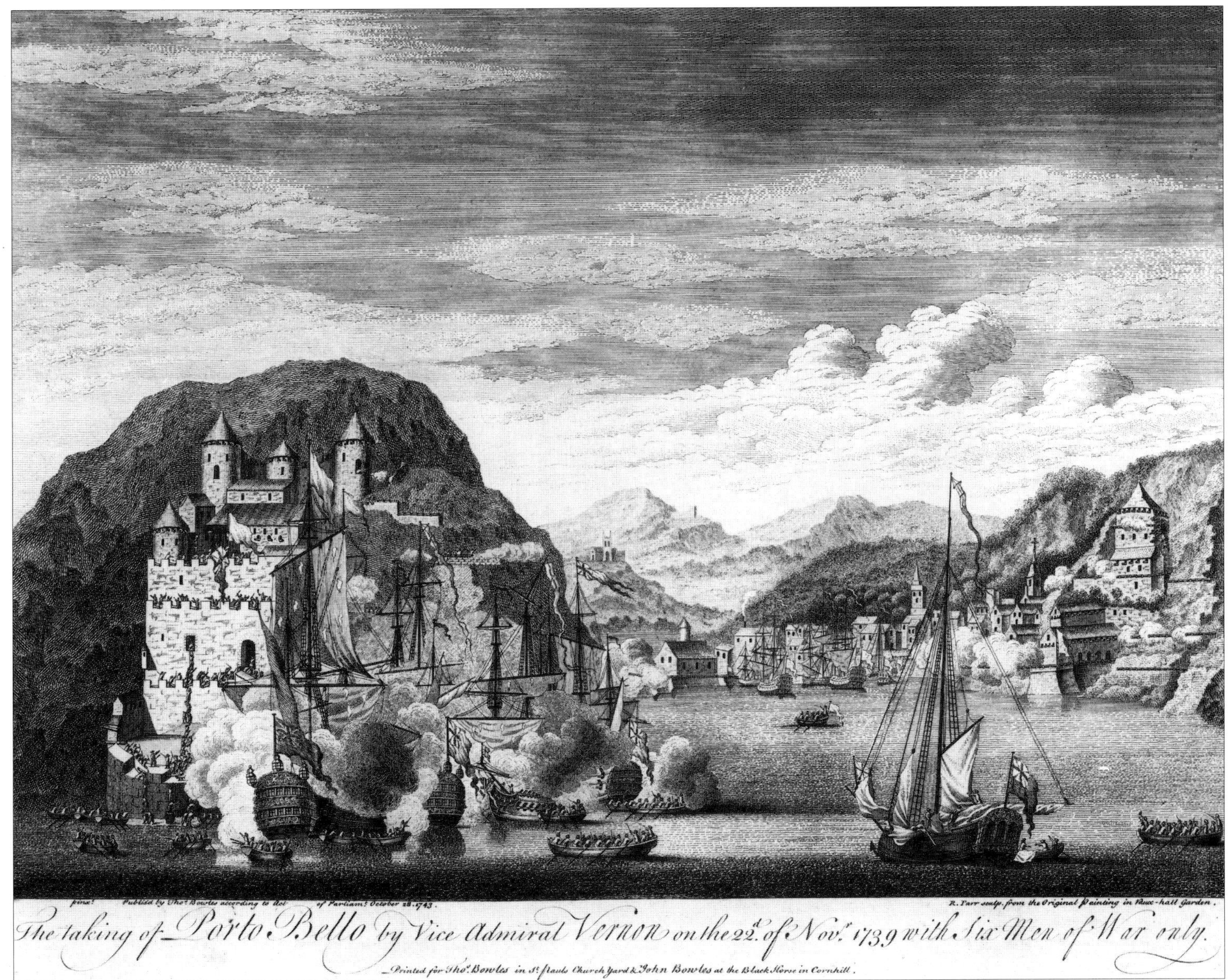

Plate 22. *The taking of Porto Bello by Vice-Admiral Vernon on 22 November 1739 with six men-o'-war only. Engraved by R. Parr after the original painting in Vauxhall Gardens by Peter Monamy. Published in 1743.* BRITISH MUSEUM (PRINT ROOM)

Peter Monamy's pictures were popular subjects for engravers and this is just as well because the four major paintings which he did to decorate the boxes in the Vauxhall Gardens towards the end of his life have all been lost. They were all engraved, however, by first class printmakers and the four very fine engravings are illustrated here (Plates 20 to 23). They were issued in 1743 and produced and sold by the publisher John Bowles.

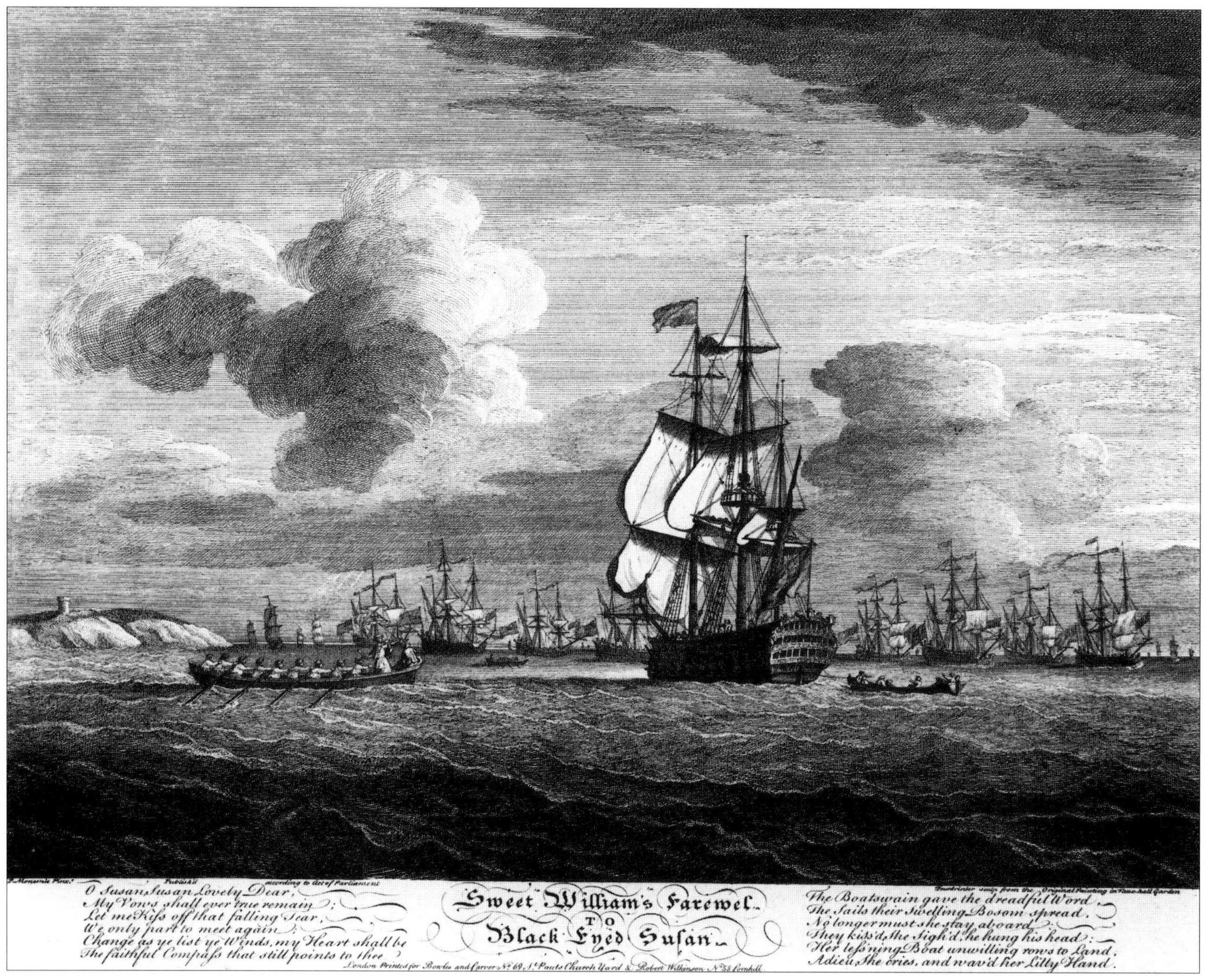

Plate 23. *Sweet William's Farewell to Black Eyed Susan, engraved by Fourdrinier after the original painting in the Vauxhall Gardens by Peter Monamy. Published in 1743.*

BRITISH MUSEUM (PRINT ROOM)

The verses below the print, run as follows:

> *Oh, Susan, Susan, Lovely Dear*
> *My vows shall ever true remain*
> *Let me kiss off that falling tear*
> *We only part to meet again*
> *Change as ye list ye Winds, my Heart shall be*
> *The faithful compass that still points to thee.*
>
> *The boatswain gave the dreadful word,*
> *The sails their swelling bosom spread.*
> *No longer must she stay aboard*
> *They kissed, she sighed, he hung his head.*
> *Her less'ning boat, unwilling rows to land.*
> *Adieu, She cries, and Waved her Lilly Hand,*

On the whole as fine an example of early eighteenth century doggerel as you could wish for! You can see Susan 'waving her lilly hand' from the stern of the rowing boat on the left.

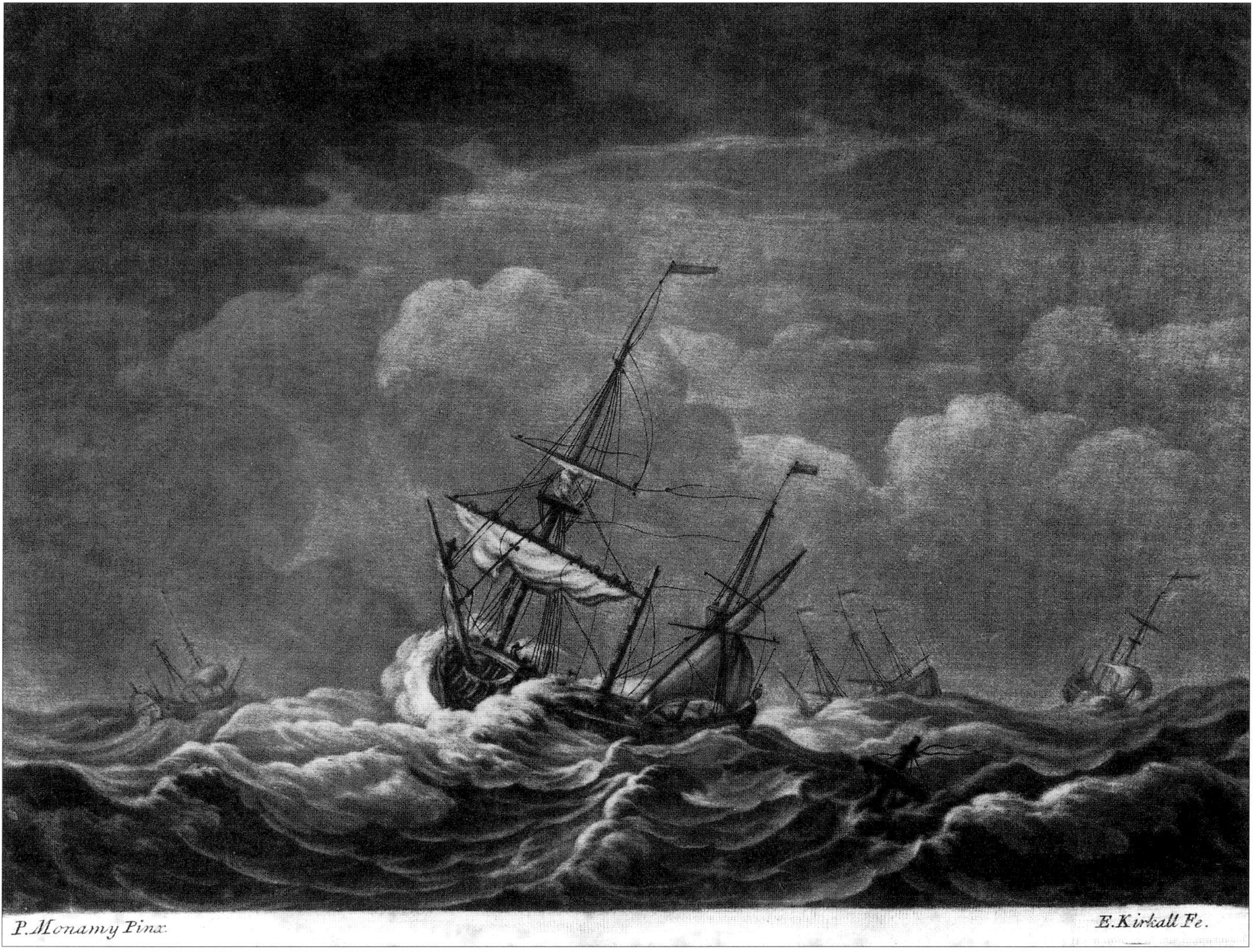

Plate 24. *A storm, engraved by Elisha Kirkall after a painting by Peter Monamy.*
BRITISH MUSEUM (PRINT ROOM)

This, and the next plate, are examples of the so-called 'green mezzotints' done by E. Kirkall and issued some time just before 1735.

Of course the quality of the engravings after Monamy paintings is very variable. At the lower end of the market a brisk trade in cheap and ephemeral prints, done by many less accomplished engravers, continued throughout the century.

Elisha Kirkall, one of the best early mezzotinters, produced a series of 'green mezzotints' after Van de Velde in 1725. He also produced some after Peter Monamy, two of which are shown here (Plates 24 and 25). In 1746 John Bowles issued a series of ten prints after Monamy, engraved by Canot.

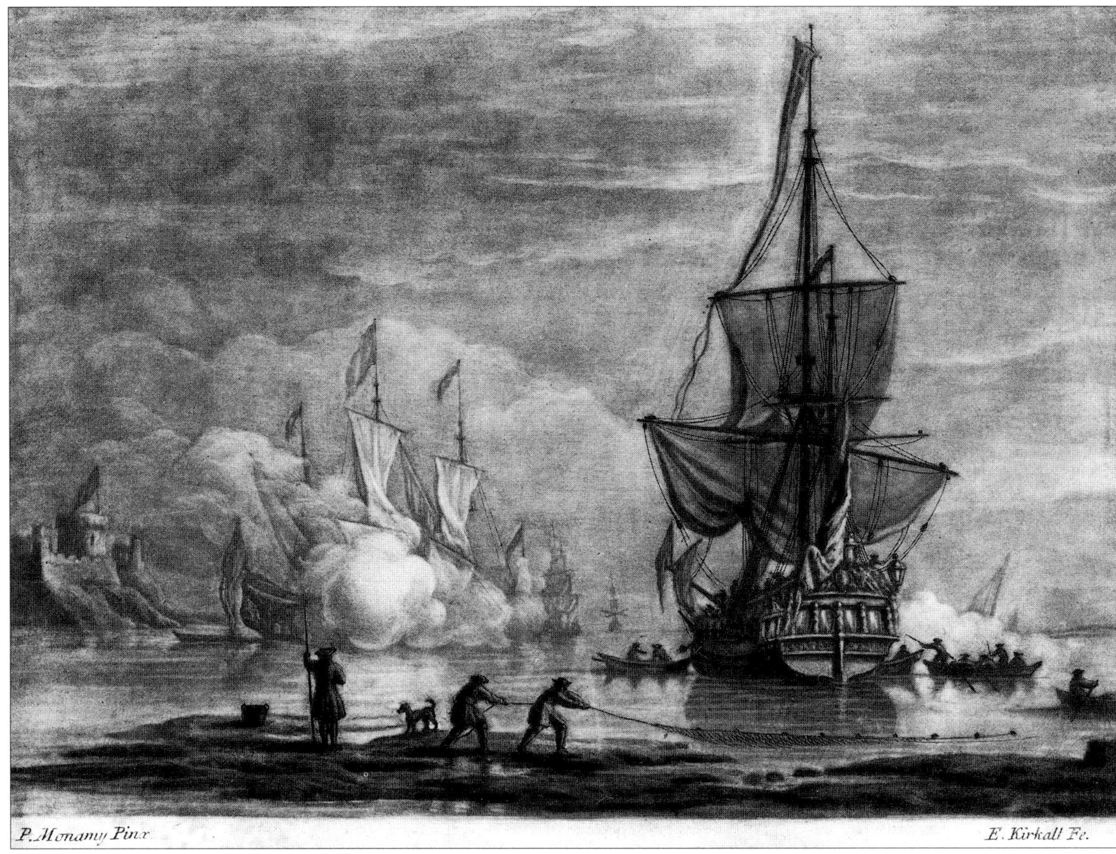

Plate 25. *Calm scene of a yacht offshore with another ship firing a salute. Engraved by Elisha Kirkall after a painting by Peter Monamy.* BRITISH MUSEUM (PRINT ROOM) *Another example of Kirkall's 'green mezzotints', issued before 1735.*

It is interesting to note that it was Elisha Kirkall's flagrant piracy of the Hogarth engravings of the 'Harlot's Progress' in 1732 that prompted the passage of the Copyright Act in 1735 (known as 'Hogarth's Act'). This gave artists, engravers and publishers sole rights for a period of fourteen years. Engravings which do not carry the inscription 'Published as the Act Directs' will have been issued before 1735.

General Sources and References

1. *A History of Engraving and Etching,* Arthur M. Hind, Dover Publications Inc., New York.
2. The *Print Collectors Handbook*, Alfred Whitman, E.P.P Publishing Ltd., 1973.
3. *Peter Monamy 1681-1749. Marine Artist,* C. Harrison-Wallace, Catalogue of Pallant House Gallery Exhibition, Chichester, 1983.
4. British Museum. Print Room.

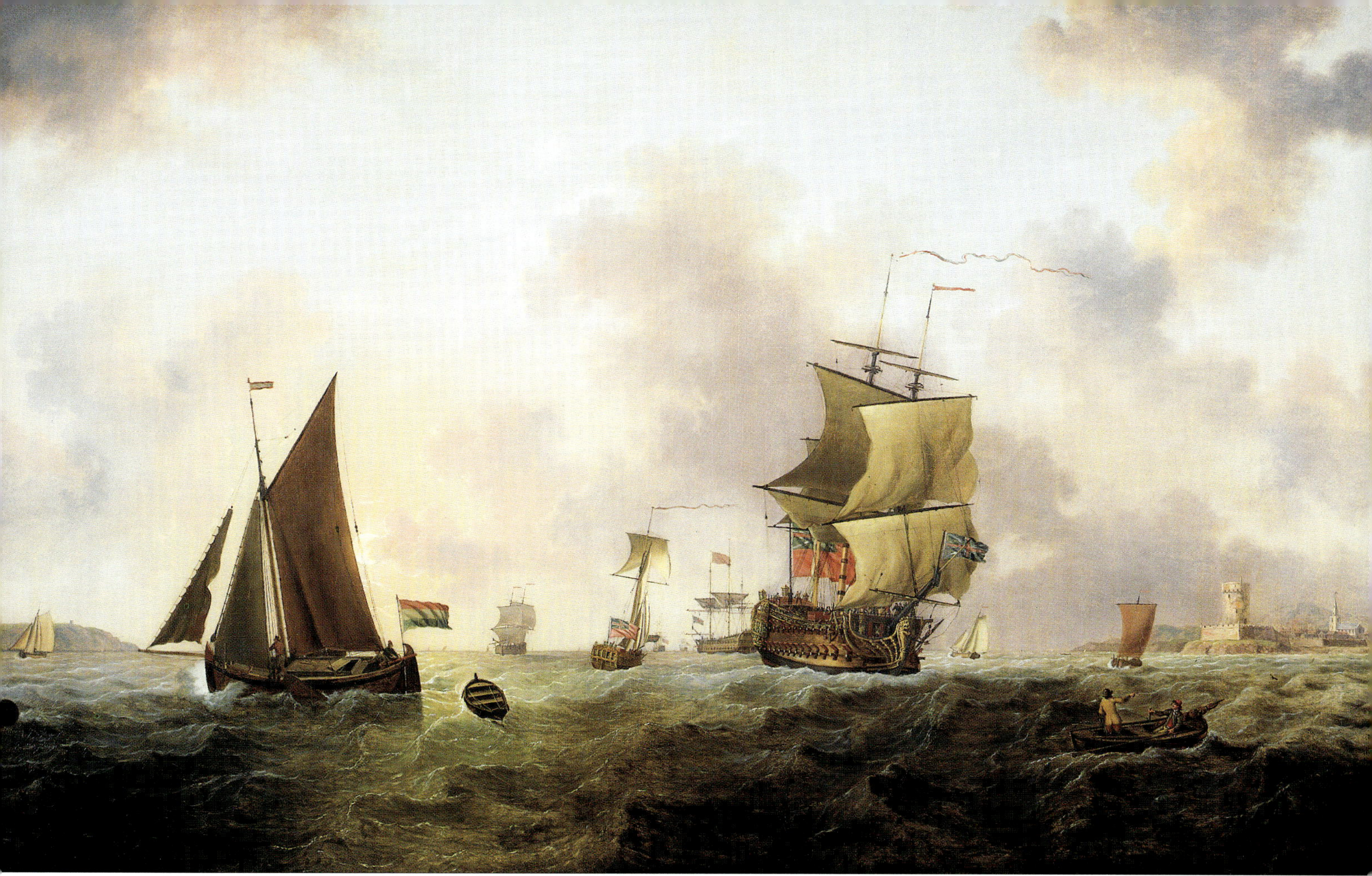

CHAPTER 5
Francis Swaine 1720-1783

Francis Swaine was the natural successor to Peter Monamy in two
different ways.

Firstly he knew the Monamy family in their later years well enough to
marry their second surviving daughter, Mary, just five months after Peter
Monamy's death in 1749. Moreover, he named his first born son Monamy
Swaine to signal this connection. Young Monamy Swaine was later to
become a marine painter, thus becoming number three in this distinguished
painting family, spanning nearly the whole of the eighteenth century.

Colour Plate 41. *A two-decker of the Royal Navy and other shipping off St. Peter Port,
Guernsey. Oil on canvas. 35in. x 54in. Signed and dated 1764.*
RICHARD GREEN GALLERY

*This work was submitted in 1764 to the first competition held by the Society of Arts for
the 'Best original Sea piece on Canvas'. Francis Swaine won the second prize with this
painting and was awarded 15 guineas.*

*What the little Dutch boat, with lee boards and Dutch flag, is doing down in Guernsey,
we do not know – perhaps one of the competition judges was a Dutchman!*

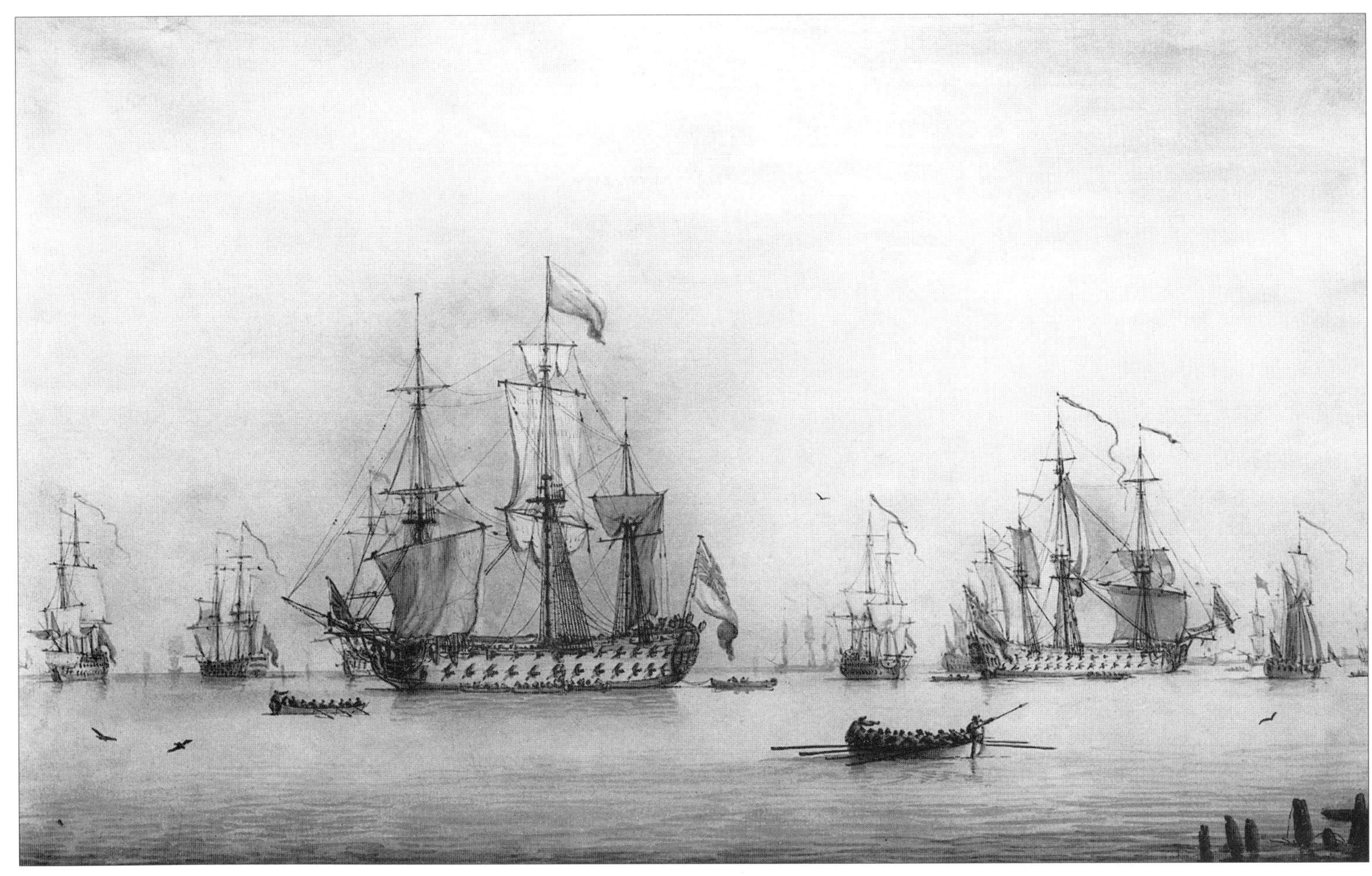

Plate 26. *A drawing of a fleet at anchor. Pen, pencil, and wash. 14in. x 21in. Signed.*
EX INGRAM COLLECTION. PRIVATE COLLECTION
This large and very finished drawing is a tribute to Swaine's excellent draughtsmanship. It is a complete work of art in itself.

Secondly Francis Swaine inherited much of Monamy's style of painting and his light and colourful palette. This is so noticeable that it leads to the inevitable deduction that he was a pupil of Peter Monamy and probably worked in his studio with him in his later years. He must have learned a lot from Monamy because many of the Monamy 'tricks of composition' are easily recognisable in Swaine's later paintings. It also seems likely that Swaine may have 'finished' some of the unfinished paintings which were left in Monamy's studio after his death.

All this has had the unfortunate result that, in the case of unsigned paintings, it is sometimes quite difficult to assign the origin correctly.

Swaine is first recorded as a messenger in a list of clerks and officers working for the Treasurer and Commissioners of the Navy in 1735. He must have taken up painting soon after this as he was working with Monamy five or six years later.

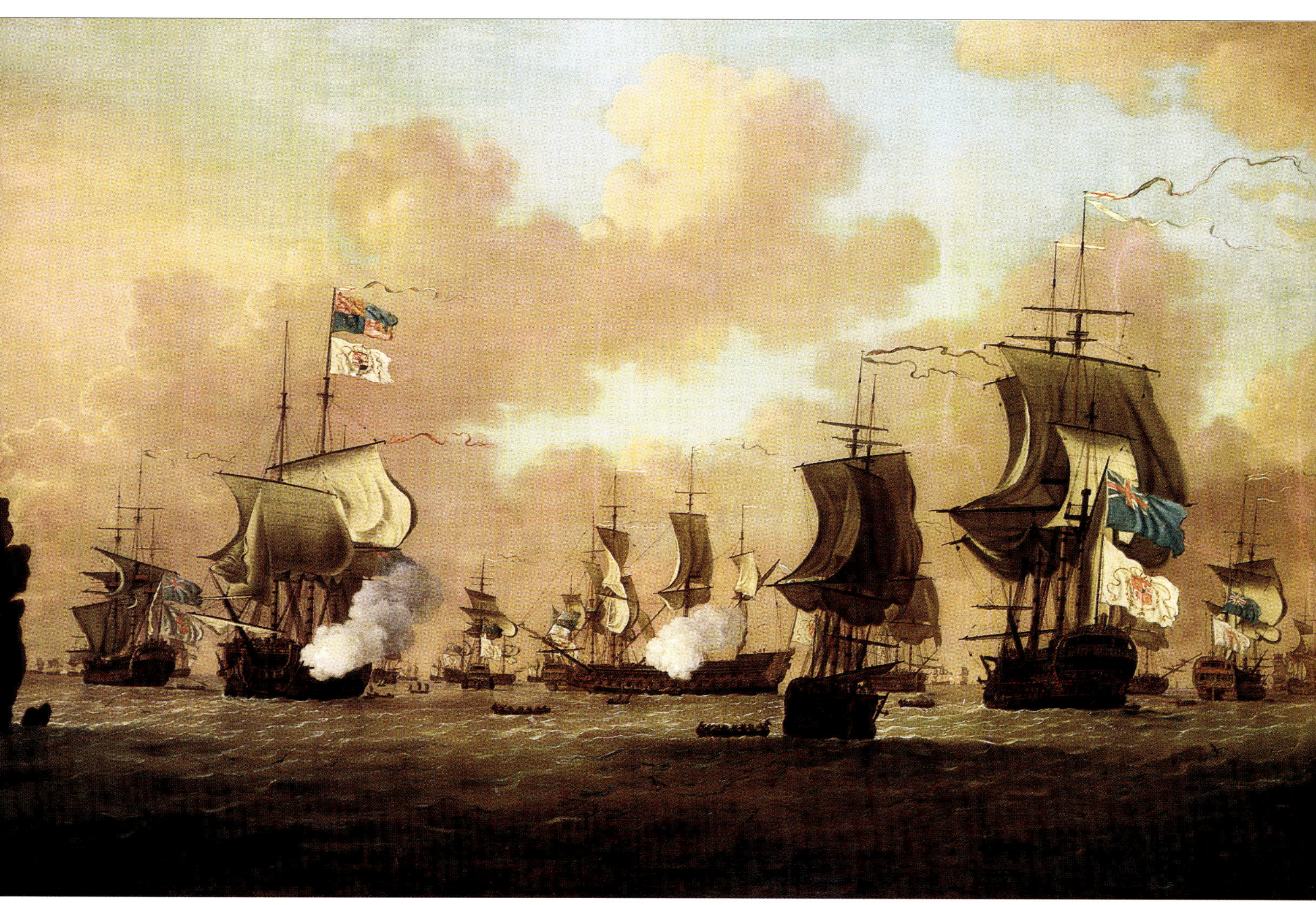

Colour Plate 42. *The surrender of the Spanish Fleet to the British at Havana, 13 August 1762. Oil on canvas. 54in. x 88in. Signed and dated 1768.*

CHRISTIE'S LOT 390. 7.10.93

This sort of very large post-battle scene is unusual for Swaine. The main part of the Spanish Fleet has been taken over by British commanders. Their flags have been hoisted above the Spanish colours to signify the surrender.

He probably had some connection with Charles Brooking as well as they are direct contemporaries and Swaine is known to have made copies of some Brooking compositions.

Swaine was lucky in that by the time he came to maturity the societies for the encouragement and exhibition of painters' works were just beginning to appear. Swaine exhibited his work regularly at the Free Society from 1761 to 1782 and at the Society of Arts from 1762 to 1782 but, oddly enough, not at the Royal Academy. Colour Plate 41 shows a painting exhibited at the Society of Arts in 1764 for which he won second prize and the painting was awarded fifteen guineas! He exhibited from an address near Avery Farm in Chelsea.

Colour Plate 43 *(Opposite). A royal yacht and small naval ship in a calm, and a royal yacht and a merchantman in choppy seas. Both 4½in. x 6in. Both signed.*

RICHARD GREEN GALLERY

This attractive pair of small paintings, both on copper panels, was the sort of thing which Swaine really specialised in. No other artist of that era did these miniature paintings quite as well as Swaine. Note the wind vane pennants at the masthead and compare them with Monamy's technique.

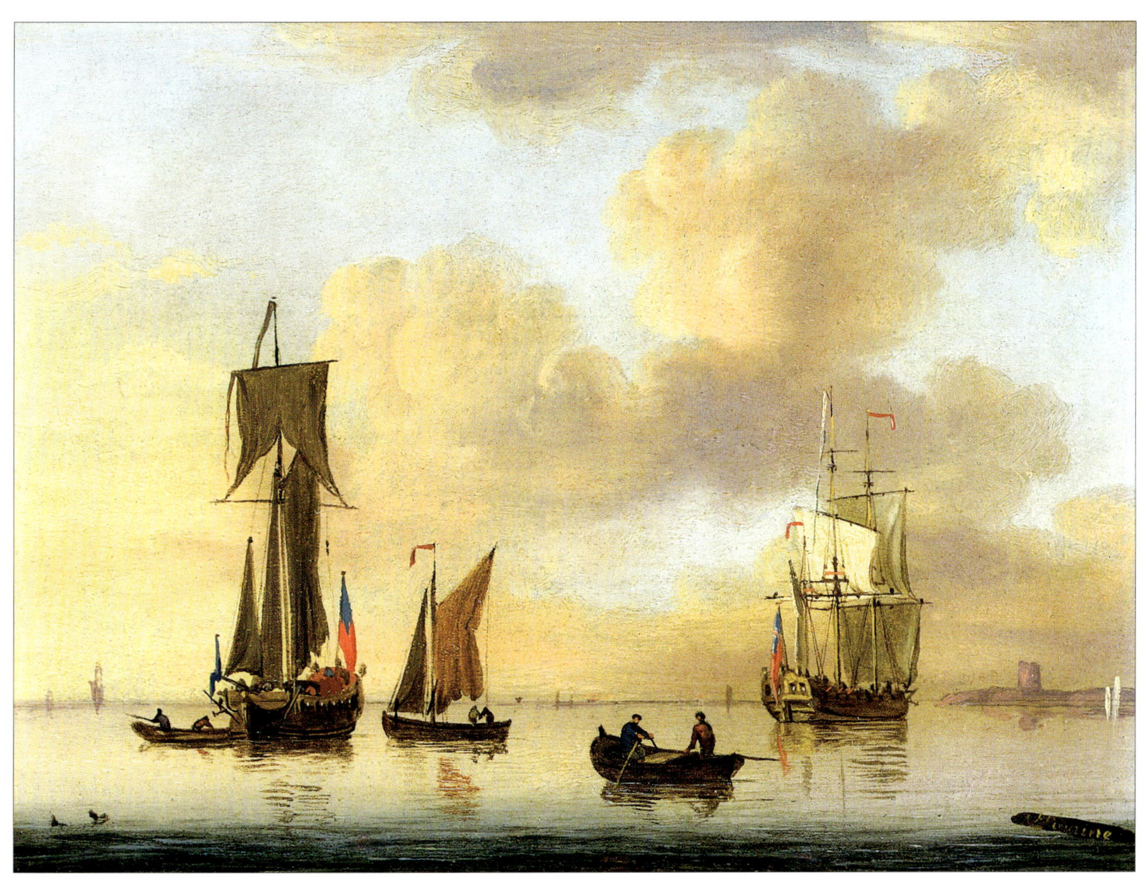

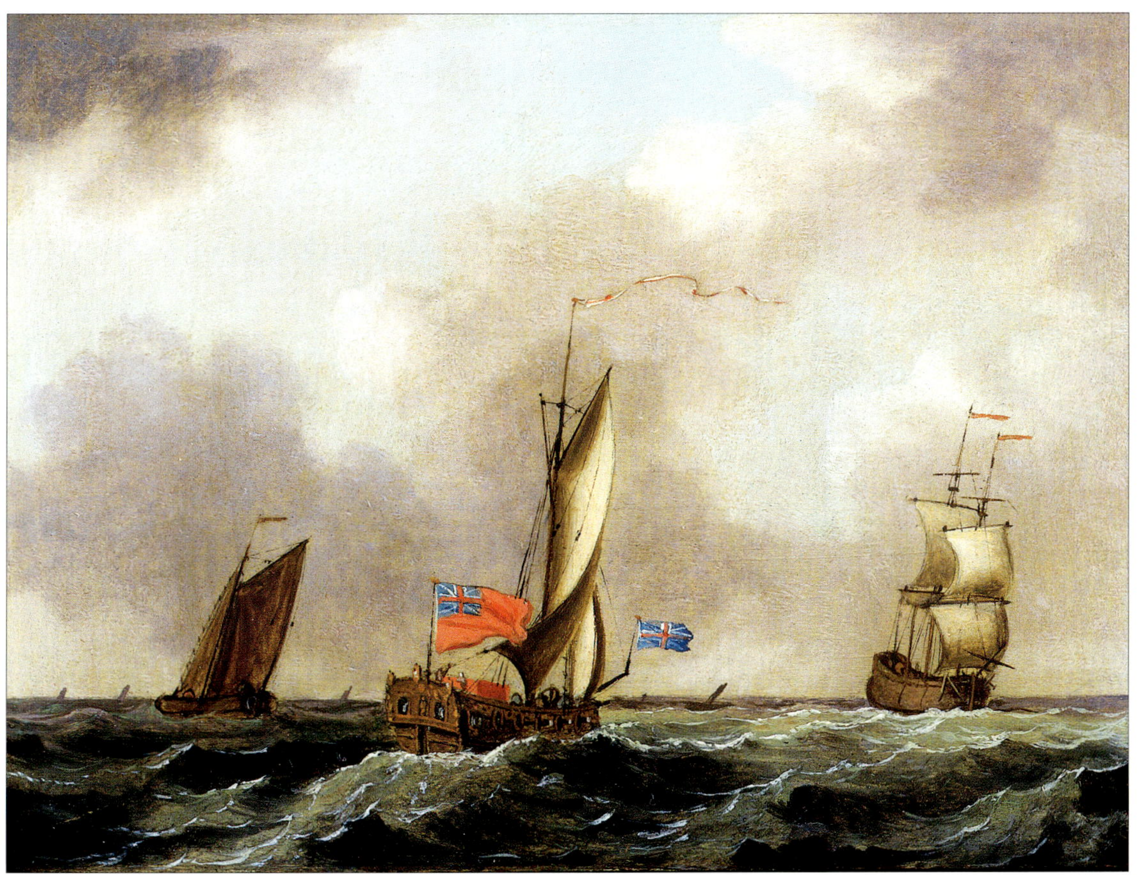

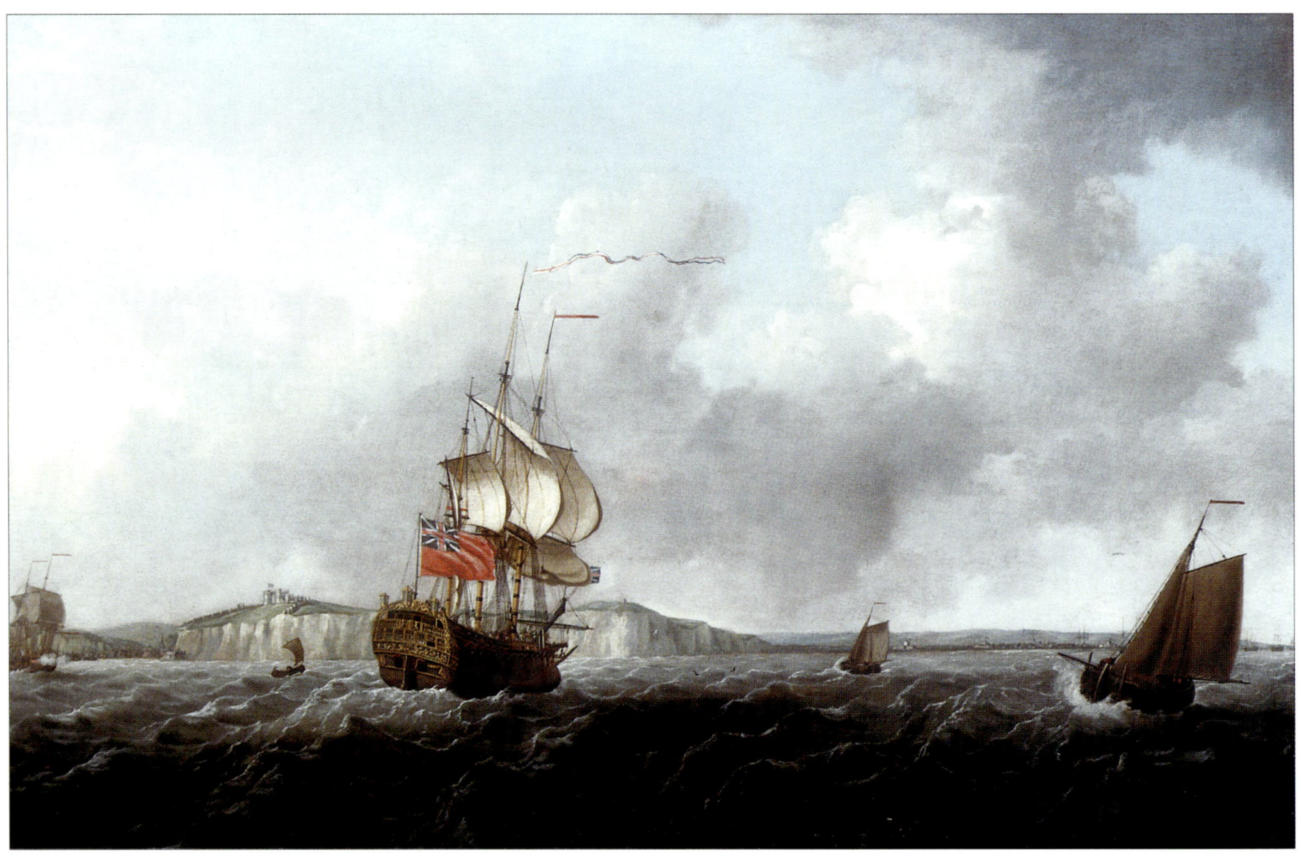

Colour Plate 44. *A large two-decker and a cutter off Dover. Oil on canvas. 36in. x 51in. Signed.*
LANE FINE ART

This is a large and bright seascape, very decorative. Swaine's rather formal depiction of a rough sea with very regular little waves all going in parallel lines is well shown here.

The Paintings

Swaine was extremely prolific and there must be at least as many paintings by him in circulation as there are by Monamy. His work is fairly rare in museums but is widely dispersed in private collections. This means that his pictures continually come up for sale and, as they are often unsigned, there is often an attribution problem.

He liked to paint general shipping scenes in rivers and estuaries. Large battle scenes from his brush as commissions are rather rare, although one good example (Colour Plate 42) is illustrated here.

His speciality was undoubtedly small, finely painted, pairs of pictures usually on copper panels (Colour Plate 43). These pairs would show Morning and Evening, Calm and Storm, or two views off a port or seashore, and were obviously very popular. He also continued the Monamy tradition of painting moonlight scenes and ships on fire. He is at his best

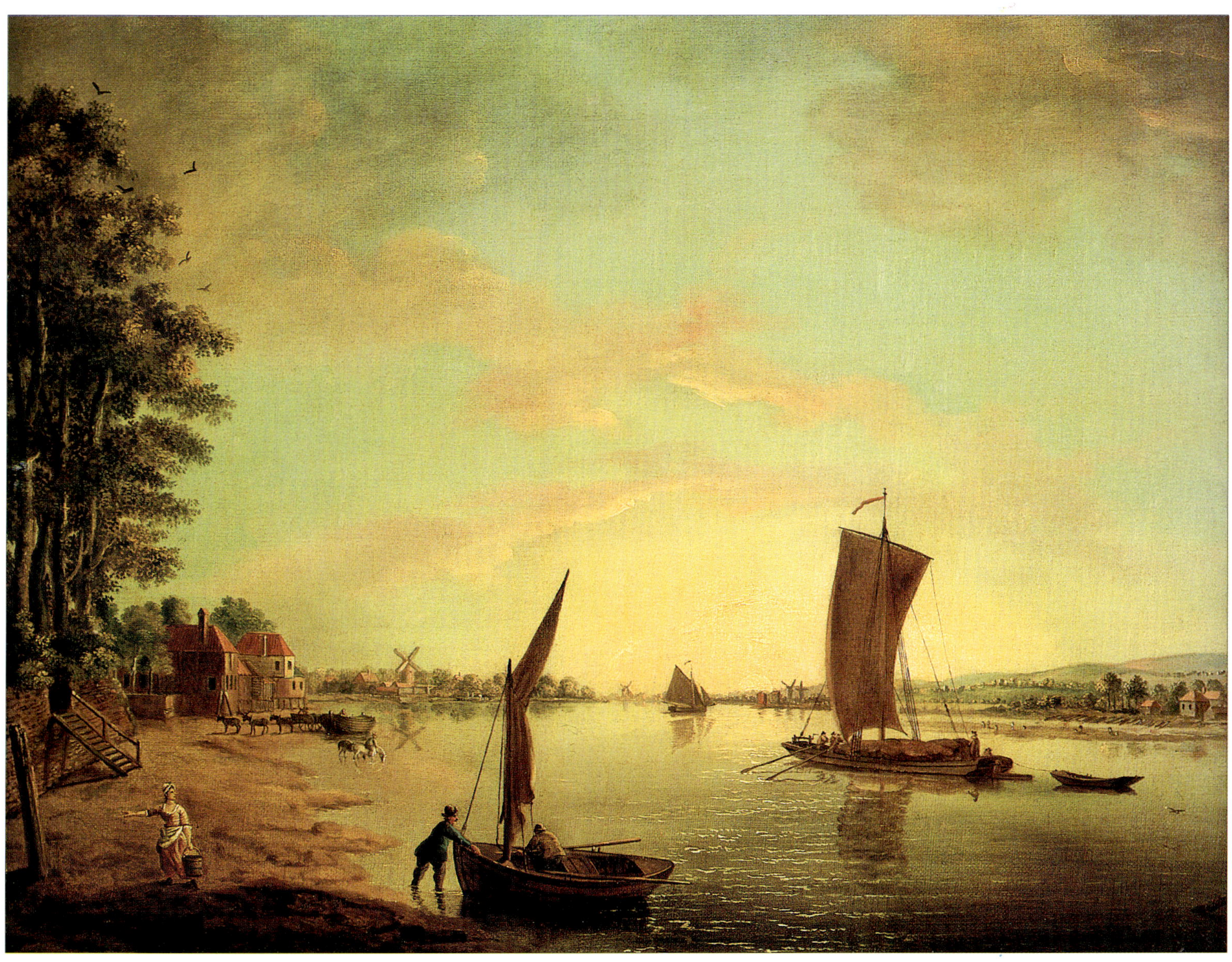

Colour Plate 45. *Scene on the Thames. Oil on canvas. 16½in. x 20½in. Signed.*
CHRISTIE'S LOT 326. 18.5.90

This calm little scene on the Thames, with plenty of interest and detail on both banks, shows Swaine at his best.

painting calm estuary or river scenes, often with a good deal of shore scenery – rather more than Monamy would attempt. However, he was definitely not at ease when it came to painting ships at sea in moderate winds with a ruffled sea. In particular his drawing of the sea in all its moods is very weak and unrealistic and his ships sit on it rather awkwardly. In this respect he is rather inferior to Monamy and Brooking. It is only necessary to compare the drawing of the sea in Colour Plates 44 and 49 in this chapter with Colour Plates 26 and 33 in Chapter 3 (which show the realistic rendering of a moving sea by Monamy) to appreciate this point.

In spite of this failing, however, his pictures are decorative and remain very popular among private collectors. His work is not necessarily in English waters. There are many scenes in Dutch rivers and waterways and there are also views in the West Indies, such as a view of Martinique, and also a view of Quebec.

Specific Recognition Features of Swaine

Many paintings by both Swaine and Monamy are unsigned, or have lost their original signatures, or in some instances have acquired false signatures. It is helpful to have a short list of points to look for in identifying a Swaine or Monamy and, indeed, differentiating them from many of the other less famous artists of the period.

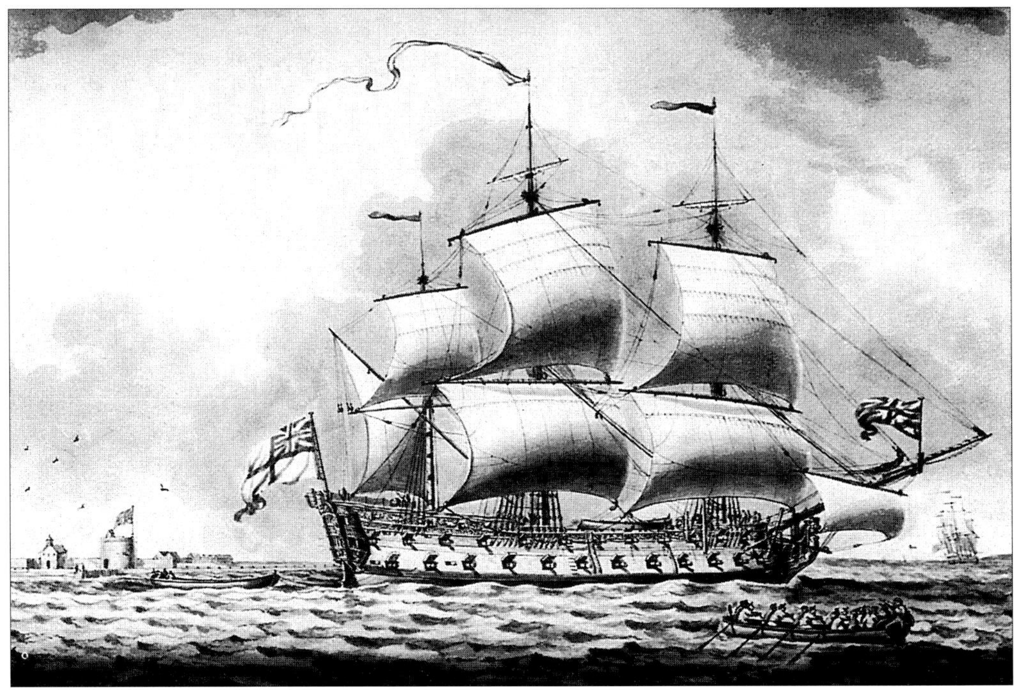

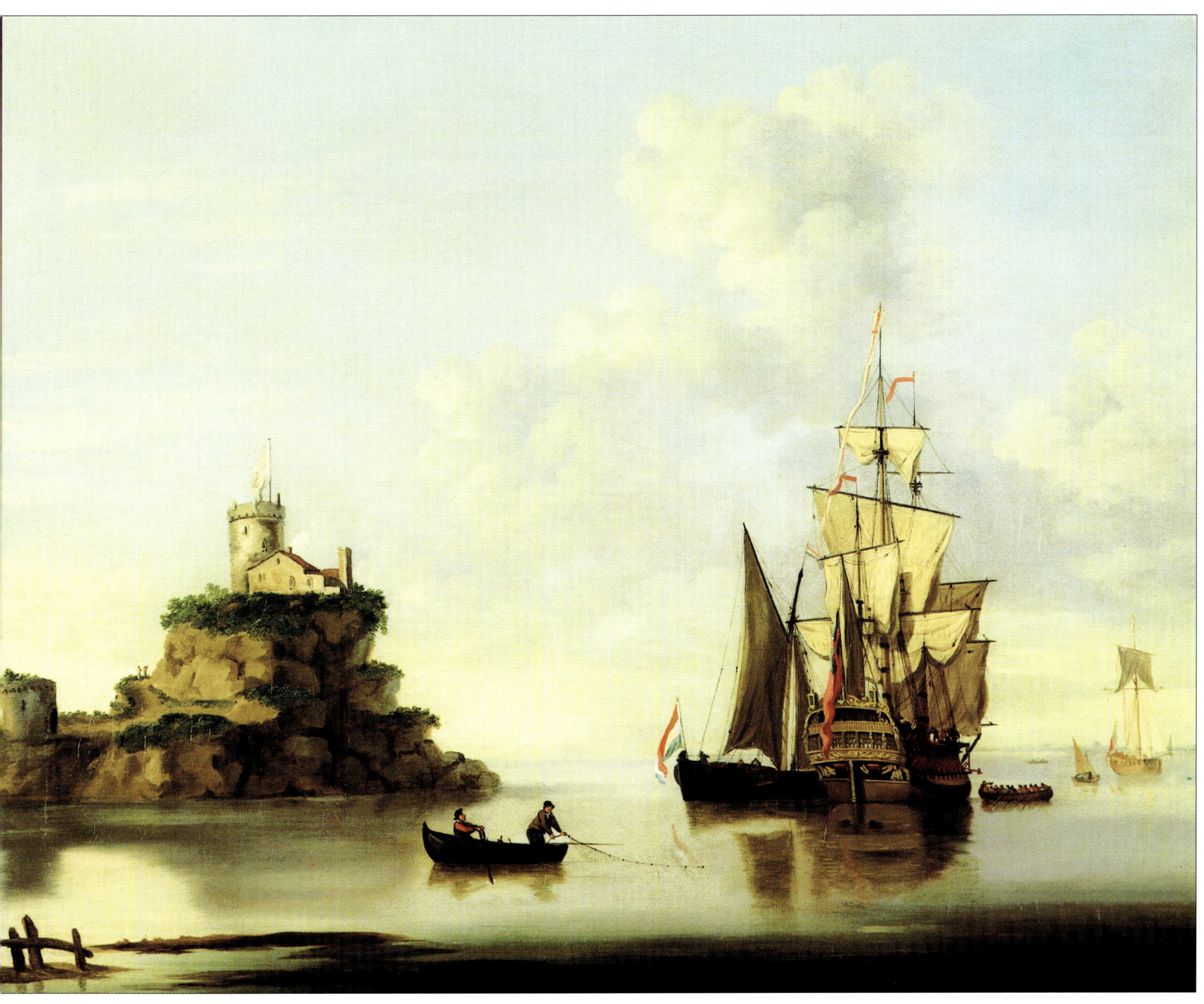

Colour Plate 46. *An English two-decker and a Dutch barge at anchor off a coastal fort.*
Oil on canvas. 20in. x 24in. Signed.   CHRISTIE'S
An attractive picture, with a glassy calm sea and some interest on shore as well. Accurate
and well painted.

Plate 27 *(Opposite). A drawing of a British two-decker off Calshot Castle. Pen, pencil,*
and wash. 10in. x 18in. Signed.   SOTHEBY'S LOT 196, 10.7.86
Another accurate and meticulous record of a British warship under sail.

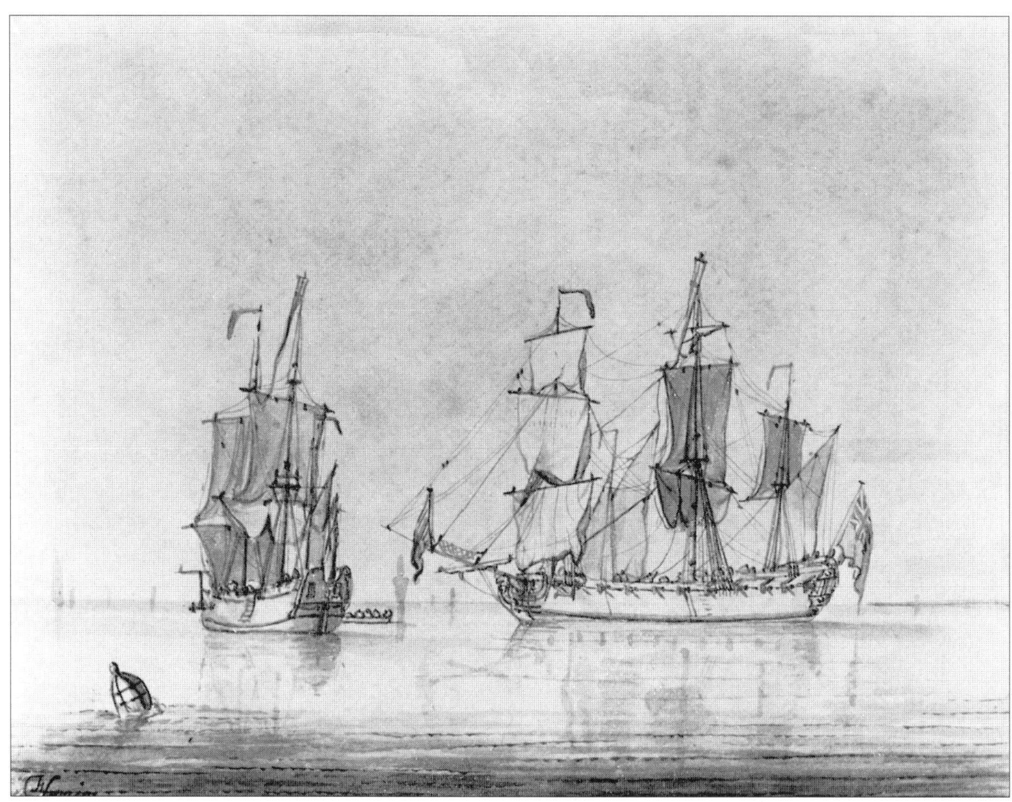

Plate 28. *A drawing of a small British sixth-rate warship, in two positions. Pencil and wash. Signed.* APPLEBY
This is a quick pencil sketch of one of the small so-called sixth-rate ships of the 1745 establishment. They were the precursors of the frigates of Nelson's day.

Colour Plate 47 *(Opposite above). A yacht and a small man-o'-war in a calm river near a church. Oil on copper. 6in. x 8in. Signed.* O'MELL GALLERY
One of Swaine's small beautifully painted miniature pictures on a copper panel.

Colour Plate 48 *(Opposite below). A fishing boat being launched off the Dutch coast. Oil on copper. 7¼in. x 10in. Signed.* SOTHEBY'S LOT 1. 14.11.90
Again a little estuary scene, but this time with a high wind and rough water.

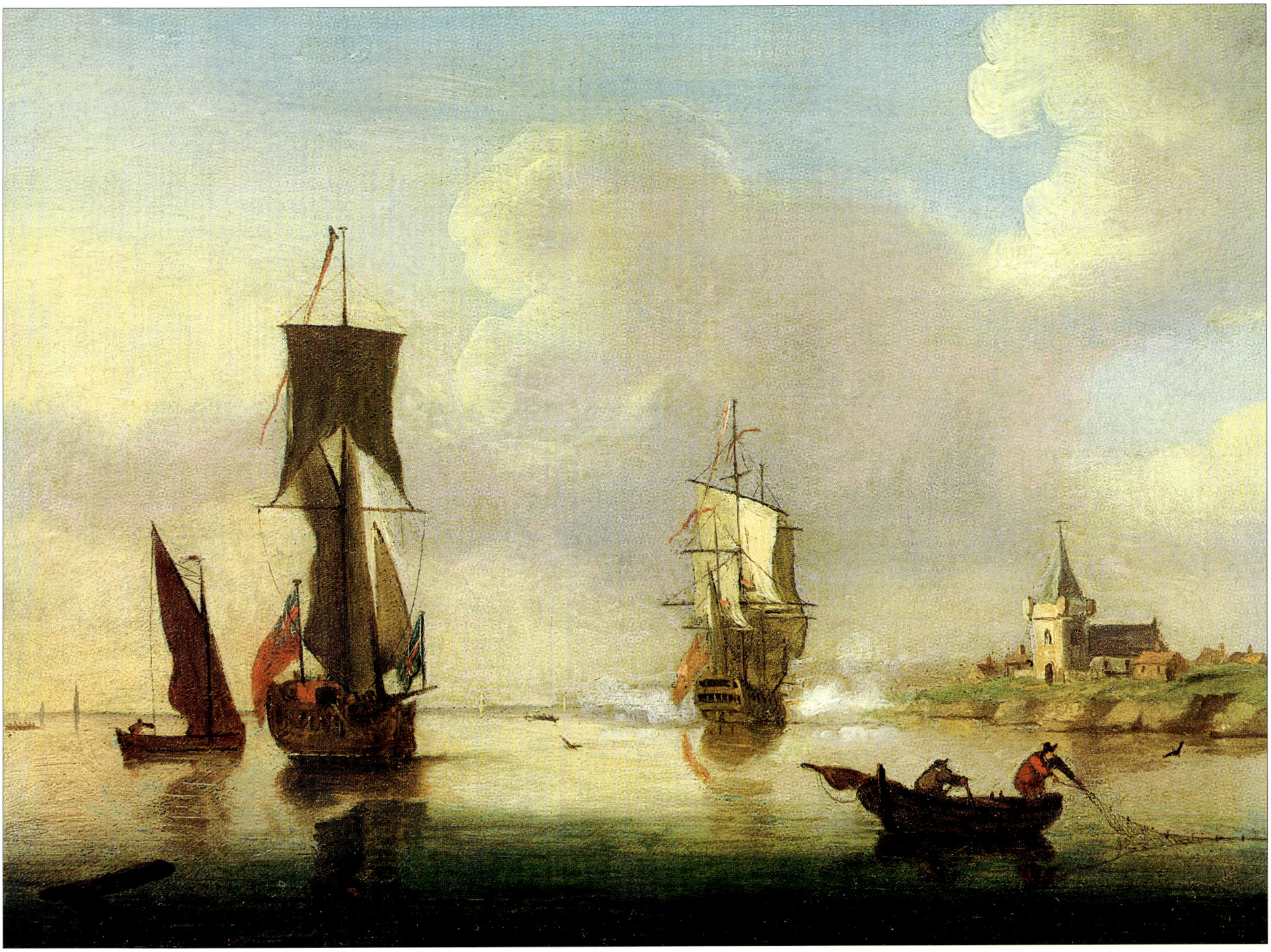

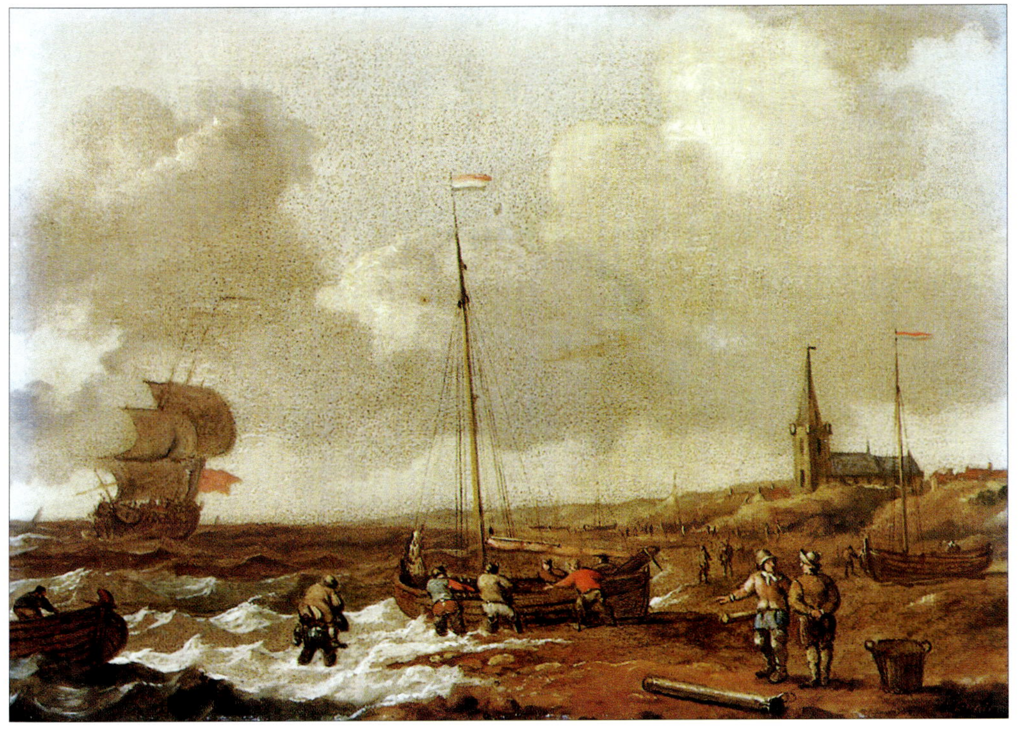

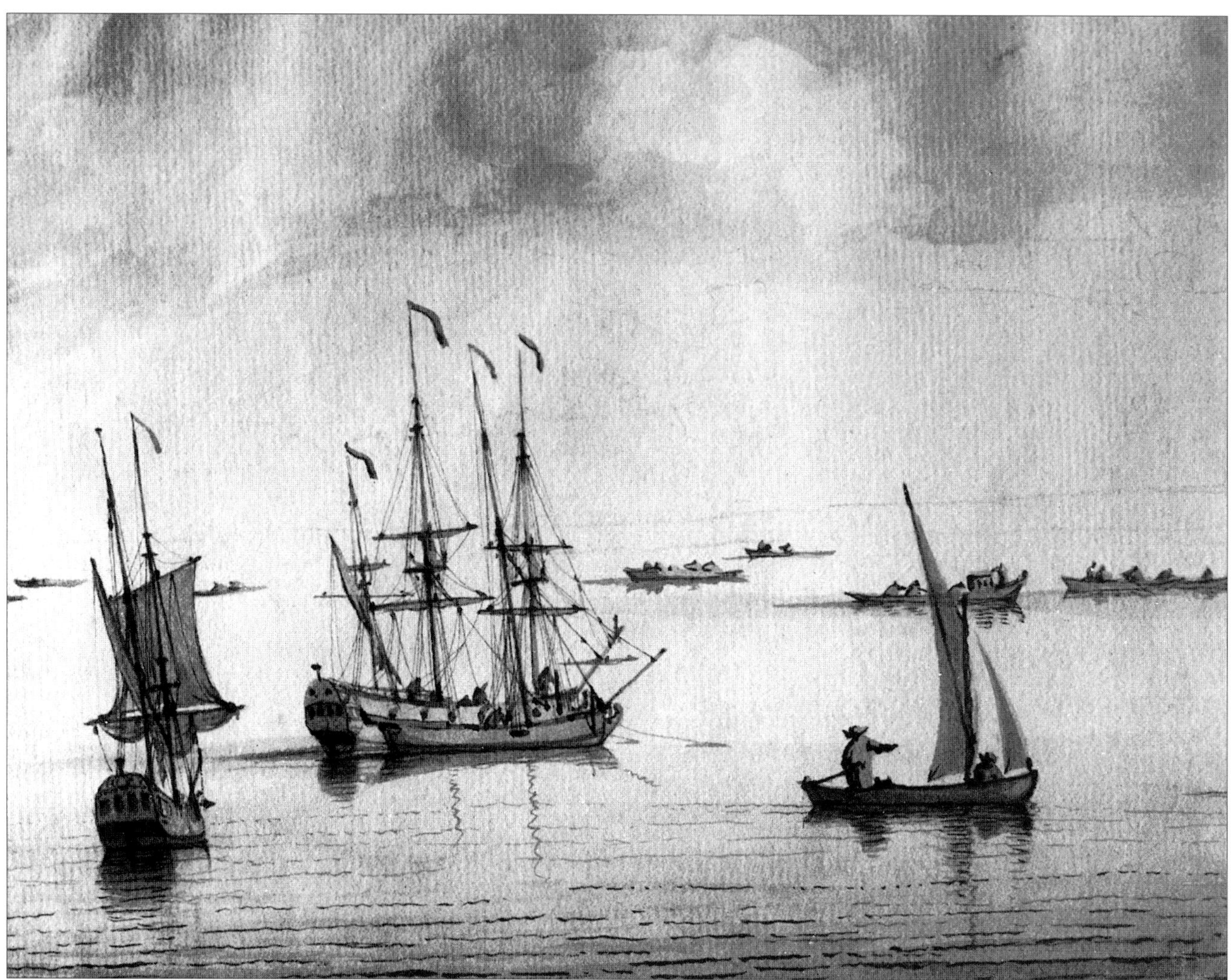

Plate 29. *A drawing of small craft on the Thames. Pencil and wash.*

EX. INGRAM COLLECTION. PRIVATE COLLECTION

This was one of a series of six small quick sketches of small craft which populated the Thames in those days.

1. *Composition and Palette.* The composition of Monamy's pictures usually shows a sense of reality and naturalness, whereas Swaine's scenes are rather contrived and the ships sit awkwardly in the water. The palette of Monamy and of Swaine is about the same.

2. *The Painting of the Sea.* As already mentioned, Monamy's seas are always much more realistic. Swaine often just indicates waves by recurrent white strokes of the brush. When he really tries a rough sea (Colour Plate 44) it appears in regular elevations and depressions rather like a regular line of little mountains. This method is often resorted to by artists who have no real experience of rough seas – which I suspect was the case with Swaine.

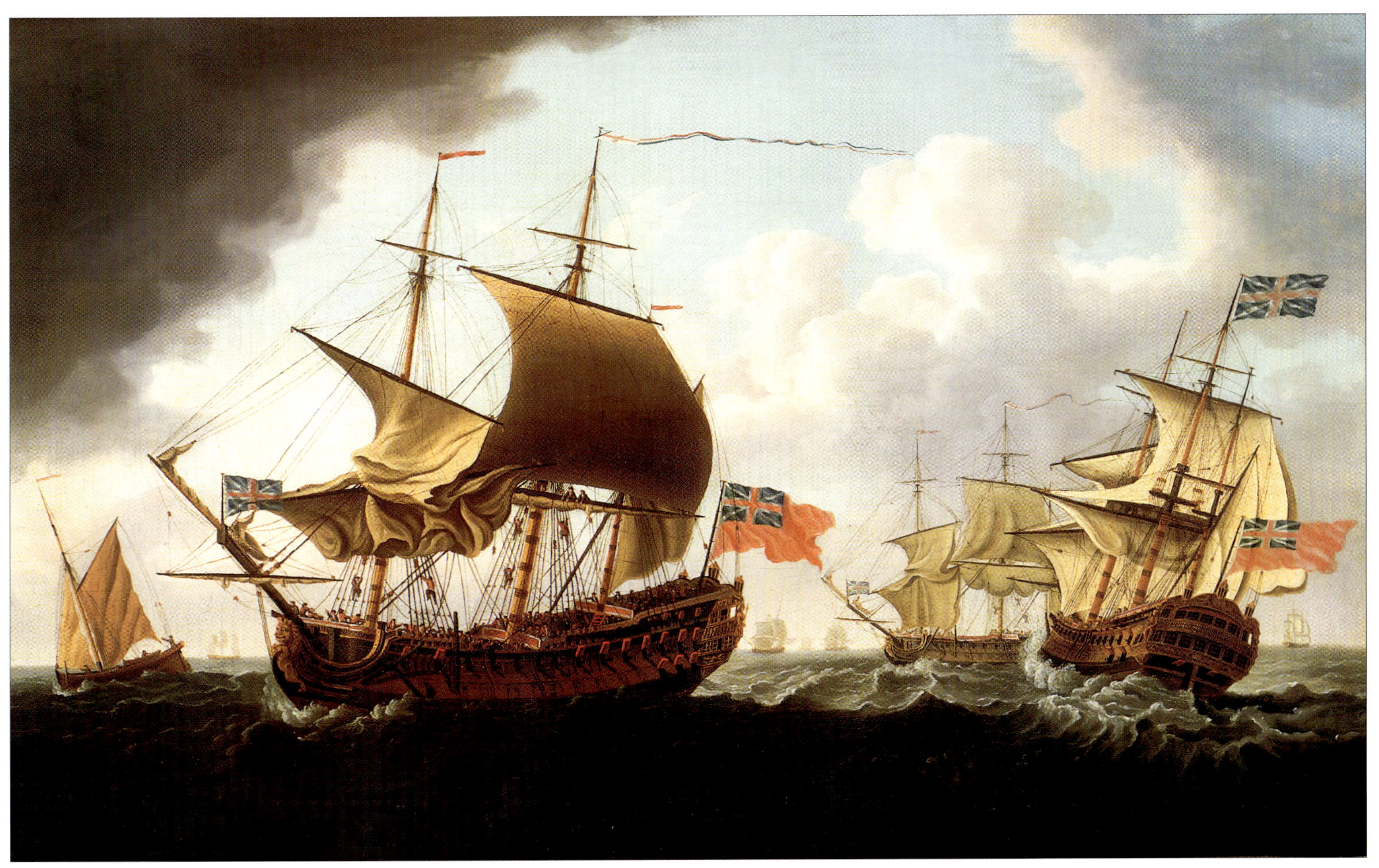

Colour Plate 49. *Men-o'-war sailing in choppy waters. Oil on canvas. Signed.*
Sotheby's Lot 133. 19.7.78

A slightly uncomfortable scene. Swaine is not at his best when painting several ships in rough seas. It looks as though a collision might be imminent!

3. *The Clouds.* The two artists paint their cloudy skies differently. Swaine has diffuse clouds, sometimes pink, or dark, but with indeterminate edges. Monamy has rolling white clouds with definite rounded edges, often with a line of impasto somewhere, which is highly typical.

4. Lastly, in the calm scenes, look at the wind vane at the top of the main or foremast. In Swaine pictures it always sticks out at a right-angle from the mast, before it droops (Colour Plates 43 and 46). In Monamy pictures it sticks out at an angle of 45° before slight drooping (see Colour Plate 30). This characteristic is so constant that it can be used as a reliable recognition feature in most calm scenes. (A notable exception to this is Colour Plate 29.)

Using these features a reasonably fair evaluation of any given painting can be achieved.

Drawings

Swaine, unlike Monamy, has left a legacy of very fine, finished drawings. He was a good draughtsman and most of his drawings are neat, tidy and accurate and are meant to be finished works of art in themselves.

They were mostly portraits of large ships at anchor (Plate 26) or at sea with sails set (Plate 27). But in addition he did a delightful series of small jewel-like drawings of the varieties of small craft to be seen on the Thames. Plate 29 illustrates one of these, taken from the Ingram Collection which had a dozen or so of the whole series.

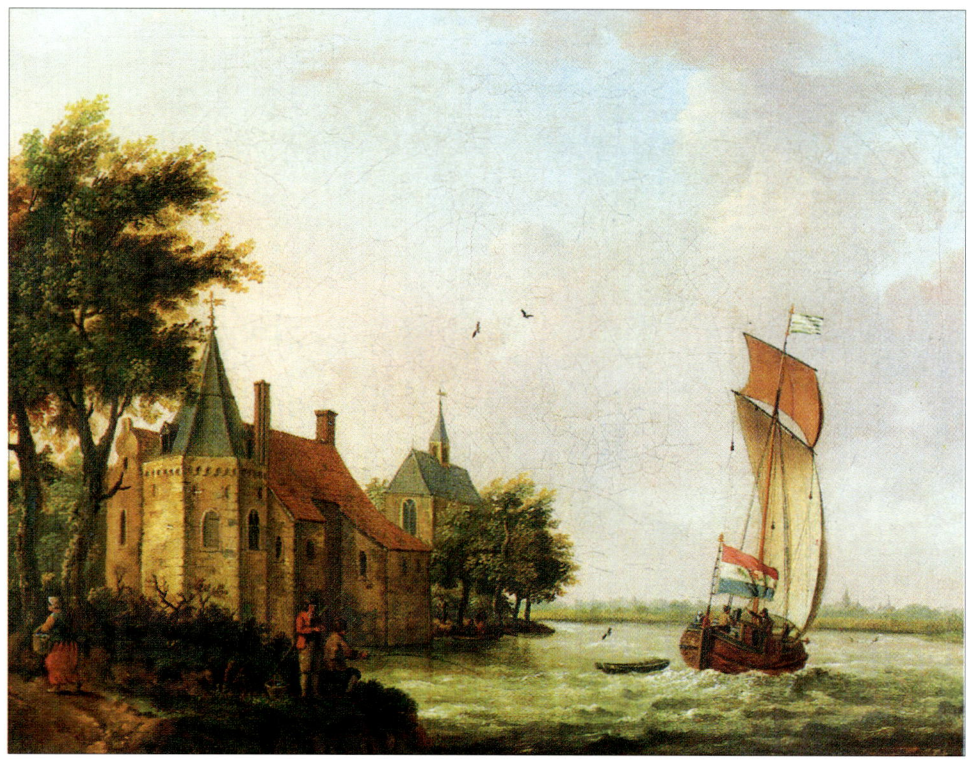

Colour Plate 50. *A wooded river landscape in Holland, with a Dutch hooker under sail in a brisk wind. Oil on canvas. 14in. x 17½in. Signed.* CHRISTIE'S LOT 54. 24.4.87 *Swaine did a number of little riverscapes like this in Holland and other locations on the Continent.*

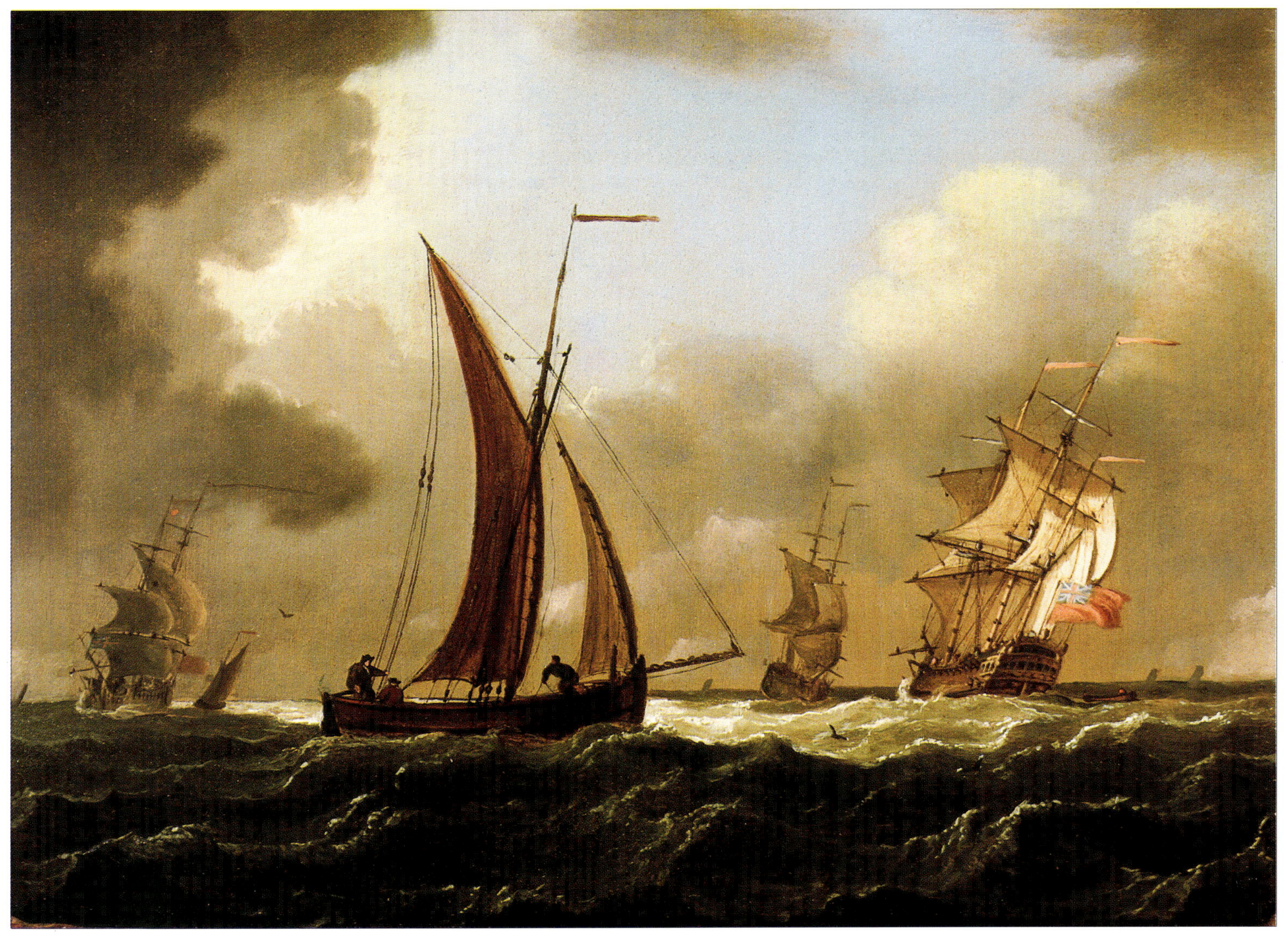

Colour Plate 51. *Small craft at sea in a stiff breeze. Oil on copper panel. 6in. x 8in. Signed.*
CHRISTIE'S

Another small very well painted seascape. A more successful rendering of a choppy sea, from his more mature period.

Prints

Like most of his contemporaries, Swaine tried his hand at line engraving and mezzotinting – but did not take it up in a serious way. There are several examples still to be found on the market, mostly prints of Monamy pictures rather than his own. Some examples, particularly of ships on fire at night, are of his own work.

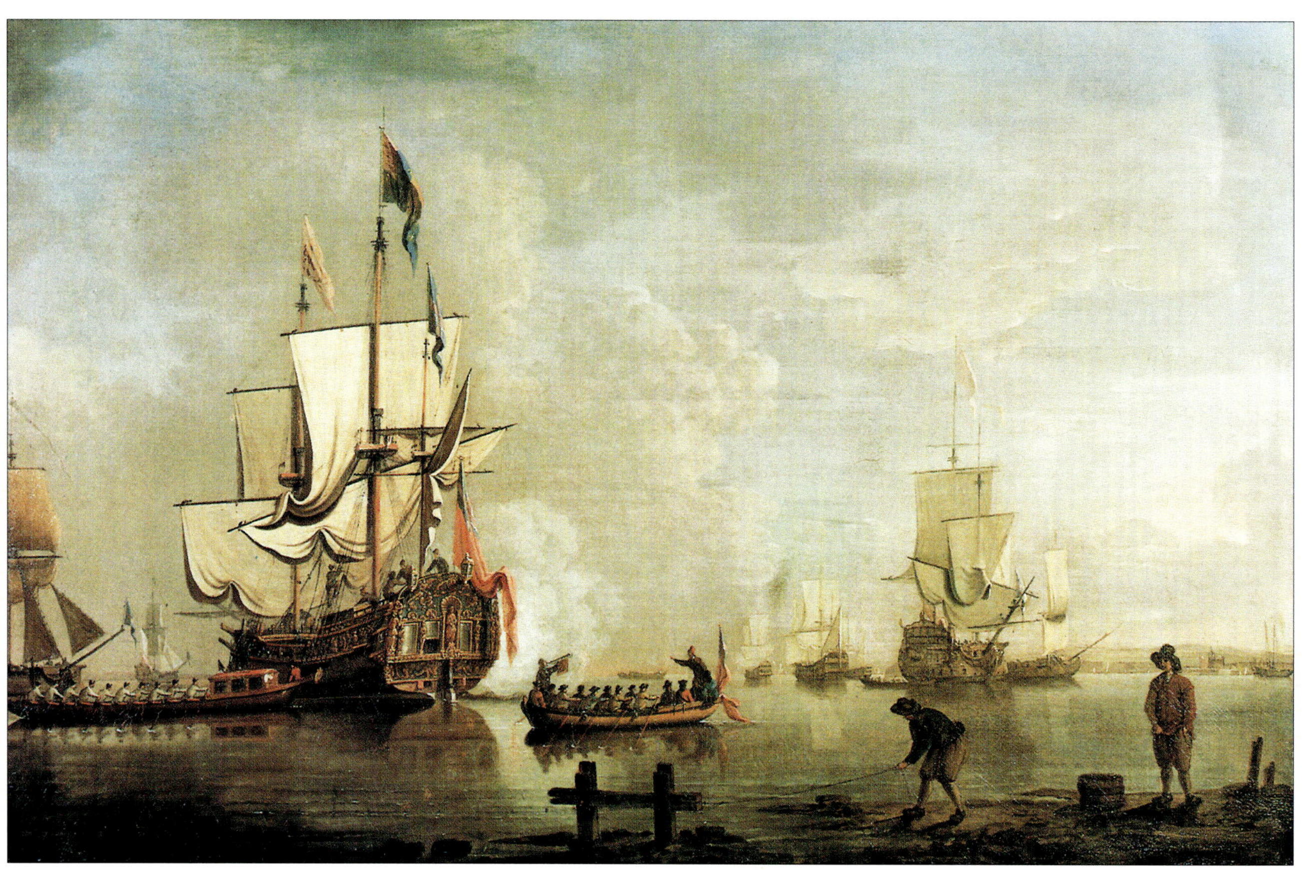

Colour Plate 52. *Thomas Mellish. The* Royal Caroline *in a calm estuary, flying a Royal Standard and surrounded by an attendant barge and other small boats. Possibly the King has just boarded the royal yacht before one of his voyages. Oil on canvas. Not signed.*

Christie's

The drawing is meticulous and detailed and the large figures in the foreground and in the small boat are done well with great detail.

Plate 30 *(Opposite). Thomas Mellish. A two-decker and other small ships off Dover. Oil on canvas. 14½in. x 22¾in. Signed.*   Richard Green Gallery

A very attractive and competent ship portrait, with an equally well painted and recognisable background of Dover and Dover Castle. The ship is perhaps a little static (rather like a model) which explains why his work is often mistaken for that of Samuel Scott.

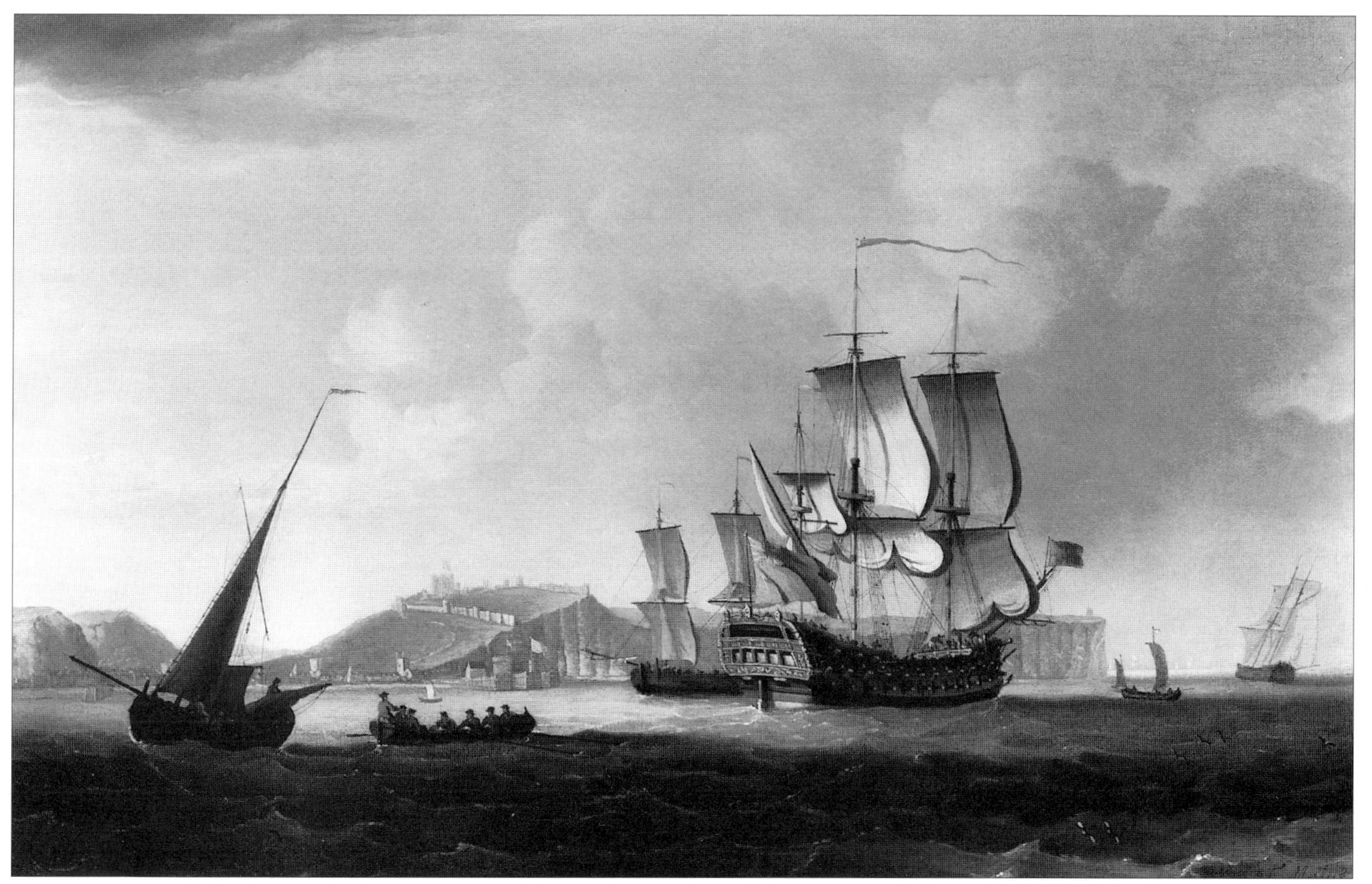

CHAPTER 6
Some Rarer Marine Artists of the Monamy Period

During the later years of Peter Monamy and Francis Swaine there was a small group of marine artists whose work is seldom seen and about whom very little is known. Their work, when it does appear, is often unsigned and unrecognised and their pictures are usually attributed to either Monamy or Swaine. There were four artists in this group who deserve a little consideration now because in fact they produced reasonably competent and attractive works.

1. Thomas Mellish   fl. c.1740–1766
2. T. Leemans   fl. c.1720–1740
3. Thomas Allen   fl. c.1739–1772
4. J. Cook   fl. c.1720–1740

Thomas Mellish   **fl. c.1740–1766**

Of the four artists named above, Mellish was by far the most competent and attractive. Details of his life and work are obscure. All that is known about him is that he lived at Hoxton Square in London and exhibited his

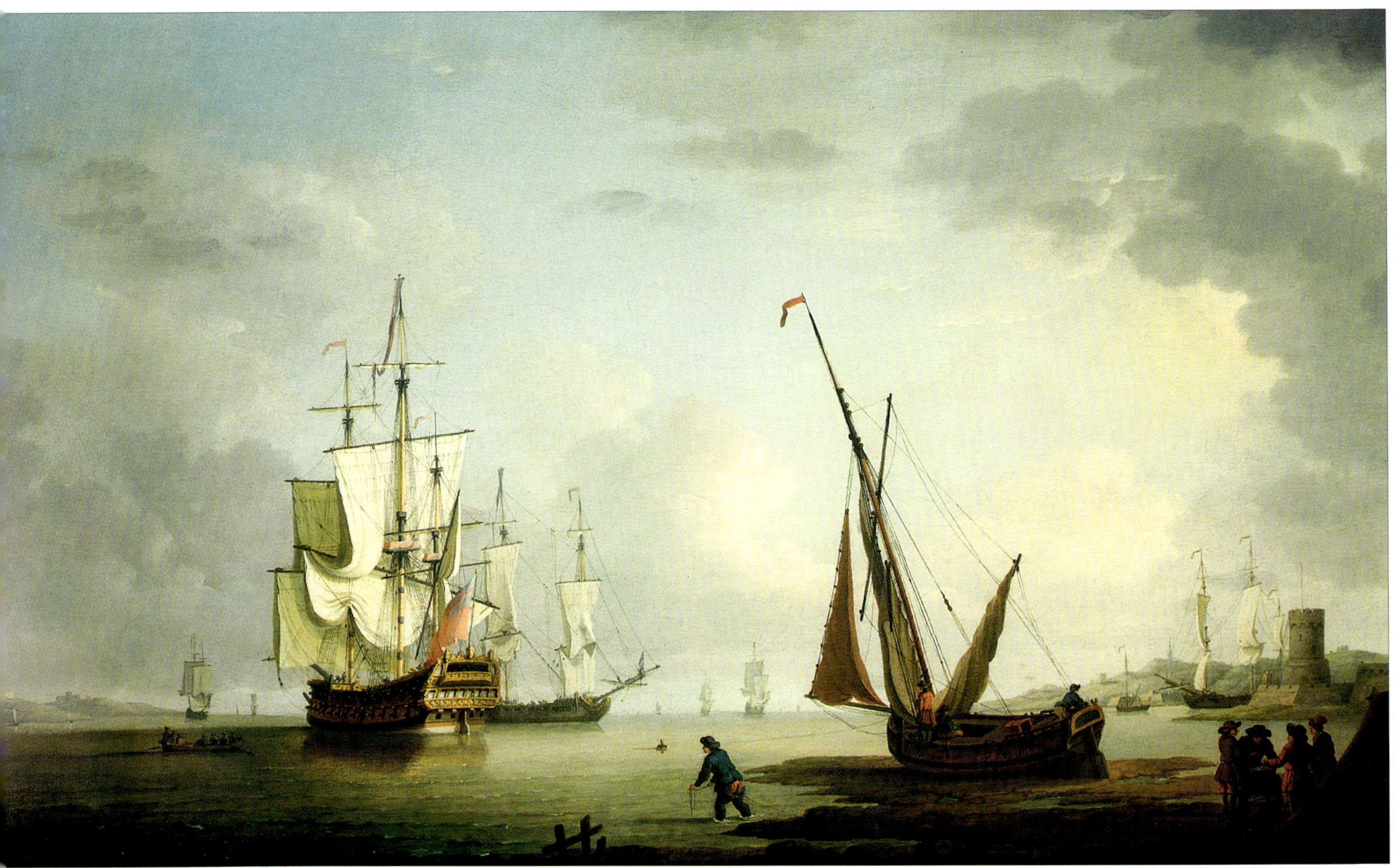

Colour Plate 53. *Thomas Mellish. A two-decker English man-o'-war and a beached hoy off a harbour. Oil on canvas. 16½ x 26in. Signed.* RICHARD GREEN GALLERY
Again a very competent and typical scene, well composed and painted with great attention to detail. All rather static, perhaps, and thus rather in the style of a Samuel Scott.

work from 1761 to 1766 with the Society of Artists. He appears to have painted marines, harbours and a number of Continental views, most actively in the 1740s and 1750s.[1]

There are only about six signed works known, but these are enough to give us a good appreciation of his style, which is very similar to the mature Peter Monamy at his best, with a very pleasant toned down palette which is quite sophisticated. The painting of the land features is very detailed and accurate, but probably the most outstanding recognition feature is his brilliant drawing of the figures on shore or in little boats. He is superior to

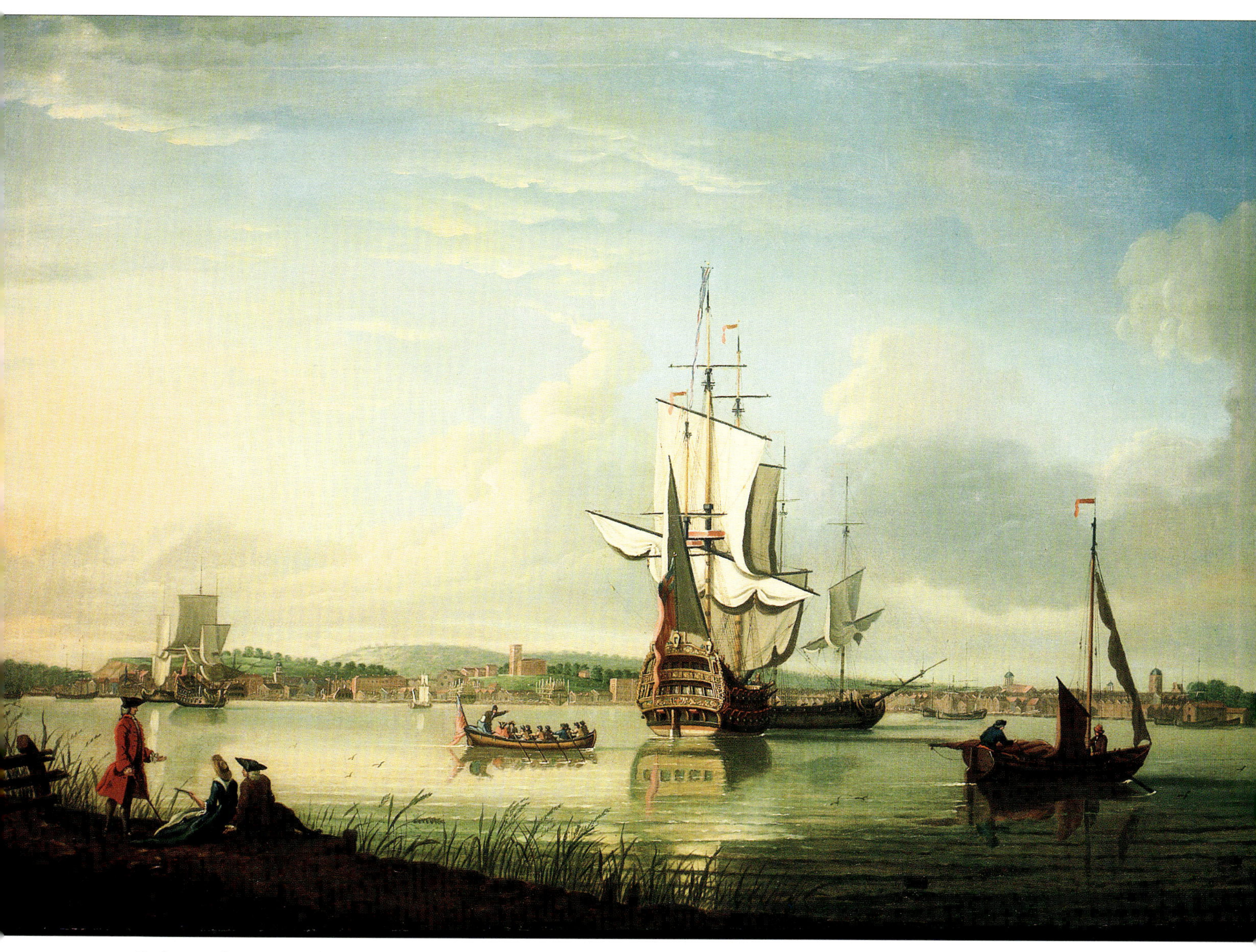

Colour Plate 54. *Thomas Mellish. A view of the Thames at Woolwich with shipping becalmed. Oil on canvas. 32in. x 46½in. Unsigned.* RICHARD GREEN GALLERY
A very similar view of Woolwich, but with the main ship turned to a stern quarter view, is owned by the National Maritime Museum. The general execution of this very detailed painting is of a high order and the detail is impressive. The gentleman in the red coat, lower right foreground, occurs in several Mellish paintings. Although unsigned, its attribution to Mellish is certain.

both Monamy and Swaine in this respect. This can be appreciated in Colour Plates 52 and 54 and Plate 30.

The National Maritime Museum has an excellent signed view of Woolwich by him which is very similar to Colour Plate 54. The Ferens Art Gallery in Hull has a signed view of Charleston, South Carolina, and the Shipley Art Gallery also has a marine by him.

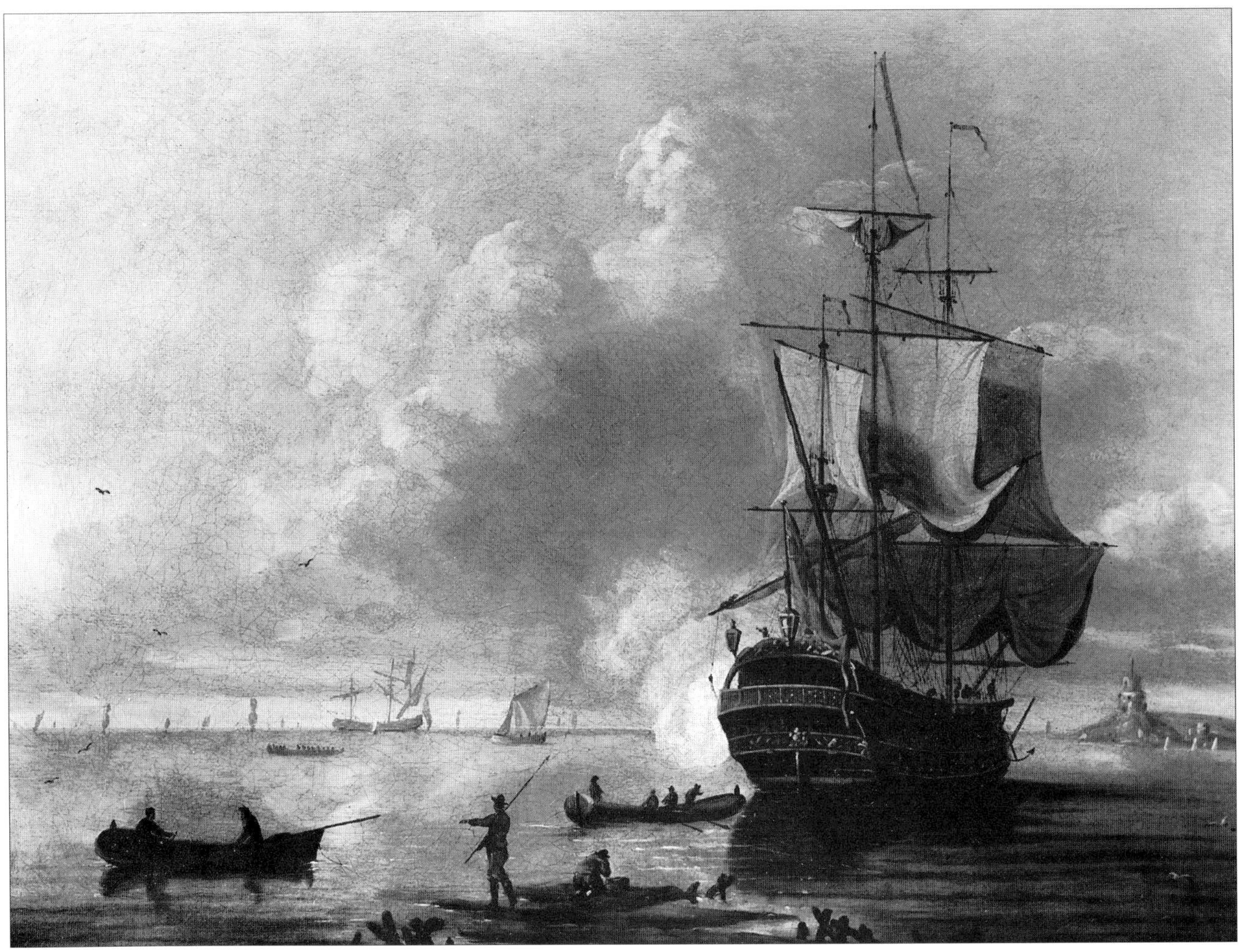

Plate 31. *T. Leemans. A two-decker warship, stern quarter view in a calm estuary. Oil on canvas. Signed T. Leemans.*   SOTHEBY'S
This is one of the very few signed pictures by Leemans to appear on the market. The tall figures in the foreground of the picture and the high masts of the ship are there, but the fact that this is a black and white photograph completely hides the high dramatic colouring which is the other important characteristic of Leemans' compositions.

T. Leemans   fl. c.1720–1740

T. Leemans is the most enigmatic and almost completely unknown of this little group of four minor painters, but oddly enough he is usually the most recognisable! His pictures are on canvas, of medium to large size, and always show a calm scene with a large man-o'-war, seen from the stern, with a vast spread of drooping sail. What sets them apart, however, is the extremely harsh palette. The sky is very blue, the stern of the ship is rather wider than it should be and is highlighted in pure gold, which makes it stand out of the picture. The masts and sails are usually much too big for the ship (excessive top hamper) and the whole composition looks theatrical, painted in harsh bright colours.

The trouble is that often the composition does show some trace of

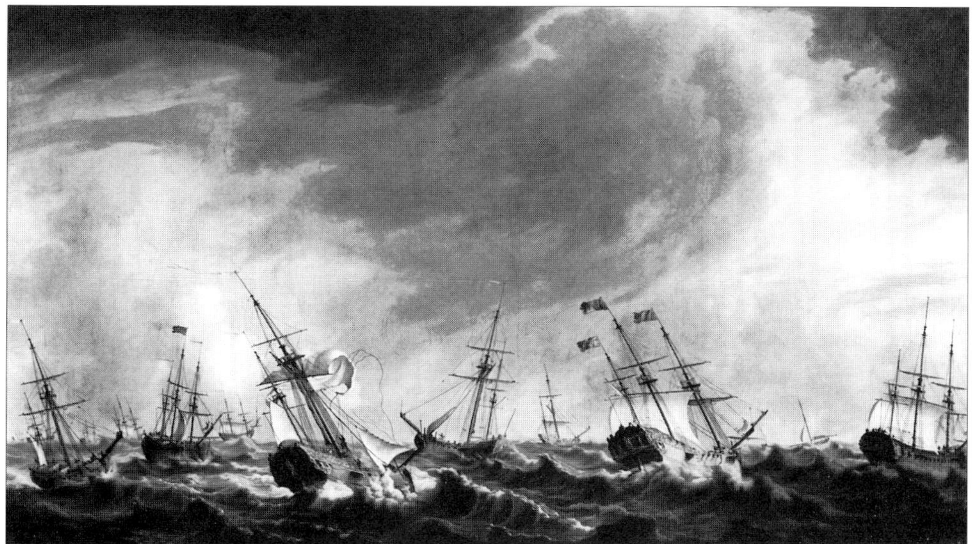

Plate 32. *Thomas Allen. The storm during Princess Charlotte's voyage to England in 1761. Oil on canvas. 15½in. x 23in. Not signed.* BONHAMS
The yacht Mary *was laid on her beam ends during this storm. This painting was engraved by P.C. Canot and published by J. Bowles.*

Monamy influence and the almost inescapable conclusion is that this artist may well have been one of Monamy's assistants for a short period. Nearly all his pictures appearing in salerooms are catalogued as 'Peter Monamy'. This is very detrimental to Monamy's reputation as they are really of rather a primitive type compared with the real Peter Monamy.

In a group of seventeen pictures seen by the author over the last twenty years only one was signed. All seventeen were flat calms and were fairly identical compositions – stern view of a major ship, possibly a small 'hoy' beached in the foreground with some small exaggerated figures either in a boat or in the foreground. In all of them the main identification feature was the harsh theatrical colour, making it look like a so-called 'chocolate-box' illustration. In black and white photographs one cannot of course appreciate this feature, and so they look slightly more Monamylike.

The three illustrations here (Colour Plates 55 and 56 and Plate 31) show all these features quite well.

In spite of all these remarks, his pictures usually do quite well in the saleroom and surprisingly high prices are sometimes achieved. I think the reason for this is that they have a decorative, colourful and eye-catching quality on the wall which can appeal to a less sophisticated taste.

Thomas Allen   **fl. c.1739-1772**

Thomas Allen's main period of activity was just after Monamy's death in 1749. He exhibited marines at the Free Society from 1767 to 1772. His best known works are his depictions of the voyage and arrival in England of George III's bride, Charlotte of Mecklenburg-Strelitz. The series

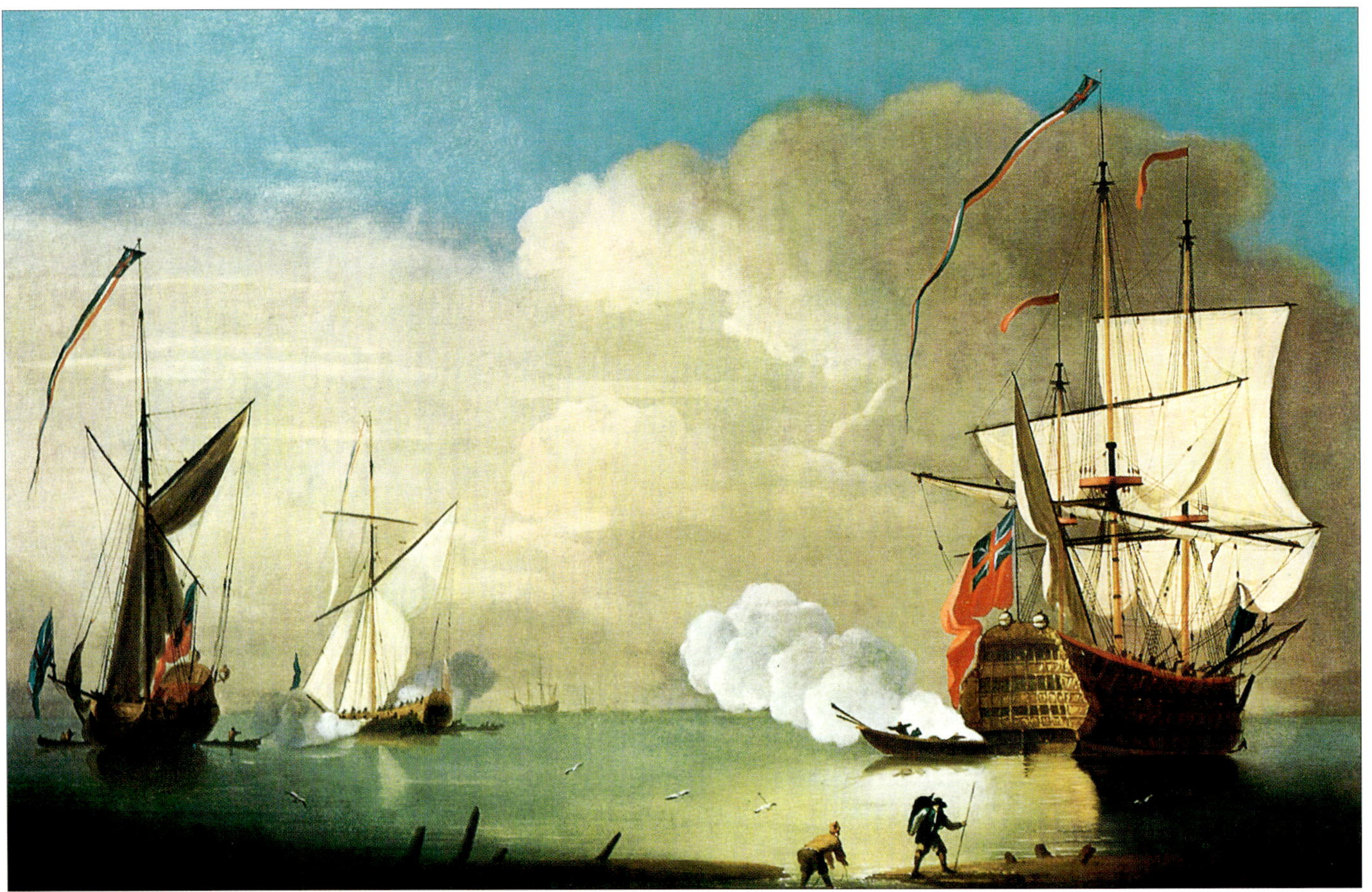

Colour Plate 55. *T. Leemans. A calm seascape with stern quarter view of a three-decker first-rate warship and two royal yachts. Oil on canvas. Not signed.* CHRISTIE'S
Again a very typical Leemans, both in composition and colouring. Very high masts and large drooping sails much in evidence.

Colour Plate 56 *(Opposite). T. Leemans. Stern quarter view of a three-decker English first-rate man-o'-war firing a signal gun. Oil on canvas. Not signed. 30in. x 25in.*
CHRISTIE'S
This picture bears all the hallmarks of T. Leemans. Dramatic very blue skies, the ship has a rather too wide, very golden stern and a vast amount of top hamper. A glassy calm and typical Leemans composition of the picture.

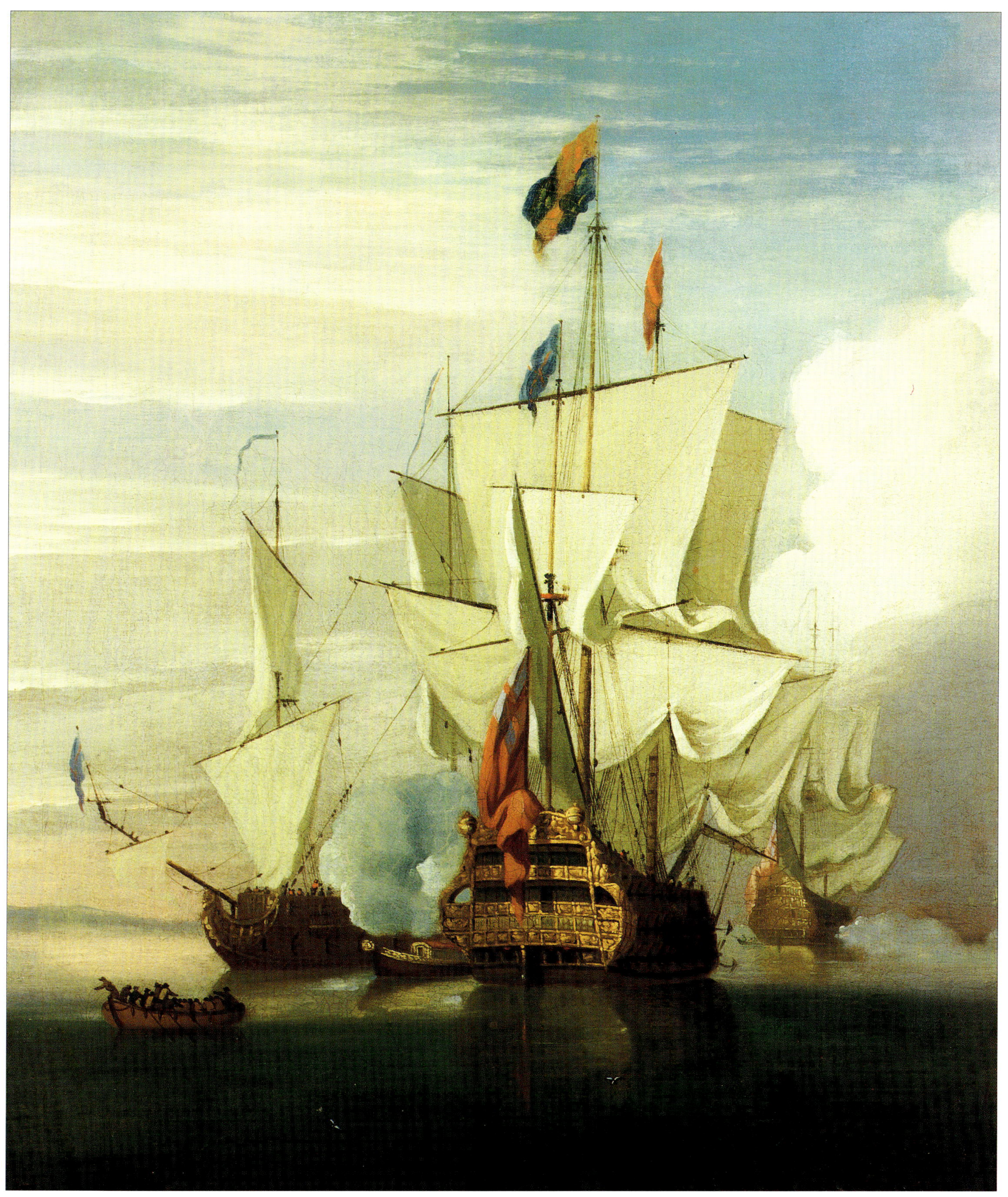

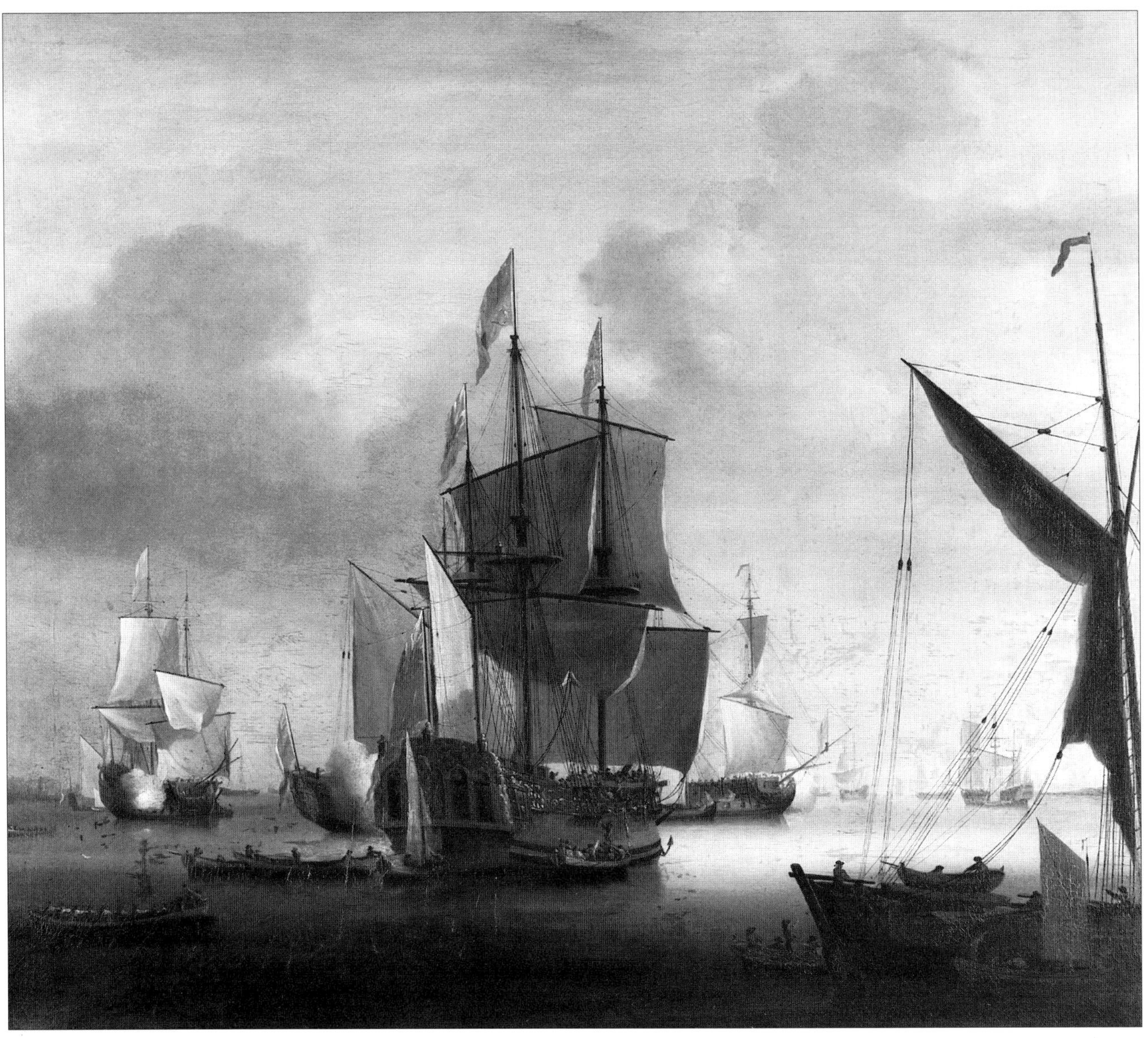

Plate 33. Thomas Allen. The Royal Caroline *at Spithead. Oil on canvas.*

This is one of four marine scenes by Thomas Allen at Goodwood. An accurate but rather dull portrait of the royal yacht. Every marine artist of those early eighteenth century years painted versions of this ship.

comprises a view of the yachts at Harwich (Colour Plate 57), the embarkation of Queen Charlotte at Stade and a lively stormy scene during the voyage across the North Sea (Plate 32). This latter painting was engraved by P.C. Canot and published by J. Bowles, which is why it is so well known.

In addition there are several of his works in the Goodwood House collection, two of which are illustrated (Plates 33 and 34).

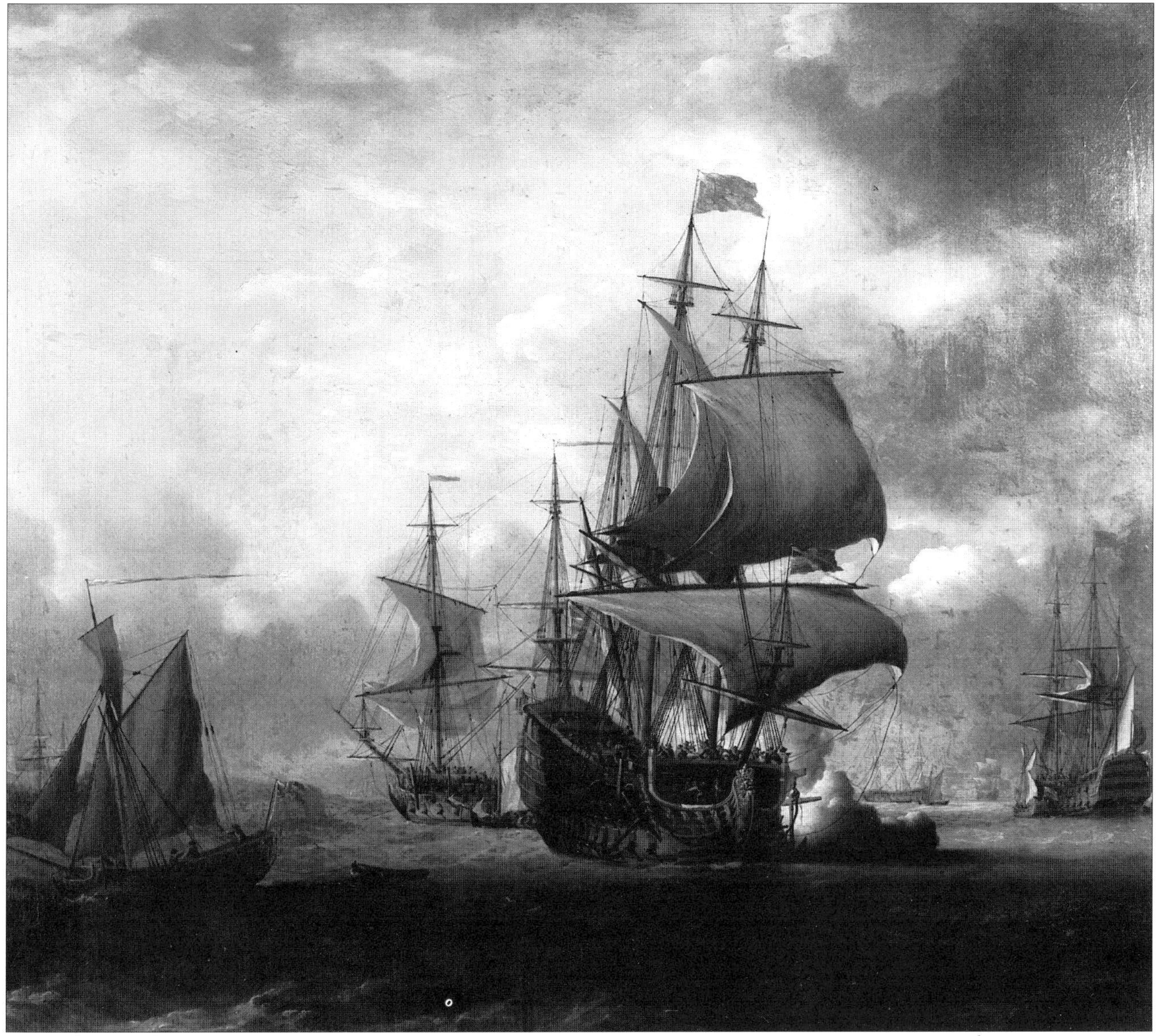

Plate 34. *Thomas Allen. The* Centurion *returning to England. Oil on canvas.*
TRUSTEES OF THE GOODWOOD COLLECTION.
PHOTOGRAPH: COURTAULD INSTITUTE OF ART
Another picture by Thomas Allen from the Goodwood Collection. This presumably shows Anson's Centurion *on its return from the famous four year circumnavigation in 1744, just about to anchor. Again the tendency of Allen to exaggerate the height of the stern in his paintings is evident.*

His pictures very rarely turn up in the salerooms and the author has seen only two signed examples in the last twenty years or so, one of which is illustrated in Plate 35. The other was signed and dated 1739.

It is probable, however, that quite a number may have slipped by unsigned and unrecognised and his life and work remain somewhat obscure at present.

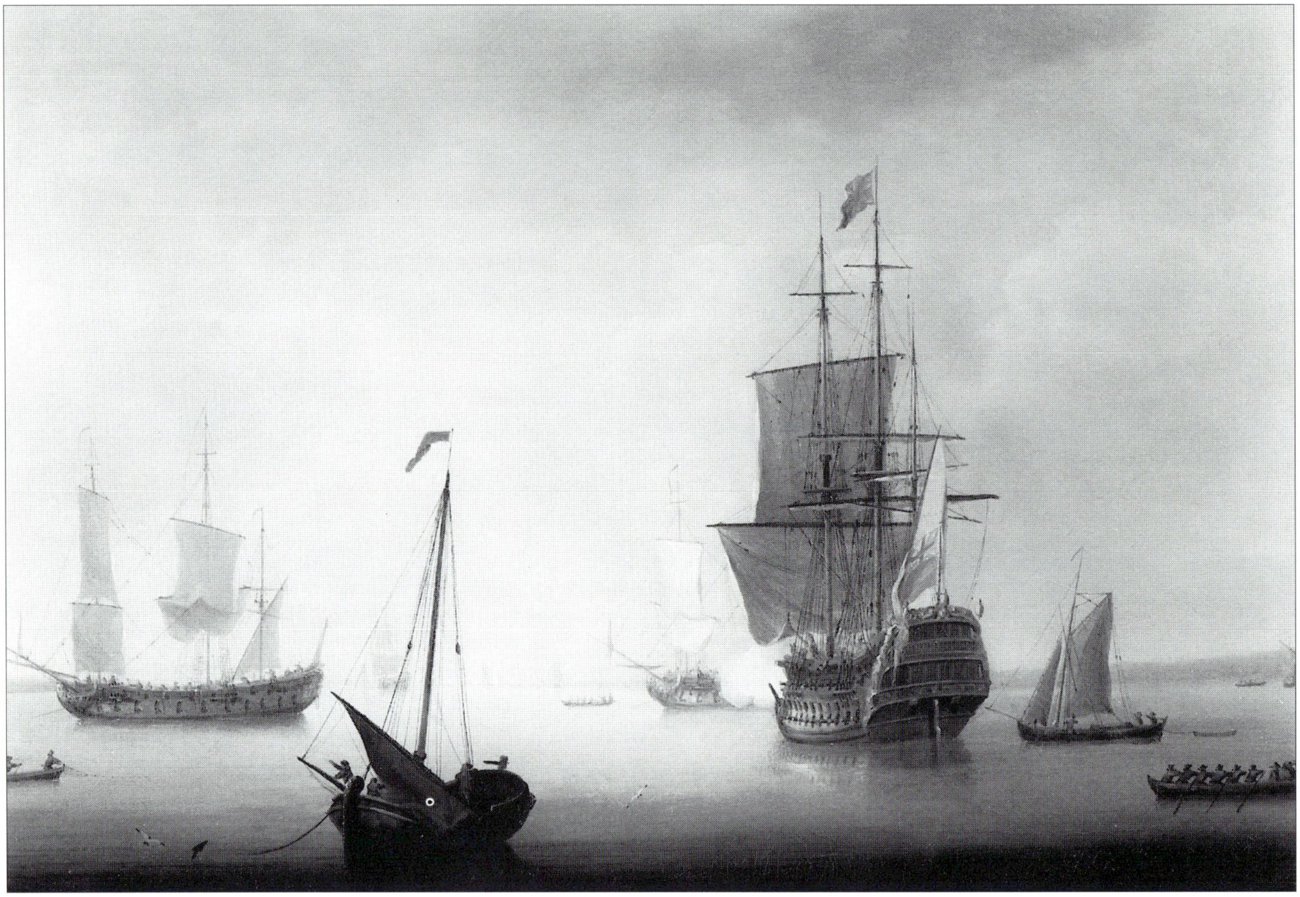

Plate 35. *Thomas Allen. A calm scene with three two-decker men-o'-war at anchor in an estuary. Oil on canvas. Signed T. Allen.* PRIVATE COLLECTION

In spite of having been painted a few years after Monamy's death, it is easy to see how a painting like this could be attributed to Monamy or Swaine. The rowers in the little boat are somewhat mechanical in appearance. Also the whole stern of the large two-decker on the right seems to be too high – a fault which seems to be typical of Allen's pictures and can easily be seen in Plate 34.

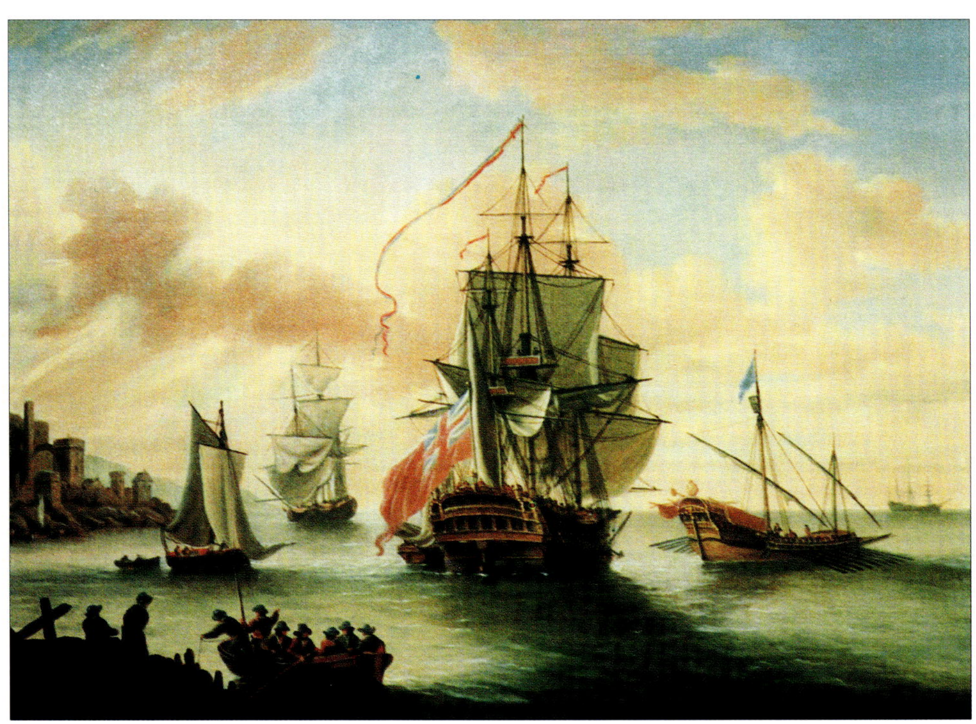

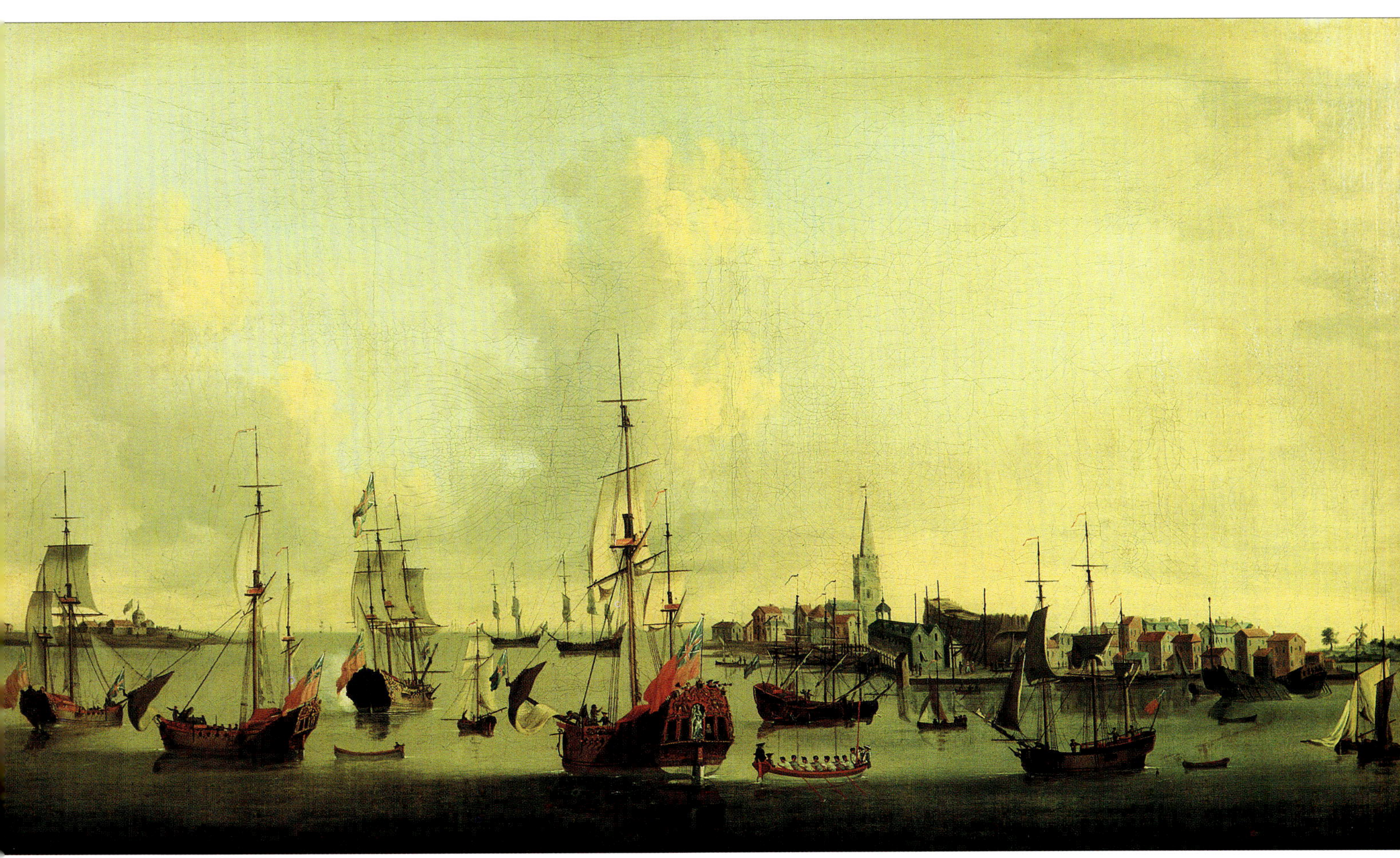

Colour Plate 57. Thomas Allen. A view of the fleet under Lord Anson at Harwich preparing to leave for Stade in Germany to bring back Princess Charlotte, the bride of George III in 1761. Oil on canvas. DAVID MESSUM GALLERY

Thomas Allen's best known works are his paintings of the voyage and arrival in England of Charlotte of Mecklenburg-Strelitz. The series includes this painting, one of the embarkation of Princess Charlotte at Stade and one of the voyage (Plate 32).

Colour Plate 58 (Opposite). J. Cook. An English merchant ship and a Mediterranean galley off an Eastern Coast. Oil on canvas, 20in. x 25in. Not signed.

PRIVATE COLLECTION

Most of his pictures seem to be of Mediterranean scenes, often with galleys in them.

J. Cook
fl. c.1730?-1750

J. Cook is the last and most intriguing of the minor marine painters mentioned here. His main known works are all of scenes in the Mediterranean, usually off Alexandria. The National Maritime Museum has a good signed example of one of these and there are at least three more close versions of this scene which have been on the art market (Plate 36). Some others which have been in the possession of the Parker Gallery are of ships in Alexandria harbour. Plates 36 and 37 are good examples of his work. He

Plate 36 (Opposite). *J. Cook. Shipping off Alexandria. Oil on canvas. 26in. x 54in. Signed J. Cook.* RUTLAND GALLERY
This is one of several very good pictures of this scene. There are also several good pictures inside the harbour. Probably painted about 1730-1740.

Plate 37 (Below). *J. Cook. An English merchant ship in Alexandria harbour, with a Mediterranean galley on the left. Oil on canvas. Not signed.* PARKER GALLERY
An excellent painting by a very competent marine artist.

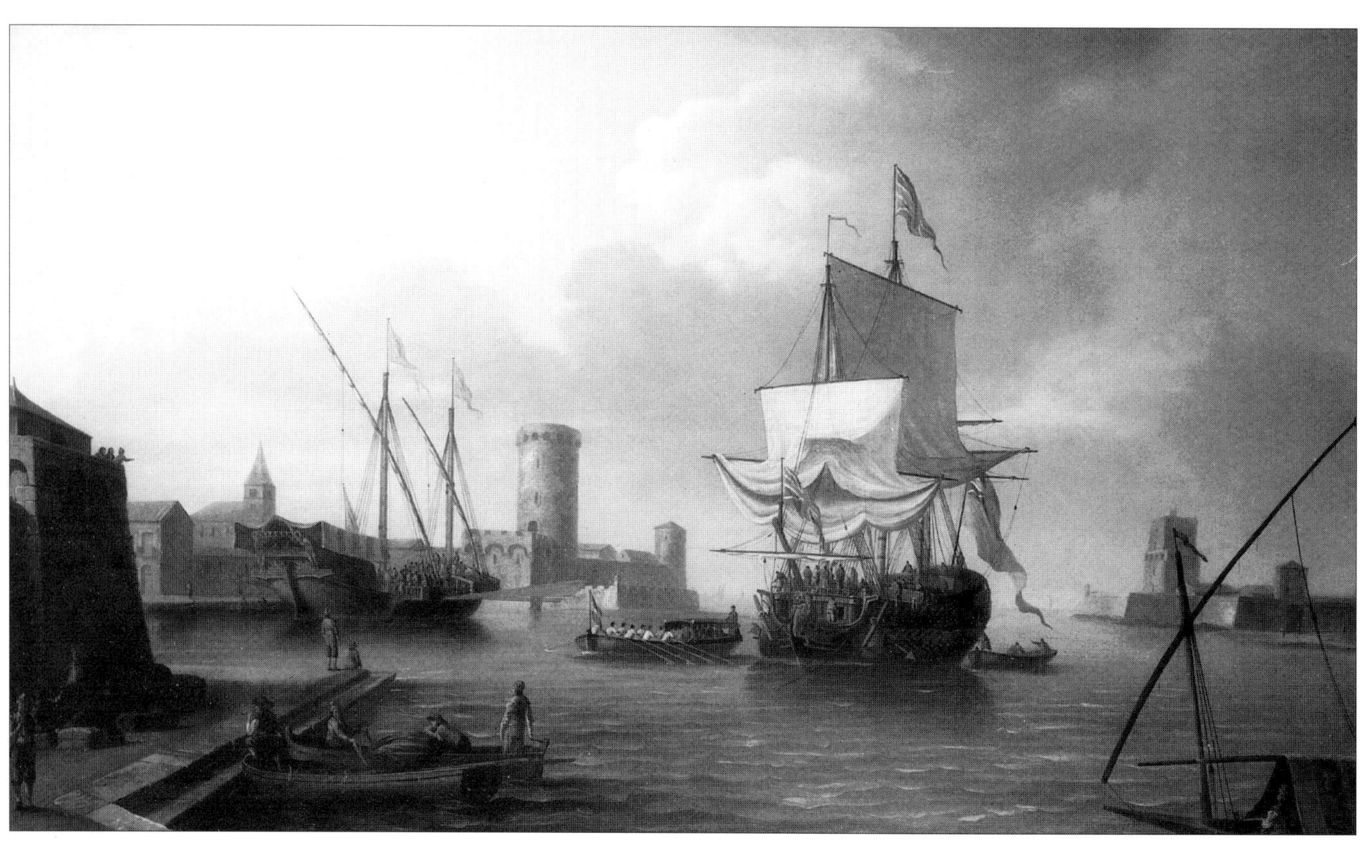

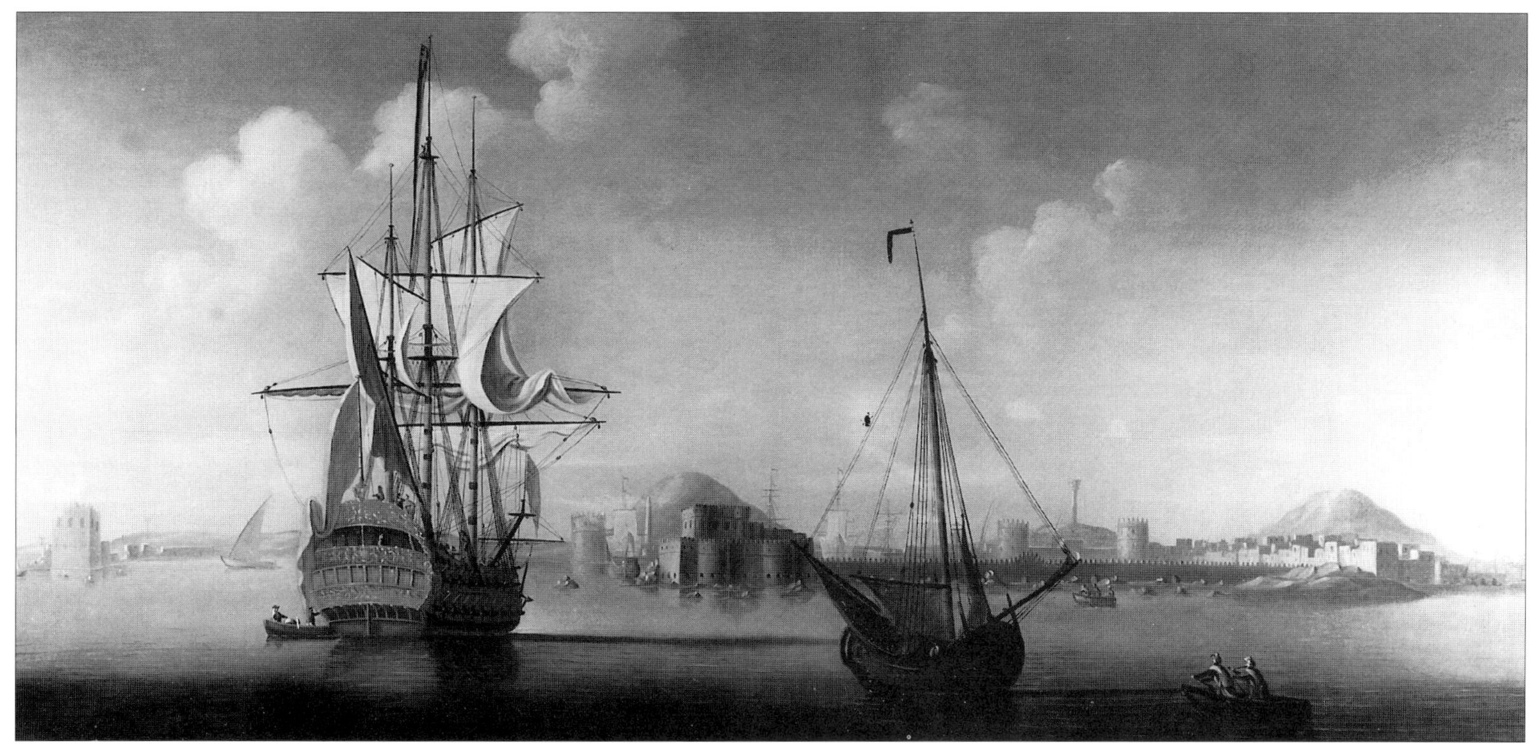

appears to have spent a great deal of his time in the (at that time) little known ports of the eastern Mediterranean and his paintings are of good quality. It is surprising that we know so little about him.

Other Rare Marine Painters of the 'Monamy Period'

In the earlier part of Monamy's active painting period there were three other artists whose paintings (especially their Van de Velde copies or versions) may be confused with Monamy's, if unsigned.

First is **Robert Woodcock (1692–1728)** who was an Admiralty clerk who developed an interest in painting ships. He was particularly known for his copies or 'versions' of Van de Velde subjects and he produced over forty of these.

The other two artists are the Vale brothers – **H. Vale and R. Vale** – who flourished between 1705 and 1730. Very little is known about them, but H. Vale produced some good pictures which could be mistaken for Peter Monamy.

All three painters are discussed in Chapters 6 and 9 of the author's previous book.[2]

---

1. *London and the Thames,* Catalogue of the Exhibition at Somerset House, October 1977 (re Thomas Mellish).
2. *Early Sea Painters,* F.B. Cockett, Antique Collectors' Club, 1995.

Index

Page numbers in bold refer to illustrations and captions